HONG KONG

香港

HONG

FIELDWORK ENCOUNTERS AND DISCOVERIES

A Series Edited by Robert Emerson and Jack Katz

Caroline Knowles
Douglas Harper

KONG

Migrant Lives, Landscapes, and Journeys

University of Chicago Press | Chicago & London

CAROLINE KNOWLES is professor of sociology at Goldsmiths, University of London, and the author of *Race and Social Analysis*.
DOUGLAS HARPER is professor of sociology at Duquesne University and the author of *Changing Works: Visions of a Lost Agriculture*.

All photographs, with the exceptions of those on pages 222, 250, and 251 (photographers unknown), are by Douglas Harper, and © 2009 by Douglas Harper
The University of Chicago Press, Chicago 60637
The University of Chicago Press, Ltd., London
© 2009 by The University of Chicago
All rights reserved. Published 2009
Printed in the United States of America

18 17 16 15 14 13 12 11 10 09   1 2 3 4 5

ISBN-13: 978–0-226–44856–5 (cloth)
ISBN-13: 978–0-226–44857–2 (paper)
ISBN-10: 0-226-44856-8   (cloth)
ISBN-10: 0-226-44857-6   (paper)

Library of Congress Cataloging-in-Publication Data

Knowles, Caroline, 1954–
    Hong Kong : migrant lives, landscapes, and journeys / Caroline Knowles and Douglas Harper.
        p. cm.
    ISBN 978-0-226-44856-5 (cloth : alk. paper) — ISBN 978-0-226-44857-2 (pbk. : alk paper)
1. Hong Kong (China)—Emigration and immigration. 2. British—China—Hong Kong—Social conditions. 3. Hong Kong (China)—Ethnic relations.   I. Harper, Douglas A. II. Title.
    DS796.H79A25 2009
    305.9'06912095125—dc22

                                                                    2009007963

CONTENTS

ACKNOWLEDGMENTS

We warmly thank the British Academy for funding the research and photography that made this book possible. We also thank Duquesne University, specifically the offices of the Provost and the Dean of Liberal Arts, for financial support. Many thanks to colleagues, friends, and family for support of various kinds, particularly Claire Alexander and Les Back for their insightful commentary on earlier versions of this manuscript. Pauline Leonard was coresearcher and guide to Hong Kong in the early stages of this project. Suzan Harper drew the maps. Most importantly, we owe a huge debt of gratitude to those many informants who took the time to tell us about their lives in Hong Kong and who treated us to their gracious hospitality during numerous fieldwork trips.

This book is the result of a collaborative effort: neither of us could have produced it alone. Douglas Harper's part of the authorship is about the photographs, which remain his intellectual property. Caroline Knowles's contribution is the writing, improved by Douglas's editorial suggestions. Two of the six or more periods of fieldwork were tackled together with lens and microphone. Responsibility for all omissions and inadequacies lie squarely with us as coauthors.

Caroline Knowles
Goldsmiths University of London
Douglas Harper
Duquesne University, Pittsburgh
May 2008

Migration describes patterns of travel and settlement. It describes a broad scale of mobilities from brief sojourns, where it fades into the social practices of travel and tourism, to permanent residencies. It describes circumstances of outward propulsion from severe deprivation to accumulation of further wealth. Migration is about survival and a restless spirit of adventure. We live in a world on the move. As well as people, objects, images, and money slide along routes and networks, making the world in these terms. Cities, like Hong Kong, provide a platform, a place to stand and take stock, of the corridors, networks, and circuits configuring the global world in which we live. This book describes a fragment of this world. Global cities like Hong Kong are fabricated through the practices of global migrants. But it is also a postcolonial city, in transition from the British Empire to the new opportunities offered in China, and is just as certainly fabricated by this. In Hong Kong, the past and the present tangle in ways that are tangible. Colonial and global routes, as well as the human traffic that travels and settles along them, intersect in Hong Kong. Its migrants live these two stories simultaneously. This book is about how they do this. It traces the routes and routines of the bodies and feet deposited in the entanglements of empire and globalization. It grinds a lens onto Hong Kong's swirling transience and transition. Think of it as a travel guide to the world of twenty-first-century migrants who live as minorities in a thoroughly modern Chinese city.

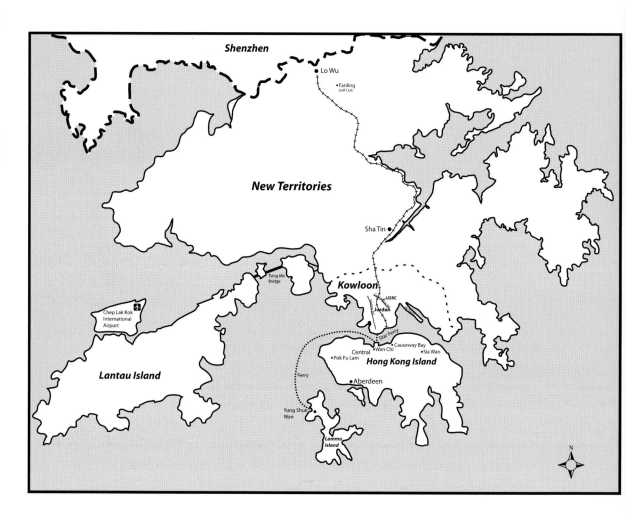

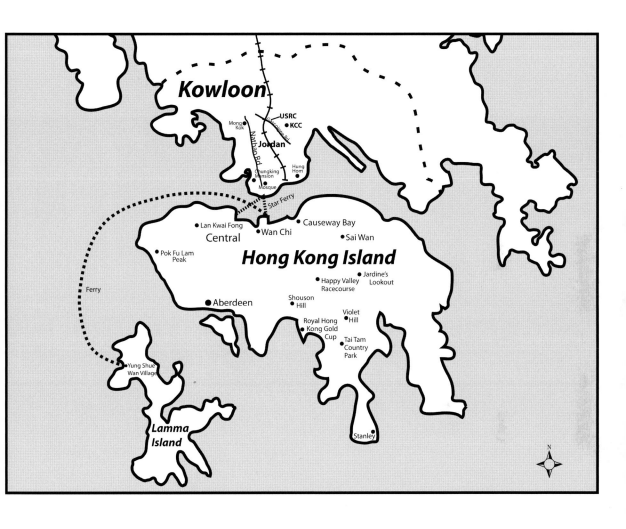

Kowloon

Mong
Kok

USRC
KCC

Nathan Rd

Jordan

Chatham Rd

Chungking
Mansion
Mosque

Hung
Hom

Star Ferry

Lan Kwai Fong

Central

Wan Chi

Causeway Bay

Sai Wan

Pok Fu Lam
Peak

Hong Kong Island

Ferry

Jardine's
Lookout

Happy Valley
Racecourse

Aberdeen

Shouson
Hill

Violet
Hill

Royal Hong
Kong Gold
Cup

Tai Tam
Country
Park

Yung Shue
Wan Village

**Lamma
Island**

Stanley

N

BEGINNINGS AND ENDINGS

Arriving in Postcolonial Hong Kong

The City must never be confused with the words that describe it.[1]

Migration begins with a single journey. The ease of contemporary travel conceals its complexity. Migration involves complex dislocations of biography, personal ontology, organization, and engagement with the practicalities of here and there. Arriving is both the end of a journey and the beginning of another; of life in a new place.

Arriving in Hong Kong—from London, New York, Manila, Bangkok, Mumbai, Dhaka—involves descending into Chek Lap Kok International Airport on the western island of Lantau in the South China Sea. Walking through connecting tubes, the new arrival will enter a magnificent vaulted cathedral of white tubular steel, designed by world-renowned architect Norman Foster. Hong Kong's beautiful new airport signaled more than a change of regime. It is an architectural manifestation of the arguments and arrangements between Britain and China over the terms on which the colony would be handed back to China in 1997. It drew a line under Hong Kong's colonial past. The most forward-looking of cities, Hong Kong routinely demolishes its past. Impatience with the past and determination to live in the present gives the airport and the city a new, gleaming aesthetic. A palace of arrivals, departures, and transits, the airport is a fittingly grand gateway to a thoroughly modern Chinese city, advantageously positioned on the shipping lanes of the Pacific Rim. Hong Kong is a significant node in the global flow of people and things.

A fast train from the air terminal building transports arriving passengers through city fractals of high-rise buildings. These form vertical cities in which lives unfurl in multiple sky capsules. In thirty minutes we will be standing at the tip of the Kowloon Peninsula—geographically part of mainland China—dazzled by the jumble of neon lights in Cantonese and English: the mix of imposing department stores and tiny market stalls selling food and other small items around Nathan Road. We are absorbed into the buzz of the street. Although Hong Kong's land area is routinely extended by land reclamation projects, seven million people in a compact space means that the average population density (6,603 per square kilometer) raises in Kowloon's Mong Kok district to (40,000 per square kilometer) among the highest in the world.[2] Population density is a sensory experience. We will join the symphony of pounding feet and the roar of traffic.

High population densities and a slum clearance program that began in 1953 rehoused 50,000 ordinary Chinese families a year, so that by 2001, 49 percent of the population lived in some kind of public housing. The majority are rental units with rents pegged at 10 percent of median income. Rent control plugs the gap between high land values and rents on the one hand and wages on the other. Sustaining lower wages ensures a competitive edge in global production. Sustained development of public housing has also produced several high-rise new towns north of Kowloon in the New Territories, which abut mainland China. Hong Kong is a fractal city: a city that expands not through suburbs, but in new districts repeating the structures of the city center.[3] A megacity in the making, the Hong Kong, Shenzhen, Canton, Pearl River Delta, Macau, and Zhuhai metropolitan matrix is the largest urban area in the world.[4] Hong Kong is a place of rampant urbanization.

Some of these places extend into mainland China. We will see Shenzhen in the distance, through the barbed wire fence separating mainland China from the New Territories, later when we go on patrol. This border, and Hong Kong's relationship with China, is important in producing Hong Kong's landscape. There is a close (mutual) economic interdependence between China and Hong Kong, with investment flowing in both directions.[5] China is also a key source of migration. Hong Kong has always hosted waves of Chinese migrants, dissidents, and those seeking new lives. The Communist Revolution (1949) and the Cultural Revolution (starting in 1966) increased this flow. One hundred and fifty mainland Chinese a day (54,750 a year) now cross the border and settle in Hong Kong. Arrivals from London, New York, or Manila—migrants in a city of migrants—make little impact. There is also close political association between China and Hong Kong. Since 1997, when it ceased to be a British colony, Hong Kong is a special administrative region (SAR) of China. It has its own miniconstitution in the Basic Law and its own Legislative Assembly (LEGCO). Hong Kong's active prodemocracy movement monitors China's relationship with its newly reacquired SAR. Hong Kong lives in interesting times.

If, instead of getting off the airport express in Kowloon, we stayed on the train for one more stop, we would be deposited a few minutes later in the central district on Hong Kong Island. Here we would be among elegant high-rise buildings designed by the world's leading architects for the world's leading global corporations: the Bank of China Tower, the Hong Kong and Shanghai Bank (HSBC), Jardine House on the harbor front, and taller than the Peak, Two IFC (International Finance Centre). Hong Kong is both a newly industrialized part of Asia's economic miracle, and newly deindustrialized as it was catapulted into the service economy, offshoring (with China) and banking, insurance, and corporate headquarters.[6] These buildings are stylishly lit as night falls and contrast with the garish jumble of Kowloon. Kowloon is easily visible from the central district's shoreline; and from the heights of the Peak, which provide views into Central and the Chinese mainland beyond. From the Peak we can gaze on one of the world's most breathtaking cityscapes as it lights up at dusk.

A fabulously modern city with a state-of-the-art public transit system, its central walkways and plazas are corporate spaces that present themselves as public space.[7] "Cities are rarely the site of disinterested practices."[8] A close relationship between the local state—as landlord-in-chief—and the local corporate elite—who lease and develop land—has shaped this city.[9] Its marble malls retail the output of the global fashion industry's luxury products—Gucci, Fendi, Prada—which add to the glitter of Hong Kong and its impression of prosperity. And yet Hong Kong ranks fifth in the world in terms of the gap between rich and poor, with half a million workers earning less than HK$ 62,400—less than US$ 10,000[10]—a year despite the fact that its gross domestic product (GDP) has at times surpassed that of its colonizing power.

More subtly marked on the landscape are inscriptions of Hong Kong's colonial past. We will have to hunt for these. They reveal their subtle inscription slowly as the eye tunes into the landscape. They are fading, peeling, covered up, unannounced, subtly burned into the built landscape and street furniture. "The city. . . . does not tell its past, but contains it like the lines of a hand, written in the corners of the streets, the gratings of the windows."[11] Faded royal crests can still be spotted by the discerning eye on the front of buildings and on wrought iron gates. There are recognizably British postboxes complete with crown insignia, now painted bright green rather than red. There are London-styled double-decker buses and trams. There's the British Council spreading British culture and English language abroad, now operating in a new spirit of local cooperation that aims to strike a distance from the past. There's Government House, the old residence of the colonial Governors, now tied in with new, Chinese, public functions. There are British and Irish pubs scattered around the fashionable parts of the city. We can go for high tea at the elegant Peninsular Hotel, or get a steak and kidney pie at the Old China Hand Pub. Hong Kong's past lies in recast symbols and redirected institutions that are fading even as we write.

The significance of this colonial past in the making of Hong Kong is a matter of debate among historians.[12] But Hong Kong was the last major British colonial territory. On this account it exposes the interconnections between the colonial and the postcolonial, between empire and globalization,[13] between past and present, more clearly than other places. Hong Kong entered the modern global era under colonial rule. Its mutating urban landscape is built on a shifting, accelerated set of global economic circumstances, in which traces of the past remain visible.

Framing Migration

This section clarifies the selection of framing devices and (scholarly) conversation organizing your tour. It illuminates the assumptions and knowledge with which we practiced research and writing, and it exposes the thinking behind our methodological decisions.

Globalization scholarship describes the networks, corridors, and circuits that span the surface of the earth, connecting distant locations, people and objects while simultaneously disconnecting them from hinterlands and immediate social contexts.[14] New maps, new geographies, connecting subnational spaces across borders, have resulted from this scholarship. Migration, and the translocal household strategies it creates, is one of globalization's key constituting processes.[15]

A growing number of lives are cast in migration. The largest scale migrations are rural to urban inside the most rapidly developing countries, China and India. Surges in international migration are often politically generated. In 1996 we were able to log over half a million refugees, 1.2 million displaced persons and 1.4 million war-affected persons in need of assistance, in the successor states of the former Yugoslavia alone. Two hundred million people live outside of their country of birth or citizenship. At the end of the twentieth century, one in thirteen people living in the West is an international migrant, the majority from developing countries.[16] A significant scale of migrant traffic moves *out* of economically developed countries, too, most of it to other economically developed (or rapidly developing) regions. Six million British citizens, 10 percent of the population, live overseas.[17] This combines with a democratization of migration: an increase in the type of people for whom it is a viable strategy. People in ordinary occupations, students, pensioners, and second-home owners cast their lives in global terms. Other Europeans are doing likewise. While half a million British citizens live in France, London is now the seventh largest French city.[18]

Migration literature and debate in Britain and other European countries and the United States focus on *in-* rather than *out-*migration: immigration. It focuses on asylum seekers, on undocumented and economic migrants: on those fleeing famine, war, human rights violations, and disaster to live in economically developed countries.[19] Like other economically developed countries, Britain differentiates (undeserving) economic migrants upgrading their circumstances from (deserving) asylum seekers fleeing persecution and execution. British social policy is also preoccupied with the consequences of migration. Migrant settlement practices are scrutinized through the lens of social cohesion. Anxieties about social cohesion have generated renewed concern with ethnic segregation. This combines with post–9/11 fears about terrorism to target British Asian Muslims for a failure to integrate into British society.[20] Concern with settlement practices centers on the habits of (new and old) arrivals. Meanwhile, the habits of the six million Britons who live in other countries have escaped detailed attention.

An expanding new literature explores the affairs of migrants from economically developed countries. This is described as "skilled" or "transient" migration.[21] It is also described as "elite" transnational migration, brokered by intracompany transfers. This kind of migration is suspected of creating only minimal disruption to migrants' lives.[22] Acknowledging the democratization of migration beyond elite skilled transient workers, a growing literature thinks about migration in terms of the ordinary lives, of "middling transnationals."[23] These interventions have exposed the geographies and motives of a range of migrants—ordinary workers, expatriates, gap-year students, pensioners, and temporary and long-term lifestyle migrants—to analysis.[24] The British in Spain, Portugal, Cyprus, and Turkey are described as distinctive, self-servicing, circulating communities with strong ties to Britain.[25] Similarly, American and European corporate elites are described as living in "symbolically segregated communities" of standardized luxury.[26] These migrants from economically developed countries share their framing in migration literature as a small, invisible, adaptable, uncontroversial segment of migration.[27] They are the bearers of crossborder flows of knowledge and skills.[28] They follow the opportunities opened by international labor markets, or of housing equity, cashed in on highly priced real estate markets like the UK. In this they stand in stark contrast to migrants *into* economically developed countries.

This book is about ordinary British migrants in Hong Kong and the American, subcontinental Indian, Nepalese, Filipino, and Thai migrants with which their lives intersect. We study these migrants by tracing social networks and by observing places where networks intersect. Placing these migrants together highlights significant differences between their lives, their circumstances, and their relationship to the city. This book explores simple but fundamental things that we don't know about migration. Migration literature's focus on "flows," "circuits" and the production of social fields that cross nation-state boundaries[29] has prioritized migrations' travel and connectivity over detailed examination of dwelling. As a number of authors have noted,[30] we don't actually have detailed accounts of migrants' routine settlement practices. We lack up-close portraits of how migrants actually live in landscapes of new belonging. Subsequently our accounts of what it actually *means* to migrate are rather thin. This book attends to this gap. Migration is as much about dwelling in the routines of travel, as travel in the routines of dwelling. Dwelling embeds connectivity and mobilities, too; ours is a change in

emphasis. We explore rhythms of arrival, departure, dwelling, and settlement; the ways in which lives are mobile and the ways in which they are recast in culturally unfamiliar landscapes. It is about transience and transition on different scales; individual, social, and global. And the book explores how transience and transition become the substance of routine lives and social relationships. We explore how migrants 'do' migration: ontologically, biographically, and socially. We are concerned with the adaptation, concessions, and bargains that are struck in living in new places: circumstances a growing number of people face.

Stories of people-in-motion and their relationship with a city-in-process work with two fabrics. The first is people and bodies and feet kinesthetically engaged with the material social world: "the footwork of dwelling."[31] The second fabric is the city's shifting materiality in its architecture, street patterns, and modes of circulation. In the interconnections between urban landscape and its migrant bodies we find points of access to their world and the skills it takes to live in it. The idea of fabrication is central to this book. Lives, people, and places are all *made* or produced. Equally important is the idea of fabric. Fabric suggests the social and material world that lives and landscapes are made from.[32] Architecture is used to suggest the design and production of buildings and built landscapes as well as the design and production of the social world as architecture: social architecture.

How shall we describe these migrations from Britain, the Philippines, the Indian subcontinent, and other places? Most definitions of migration stipulate that this term refers to stays of at least a year outside of someone's country of origin or citizenship. Applying the categories used in migration literature, none of these migrations are "forced." Voluntary migration, however, describes divergent circumstances and scales of necessity. The distinction usually made between temporary and long-term migration is not particularly useful either. In the unfolding of lives, temporariness often just accumulates to long term. And even long-term migrants live in temporary ways, as we will see. These are legal migrations.[33] But this category too frays at the edges when migrants overstay or break their conditions of entry. In the terms used by the literature, they are "economic migrants" who have employment-related reasons for moving.[34] They are also "skilled migrants," although they are processed differently by Hong Kong's immigration authorities. Only some migrants are permitted to transfer their skills; others have to fill unskilled jobs in spite of their skill. These categories of migration lead into the murky waters of migrant motivation. This is complex, overlapping, and contradictory. The use of "economic migrant," for example, imputes limited intentions that support the priority of labor markets. Economic gain may be one among many motivations to migrate. And is this term usefully applied to migrations avoiding poverty and starvation as well as those that turn a high wage into a higher one? This kind of slack and slippage in terminology is noted by a number of authors.[35] Finally, the term "lifestyle migration" has crept into a small number of recent studies to describe a range of circumstances and motivation that is broader than employment. Some of these use the term lifestyle migration to describe the exercise of environmental preferences. Here the primary motivation for moving is landscape or natural environment, better weather or a less-pressured lifestyle. These are migrations where aesthetic qualities including quality of life are prioritized over economic factors like job advancement and income.[36]

We take this term "lifestyle migration" and elaborate it as an entry point into thinking about (British and American) migrants from economically developed countries. Our usage of lifestyle migration is not intended to flatten migration motives to a single dimension. On the contrary, it acknowledges the shifting multiplicity of motives and adds something we consider more important: the operationalization of motives in concrete settlement practices. We think about lifestyle migration as constituted in its settlement practices. Our use of lifestyle migration also acknowledges the inseparability of economic factors like income, and the quality of life it supports. In the global scheme of things, those who are already economically privileged are able to prioritize qualities beyond life's financial elements. So we use this term because it includes economic factors in concert with a range of others. It is broad and inclusive, and it acknowledges the things migrants have told us about their lives and the things we observed about them during our investigation. It supports elaboration of divergent conceptions of migration we found between migrants in our study, including those in the same household or family. Lifestyle migration allowed us to explore household and family practices for what migrants like about migration.

Our use of the term "lifestyle migration" also allows elaboration of a sliding scale of differences between migrants that are otherwise obscured by terms like "economic migration." Elements of settlement practices constituting lifestyle migration are evident in the mobilities of exotic Thai dancers, Filipino maids, and Nepalese and Indian waiters. This is not a sealed category but an open matrix. But among these groups, key elements of lifestyle migration are constrained by the ways in which they are administered by immigration authorities. They are governed by contracts, which grant admission and channel them into a range of service capacities. These groups are not adequately covered by the term "contract labor migration," which equally applies to some lifestyle migrants. This is because the channels organizing their entry and subsequent disposition are quite different. Our starting point is to think about these groups as "serving-class migrants." This term sums up their relationship with the state and its immigration policies, the local Hong Kong Chinese population and their interactions with lifestyle migrants. Inevitably this categorization of migration oversimplifies. It will unravel and be elaborated by the diverse biographies and circumstances we will encounter as our tour proceeds. These terms are entry points.

Framing Migrants

Migrants themselves animate migration categories. "Expatriate" (short form, "expat") is the term (some) migrants in our study use to refer to themselves and their networks. In migration literature this term is used interchangeably with the tangle of terms just noted to refer to those who we are calling lifestyle migrants. "Expat" is a widely contested term. At its simplest it literally means those who live outside of their country of birth, citizenship or (some other calculation of) belonging. But it is commonly used more narrowly than this to refer to migrants from economically developed countries. It is used in this volume because it captures the way (some) migrants refer to themselves. They use it to establish common cause; inclusion and exclusions around origins and settlement practices. They use it to differentiate types of migrants and to differentiate migrants from locals. Those who have expatriated themselves from the Indian subcontinent, for example, are not referred to, nor do they refer to themselves, as expats. Australians, Americans, Europeans, British, and sometimes, British citizens of Indian descent refer to each other and to themselves using this term. The boundaries drawn around the application of expat appear to have something to do with citizenship, culture, and ethnicity. What, we will have to wait and see.

British lifestyle migrants' stories form the spine of this book. They are a tiny speck on a tide of in-migration from the Chinese mainland and out-migration of Hong Kong Chinese entrepreneurs to North America and Australia. British migrants in Hong Kong are a small capsule of the (insufficiently researched) 10 percent of Britons who live abroad. Their investigation exposes the settlement practices of the ex-colonial tribe. The significance of the British in Hong Kong lies in their insignificance. There are now less than 19,000 British migrants in Hong Kong, only 0.3 percent of a population that is 95 percent Chinese. This compares poorly with other foreign migrants. The 143,000 Filipinos and 42,000 migrants from the Indian subcontinent form more substantial groups.[37] There are more American than British migrants in Hong Kong (50,000); a figure resonating with US influence on globalization. Numeric insignificance should not be underestimated. It was one of the drivers of the British Empire. In 1820 Britain ran a landmass 125 times bigger than Britain and governed one in five of the world's population with a domestic population of only twelve million.[38] Insignificance is lethally deceptive. It can also be instructive.

The British migrants in this book are from varied social circumstances, migrant histories, and migrant genealogies. Some are recycled colonial functionaries who arrived in the seventies to work the apparatus of empire and its attendant enterprises as police officers, civil engineers, or teachers. Others arrived after the future of Hong Kong was settled in the Sino-British Joint Declaration (1984), and still others arrived in the service of multinational corporations and as teachers in the years after 1997. They have lived in Hong Kong from three to thirty years; a mix of long-term belongers and temporary contract workers. Some plan to stay and some to move on. They have vague, and sometimes more definite, plans for future posts or retirement. A mix or men and women, they fall between the ages of seventeen and eighty-five. In occupational terms they are teachers, classroom assistants, self-employed workers in a range of not particularly well-paid jobs, corporate lawyers, surveyors, urban planners, office administrators, ladies who lunch, clergy, high-ranking police officers, and successful entrepreneurs working global financial systems.

We recorded diverse voices of the ordinary as well as the elite. Hong Kong is a place of opportunity and high rewards. But those outside of the main corporate matrix of global business operate in a small niche. This is closing with the Chinesization of business and public services, only parts of it being kept open by the demand for English-language and other services, on the fringe of the global mainstream. Some of the people we interviewed were not especially privileged and some had difficulty in maintaining themselves in employment.

As we followed them and traced their networks, we recruited other migrants they came into contact with. Serving-class migrants—waiters from the Indian subcontinent, exotic dancers, bar girls and domestics from Thailand and the Philippines—support the lifestyles of the local Chinese population and lifestyle migrants alike. They provide the substance of what many migrants particularly liked about living in Hong Kong. Including their voices, journeys, and settlement practices, this book reveals social inequalities operating on a global scale.

Framing Hong Kong Chineseness

Urban centers are powerful sites of dwelling and travel.[39] Four factors support Hong Kong as a platform from which to audit fragments of migration. It is a significant magnet drawing from China, Southeast Asia, Europe, and other Western countries. It has accumulated a stratified migrant labor force—Indian, Philippine, European, and American—that resembles other migration magnets in the Asia Pacific region (including Shanghai and Singapore) and the Middle East (especially Dubai and Saudi Arabia). Despite fluctuating economic fortunes, Hong Kong attracts global corporations and their labor forces. Third, it is closely connected with China, the growth hotspot of the early twenty-first-century set to become (along with India) a major force among global economies. Fourthly, Hong Kong is a place in transition between an old (colonial) and a new (postcolonial) global matrix. As a place it repeats its migrants' situation of transience and transition. Hong Kong's transition from colony to a Chinese SAR gradually impacted on the lives our research investigated, and beginning in 1998 just after the handover, it captured a significant moment in a gradual process. Hong Kong's past is buried in a shallow grave. We anticipated that the city and its migrants would reveal the colonial in postcolonial. It did not disappoint and adds a crucial dimension to a study of migration that is inclined to overlook its past. The stories in this book are Hong Kong stories with resonance beyond for the analysis of migration.

We use the term "Chineseness" carefully. We do not intend to impute a center, essence, or uniformity to Hong Kong as a place, or to its people. We acknowledge that "Hong Kong Chinese" is used to confer common "ethnicity" on the local population as well as to acknowledge their historic and recent origins in mainland China. We also acknowledge that distinctions are made by local Chinese people between historic and recent migrants from the mainland. We use "Chineseness" as a shortcut to naming the multiple dimensions of otherness migrants encounter when they arrive. We use the term to refer to the multitude of events, activities, social relationships, structures, objects, places, people, and things composing the fabric of Hong Kong. It is a way of naming what migrants join when they move to Hong Kong. Its use acknowledges that Hong Kong struggles with the Chineseness of mainland China, pursing a distinctive path, culturally and politically. Hong Kong's innovative art and cinematic traditions, its comparative freedom of political and other forms of individual and collective expression, chart a different path from mainland China and provide a distinctive version of Chineseness with which it is nonetheless intertwined. Thinking about Chineseness takes us to the heart of migrant settlement practices: the skill of living as a minority among multiple dimensions of difference.[40] This book is about migrant interpretations of, and intersections with, Chineseness.

Framing Whiteness

Migration scholars are hesitant in using race and ethnicity to frame their investigations. These terms are left to sociologists who seek to understand the disposal of (mostly black and ethnic minority) migrants settling in economically developed countries. This separation of travel and settlement turns migration into an event rather than long-term social and biographical processes shaping lives and landscapes. In analyses of "skilled" migrants leaving economically developed countries, race and ethnicity (as whiteness) are insinuated in claims that they are "invisible in terms of ethnicity";[41] and that their migration is unproblematic in host countries because of their "adaptability" and "acceptability."[42] This alerts us to the importance of taking a closer look at whiteness. How has whiteness been thought about in relationship to migration? How might it be thought about more effectively?

"Whiteness" is a term used to identify those who use race and ethnicity to name others without applying these terms to themselves.[43] Whiteness ends invisibility. Like other uses of race it has no genetic basis, although it is popularly attached to pale skin and European ancestry. Whiteness—like other racial categories—is widely understood as constituted in the social and political contexts where it is used to categorize and administer people.[44] Grouping loose and shifting assemblages of subjects, race operates in places where it has come over time to form a basis for the allocation of resources, differential opportunity, rights, and social justice.[45] Britain, the United States, Western Europe, Canada, Australia, New Zealand, and other places too provide examples of places where this happens. These are societies organized by "racial formations."[46] In places where race matters, the rewards of whiteness are considerable.[47] Various theorists[48] have pointed out that being counted as white hangs on assembling social and personal resources[49] and mobilizing them through performance and light-colored skin. So race/whiteness is plastic.

But these general notions of whiteness are only useful up to a point. In acknowledging that race and ethnicity are fluid categories with powerful histories we add the insight that race is continuously produced. Race and ethnicity are generated in concrete relationship with places, with other people, with activities and objects of material culture. Race and ethnicity are made, literally produced, in the scenes of everyday life.[50] As we live so we make race/ethnicity on a daily basis. It is embedded in our ways of being and operating in the world.[51] It is embedded in the way societies, and the matrix of networks connecting them, operate. In other words, race and ethnicity are personal and structural features of social organization worked up and worked on by people on a routine basis. They are not the same. Ethnicity is framed in cultural performances, language claims, among others, but rarely in terms of phenotype.[52] But they often operate in tandem, as fluid, indefinite, but powerful resources in societies where they constitute people and places.

It amounts to this: Race and ethnicity are not objects, although they may be implicated in the arrangement of objects. They are ways of thinking about, categorizing, and organizing people, logged in an array of visible differences. They are embedded in the subtleties of the organization of the social world and in how we think about ourselves and interact with each other. Race and ethnicity work with other social distinctions, subtly inflecting who we are and everything we do. Migration circulates the operational surfaces of race and ethnicity around the world. In new social contexts they recombine with other categories that are also important and used to think about people, such as national origins, class, age, and gender. They settle in new places along with the bodies and social practices that transport them. They take new forms and new meanings in new contexts. Migration circulates whiteness and otherness. In this volume we are concerned with the forms of whiteness produced using the material furnished in the bodies, habits, journeys, social relationships—the settlement practices—of British migrants. Our focus is not some general notion of whiteness, but British whiteness in this place and this time: a category we unfold in the biographies, movements, expectations, and settlement practices of the migrants we investigate. Migration provides critical exposure to difference in proximity. It exposes the skills and competence of white Britishness as ethnic minority.

Framing Empire and After

Eighteenth- and nineteenth-century empires were global racial hierarchies in action: manifestations of the architecture of European racial superiority. This is not to diminish the complexities involved in maintaining racial distinctions in empire governance. A number of writers on empire and postcolonialism have pointed out that these were easily breached in sexual liaison with locals and low standards of (European) whiteness in the behavior of the ranks.[53] "Empire" meant different things in different places, and Hong Kong historians are divided on its impact in Hong Kong.[54] Britain seized Hong Kong from China in the Opium Wars (1841 and 1856) in order to protect the trading of opium grown in British India. Empire and the business it sustained generated routes from Britain to Hong Kong for a range of elite and ordinary people. Policemen, soldiers, civil servants, and governors moved in and out of the colony. Hong Kong provided them with jobs and opportunities. It guaranteed them decent subsidized housing, home leave, and pensions when they retired. It allowed them to raise and educate families; and it provided many ordinary people with round-the-clock domestic labor. Empire business also generated routes between other British colonies and Hong Kong. Regiments of soldiers, police, and lower-ranking civil servants were deposited from the Indian subcontinent and Nepal.

The era of European empires is over; even in Hong Kong, where it only formally ended in 1997. An enormous (postcolonial) literature ponders the intellectual, political, and economic legacies of empire and its racial business.[55] Those who ponder the posts in postcolonial point out the many ways in which mainstream globalization reinstates empire's power geometries in new forms.[56] There are few satisfactory accounts of the ways in which empire persists. Postcolonial studies have treated this issue in overly abstract terms. These leave us with the impression that empire is embedded in people's mental furniture, or that it somehow hangs on as a system of ideas, disconnected from its material basis. Postcolonial whiteness is considered a vector to this dark history. It may be. But some of these theorists make insubstantial connections between past and present. Thinking these things through concretely, as we do in this book, requires us to be clear about how the past disturbs the present. We examine white British migrants' settlement practices for evidence that empire still animates them. In this reckoning of history, past, and present are less chronologically arranged than intertwined around crucial social practices that act as vectors. Sidestepping complex debates that add little to the investigation at hand, we use the term "postcolonial" descriptively to discuss social scenes that followed the formal end of empire in Hong Kong in 1997.

Framing the Investigation

The fieldwork for this book was accumulated in six trips to Hong Kong between 1998 and 2005. Using a digital recorder, we interviewed fifty migrants between three and six times each to establish their relationship with their countries of origin, their migration biographies, their daily activities, and their use of local space in Hong Kong (we have changed their names, apart from Jack, who prefers to use his own). We followed people around the city, observed them, ate with them, and joined in their activities. We established e-mail correspondence with them between periods of fieldwork. From only three initial contacts in the UK we roamed around their networks and made new contacts in places where migrants' lives intersect, places like social clubs and bars they frequented. When these networks became too homogenous we found new contacts, diversifying our reach to include new social groups. Through these routes we branched out and contacted new groups of migrants from other countries as well. Our methods included observation, interviews, mapping personal routes through the city, and photography. Combining these methods we collected three kinds of stories. The first were spoken into the tape recorder in the context of mobile and other kinds of informal interviews. The second were the stories told silently in migrants' routine movements rather than in words. Ways of walking, comportment, and habits provide important clues about their relationships with places, material objects, and people on routes through landscapes of new settlement. We logged these stories in field notes and photographs. Equally silent were the third kind of story. These were displayed in its architecture and in its arrangement as urban space. They were also told in the personal cartographies migrants charted through the city. Space is never ontologically given, it is corporeally mapped.[57]

To photograph and to write is to arrange the world through a kind of alchemy. This book is a staging of the world of Hong Kong migrants using the material we found. The microworld we present resonates beyond it;[58] Hong Kong is a capsule of contemporary migration. The camera lens picks out the particular and issues an invitation to establish connection with the bigger landscape on which it sits. Small things accumulate to bigger things. They offer a way into the macrosocial process through which the global world is organized.

We now begin our tour of Hong Kong migrants' lives. We begin with an elderly man who is near the end of his life and able to review its eight decades. Such stories are a precious resource. Like all the migrants we will meet, he has a connection with Hong Kong and Chineseness that is both unique to him and part of bigger history. At first he looks like a colonial caricature traded in early postcolonial studies. But closer examination reveals that things may not be quite as they seem. The organization of his life in Hong Kong demands careful consideration of the relationship between the past and the present. As suggested earlier, Hong Kong's past is buried close to the surface of the present.

Arranging the Dead

Take the bus north from the southern tip of the Kowloon Peninsula to one of the many new high-rise towns created through the expansion of public housing, a part of Hong Kong that abuts the border with China. This is part of a seamless urban landscape stretching from the central business district on Hong Kong Island to Shenzhen in mainland China. This journey will take more than an hour and involve changing buses. Both double-decker buses will move slowly through the busy traffic. Get off and confront rows of identical thirty-story apartment buildings in a vertical town of fifty thousand people that is Shatin. Locate the collection of apartment buildings that are called the "City One Estate." Identify the correct building by the numbers and letters above the doorway. Negotiate an entryway guarded by a curious concierge and then take the lift to the twenty-seventh floor. You will be looking at a heavily secured front door covered by a metal grille. This is for show, no one is really worried about security; everyone agrees that Hong Kong is a safe place. Ring the bell and there sitting in an armchair facing the window is a lively octogenarian. "My name is Jack Edwards."[59]

All migrant stories are uniquely personal. Jack's story begins in a central trau-

matic narrative. This includes his captivity in Japanese POW camps in the area around Singapore and Taiwan and arranges his other stories: the story of his youth, his soldiering activities in the beginning of the Second World War, the circumstances of his capture by the Japanese. He will tell you these stories, given time. But he has also published them in a book called *Banzai, You Bastards!*[60]: such was his need to bear witness. This is how the story he told us begins.

> I was at Changi the first six weeks [in a Singapore POW camp]. But we weren't in
> the jail, we were marched up every day to the beaches to do the burial of the dead of
> the people who were being massacred on the beaches . . . Kinkaseki, that was my last
> camp . . . it was a copper mine, it was the end of the road for us. We went in 530-odd
> strong and ended up the war about 80 of us left . . . there's only five of my little section
> left. All of us are not 100 percent men, there's something wrong with us . . .

He tells this story as a tale of captivity-as-the-daily-trudge-of-human-existence in dehumanizing conditions. It highlights wars' corporeal dramas. He describes the daily production of soldiers' bodies in a context of forced labor and limited food. He details the gradual and sudden deaths prison conditions secured. His

book substantiates this with photographs of emaciated bodies of survivors taken after American liberation of the camp. He challenges the Japanese prosecution of war. He provides a subtle, indirect discussion of the (ethical) conduct of war and the circumstances in which war is a legitimate strategy.

Released, emaciated, from the POW camp at the end of the war, Jack tells us that he is put on recovery, identification, and burial duty. He will find, tag, and bury his fellow prisoners. This duty takes him all over the Far East and then to Hong Kong.

> Had to search all over the Far East for them [the camp victims] of course . . . We based ourselves on Shanghai and operated . . . into Taiwan mainly . . . wherever they were being picked up, because they spread themselves all over the Far East. Not many people know the story [This is the rationale behind its telling; a story that must be told by those who survived on behalf of those who did not]. I'm talking about '45, '46, because the Japanese gave an order that all top Japanese who caused problems for the POWs were to take care of it and flee. Not many people know about these things [and Jack is one of a dwindling number of witness to a hidden history] . . . they brought their bones and remains back from Taiwan to Hong Kong while I was here, you see . . .

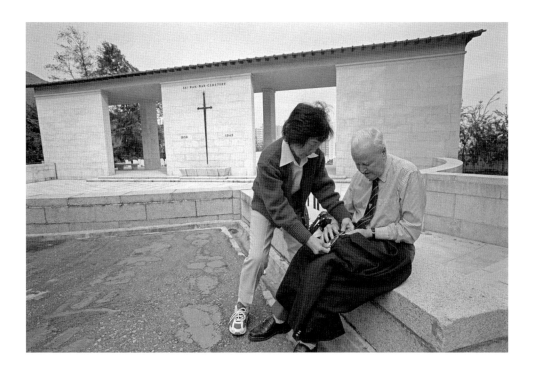

in huge containers . . . I had to go to the ship and meet it with my colonel . . . Suddenly we were told they were bringing them all back. We realized why, because while we'd buried them [in Taiwan and Singapore] they were near the surface and we couldn't cover them up ourselves.

Some pasts are impossible to bury: they just keep rising to the surface, and in Jack's case the past surfaced in Hong Kong, providing a unique connection.

It is 1948 and Jack, newly demobilized, returns to Britain, where he manages to live in a troubled sort of way he doesn't say much about, for fifteen years. By 1963, in his early forties, Jack tells us that he found a way to return to Hong Kong. He secured a job with the Hong Kong Housing Authority; an arm of colonial governance occupied with the work of slum clearance. Jacks works in the administration of slum clearance for four years. He then leaves Hong Kong at the end of his contract (1967) with the intention of not returning. But Jack is still unable to settle in Britain. He secures, with even greater difficulty than before on account of his age and war disabilities, another contract with the Hong Kong Housing Authority. He does this through a connection brokered by another Japanese POW. A life-shaping experience creates a network. In addition to slum clearance, the

25

housing authority is struggling to house the tide of Chinese and Vietnamese refugees pouring over the border. The Cultural Revolution and the Vietnam War are in full swing. Jack says, "I cut a niche for myself here, a specialist managing big estates [i.e., housing projects] like this"; like the one he now lives in.

Jack tells us that he had to return to Hong Kong because

we hadn't buried our pals . . . [When] we left [Hong Kong] . . . we left them behind. So to me and the colonel it was unfinished business . . . They [the British military authorities in the immediate aftermath of the war in the Far East] made a decision to bury them in Hong Kong. So they're all still in Hong Kong. They're here now, up at Sai Wan Bay cemetery.

Discussing the unresolved business of war, the military cemetery and its ghosts that Jack tells us, "kept calling [him] back" he slips seamlessly into the present.

I feel that I'm giving back. And I feel I'm remembering in a positive way . . . I feel when I go up to the cemetery, and I go so many times, that they know . . . It's a funny thing to say. I'm convinced that they know. Because when I first went back there, when I came back [in '63] . . . now I shall never forget going in there . . . I didn't know where they were . . . my 600-odd . . . It was Saturday, I was on my own . . . I was walking down the pathway and all I could hear was a Scotch voice, sort of crooning, "Sai deer to me, said dear to me, aye sai deer to me," and I thought, my God, I know that voice . . . and the further I got down the more it came louder and suddenly I heard a voice say "Natsu" in Japanese. That's number 7 . . . And I looked round and there was this stone—Anderson—7 was his camp number . . . we had to learn our numbers . . . they were all around him. All the blokes I was looking for. And I thought, my golly, you've brought me to where they are . . . so that made me think that time, that Saturday . . . there's a reason for me coming back . . . I've got to make my time in Hong Kong count . . . that place [the cemetery] seems to draw me. Always something happening to do with it . . . It's been a tool for me: given me a reason for living.

From the late sixties Jack's life continues in more settled proximity to the war memorial and soldiers' bones. The relics of an old story are woven into new ones. Jack's reason for moving to Hong Kong continues to define the organization and substance of his daily life. Jack's body has become a war memorial, cast in flesh and bones.

Soldiering On

In the service of his ghosts, his fellow soldiers who didn't survive Japanese internment, Jack turns his life into a series of campaigns. "I got myself involved in the local community . . . Everyone knows me through my work, with the ex-servicemen mainly." Jack traveled daily on a journey that requires two buses, through a ceaseless flow of traffic, to the British Legion, renamed the World War II Veterans Association after 1997. Poor health reduced his visits to twice a week. His wife, Polly, began to travel with him after he collapsed one day. His legs are now a little unsteady.

It's only voluntary now . . . I'm the chairman of the local organization . . . I'm the man who does all the fundraising for them . . . We cater for about nine hundred [mostly Chinese] men who use the clubhouse . . . It's a place where they come and play mahjong [and have lunch] . . . they're all retired now . . . we look after them when they go sick. Thankfully now most of them have got pensions so we only got to look after widows mainly, or new cases.

His work at the Legion is about

picking up the pieces . . . all the enquiries, trying also to fill in the gaps, because there is no end of gaps to be filled in . . . people who would like to find the answer . . . [There are] a lot of Americans in Hong Kong. Most of them work in construction, often ex-servicemen, not from *the* [Second World] war [but the Vietnam War] . . . lots of them [are] ex-Marines because they're good for security work. Three years [ago] I met a Marine. [He] used to come in regularly, used to sit where you are now, because he was in a flat near where the fighting [during the Second World War] was in Hong Kong. And he used to like to go wandering around there, and he'd always come in here, [with] something he'd picked up. And he picked up one day two spoons, old and rusty. [He] cleaned them up . . . and we found a name on them . . . and we traced [the owner of] one . . . He's back in the States now, unfortunately, but he still dreams that one day he'll be able to get that [second spoon] back into the hands of a relative.

Jack finds common cause with an America soldier from a different war who has his own version of war's unfinished business. He continues:

I'm like an encyclopedia, they say. I know exactly where to put my hands on the enquiries I still get, for relatives, people who were buried here . . . I keep the records . . . I get no end of letters, still. Its not from widows now, it's from nephews and sons and grandsons. Something gets given to them when somebody dies and it starts . . . I get some lovely letters back, because they are able to close a chapter. Not only able to close a chapter, they know somebody is looking after the grave.

Jack becomes the universal soldier, his remit extended to include more recent wars. He is on ghost duty. He deals with his own ghosts and directs others to theirs. Different wars, enemies, methods of soldiering, and untimely death merge in Jack's life. He is actively involved in the politics of war commemoration and restitution. He recalls his coup at the 1999 Barbados Commonwealth Conference. Here he succeeds in getting the commemorative gates on Constitution Hill in central London, intended to mark the contribution of soldiers from the Indian subcontinent to both world wars, extended to include all of the soldiers who fought with the Allies. He lobbied the Fijians and the Indians. He fixed it with the Canadians and the Australians. "I said look this is all bloody wrong it should be remembering the whole lot . . . the Chinese, the Eurasian, the mixed people." He is in London for the opening of the gates ceremony. He is a regular visitor to

Japan, where he lobbies for compensation and apology from the Japanese government to former POWs. He speaks knowledgably about the intricacies of Japanese politics, including gender politics. Wherever there is a military reunion or the commemoration of a Second World War anniversary, Jack is there. His geographic and ethnic cartographies are drawn in the alignments of this war. Britain and its allies drew on the military forces of their empires. For Jack this makes common cause out of older, more difficult, more oppressive alliances. This is what charts his path through the city and beyond, and fills his days with activity and meaning. "That's been good therapy for me, you see, getting down to the Legion, because I'm living, you see, while I do this work."

Drying the Flag

The Hong Kong (English-language) media report Jack's activities as though he is a living monument of colonial Britishness. What's it like being British in Hong Kong?

> All right, as far as I'm concerned. A lot of people don't like being British here, but I like being British here. I'm proud of my [he does not complete this thought], I'm still in the Welsh choir and I've flown a Union Jack off this balcony. When Princess Diana died that day, flew that Union Jack. And of course it was long after the handover . . . Thousands of people came to see it on this estate, and were so proud it was up again . . . they came in the morning and said, "How long are you leaving it up, Mr. Edwards?" And I said, "I'll leave it up the whole day." "Have you asked?" I said, "No, let them come here and take it down . . . I'm going to take it down—not when government tell me—I'm going to take it down as we do in Great Britain when it's sundown . . ." And people got to know me about it. I got stopped on the underground . . . It shows that they're still clinging to the beliefs [of empire] . . . I've got that Union Jack in there. [*He's nodding towards the cupboard in his flat*] . . . A real Union Jack, which worked . . . All those years during the occupation it was hidden away from the Japanese [they buried it, so local legend goes,] and Arthur May got out of captivity and got it up before the British fleet arrived. Just to show that Britain was reclaiming Hong Kong . . . before the fleet came in.

Following the defeat of the occupying force, Japan, Hong Kong's status as a British colony was swiftly reestablished against the possibility that China might try

to reclaim it. This performance of Britishness connects a Welsh choir, a dead princess, and a military reclaiming of empire. It displays divergent uses of a flag, separated by more than fifty years, connected in the routine details of a life.

Jack sends Polly to look for flag pictures. Polly's role is backstage. She is tea maker, secretary, finder of press cuttings, keeper of the war medals, smoother of the military jacket, nurse, travel co-coordinator, life partner, and soul mate. Polly—beautiful, nimble, and in her seventies—is a migrant from a bigger source of crossborder traffic. A dancer with the Beijing Ballet, she came to Hong Kong to escape the Cultural Revolution in the early seventies. Her husband, a high-ranking officer in the Chinese army, was to join Polly and their baby daughter in Hong Kong. He never did. She survived by teaching dance. Then she met Jack. Polly produces a photograph in which Jack is pictured in the *South China Morning Post* with flag and medals: an icon of empire's military campaigns.

There are more flag stories. The flag unearthed by Arthur May was also flown in the pageant marking the end of empire in the handover ceremonies of 1997. It takes Jack to Government House, the governor's official residence. He lends the flag to the last governor, the Queen's representative in Hong Kong, so that it can be flown in the ceremonies marking Hong Kong's transition to China. On the day of the ceremony it is raining heavily. All British migrants have a "handover" story. Jack's is about the flag. "It got brought back [to his flat after the ceremony] by the police, soaking wet . . . and the first thing we did was put it up on the balcony to dry it." There is a mischievous twinkle in Jack's eye at having to fly the Union flag in so innocent a cause immediately after it was stripped of its symbolic power. What does he think about empire?

> This is a Chinese place, it's a Chinese city. It's theirs. It was only ours to borrow, sort of thing, I used to say to Chris Patten, you know: We've only got a loan of it, and let's make the best of the place . . . I was very annoyed with the British Government, the way they were dealing with Hong Kong at the time of the handover. [He is referring to the denial of British passports to all but a handful of Hong Kong residents] . . . they [the British Government] were doing nothing for the people who'd fought for Hong Kong . . . I mean the local people. Chinese, Eurasians . . . and of course a few British who were here . . . I thought it was very wrong we were leaving them behind. And won that battle first only to find to my horror it didn't apply to their wives. It's ridiculous . . . Anyway, I won that one eventually . . . not only for those who had wives, but for those who had widows left from the war . . . twenty-eight of them.

Jack's stories are abruptly interrupted by the arrival of his travel agent with the tickets for his trip with Polly to Singapore. He is to attend a military reunion of an ever declining number of old soldiers. Jack conducts his business with the agent in rapid Cantonese.

Jack has a sad and complex relationship with recent history. He has reworked his military past into a commemoration and restitution enterprise. He runs the Causeway Bay British Legion Clubhouse, where old Chinese soldiers gather to play mahjong and eat rice. He speaks the language. He has made a home in Hong Kong. The most significant intimate relationship of his life is with a Chinese woman. He belongs to a (Hong Kong) Welsh choir. He keeps a flat in Cardiff where his sister lives, although he rarely visits. These concrete daily arrangements are made by his ghosts. The past is not over but now lives more easily on the surface of his life.

MAKING NEW LIVES

An Ordinary Life(style)

From Jack's flat in the New Territories, take the bus to the southern part of Kowloon. Get off on Nathan Road, as the bus leaves Mong Kok. Walk along Gascoigne Road and branch left up the hill to a group of high-rise apartment buildings. Pass the terrace and the communal swimming pool to find the right building and take the elevator to the seventeenth floor. Here behind an ordinary wooden door to an ordinary three-bedroom apartment you will find the Trent family. You will meet Peter and Mary, who, in their late forties, look young and energetic, and Jess, who is sporty and seventeen. From time to time you will meet their friends. You won't meet Emily or Will, the older Trent children (twenty and twenty-two). They are in Britain at university, studying sports science. This is the only part of the tour on which will you meet (most of) a family. The Trent family exemplifies how migration works in different ways in the lives of family members: producing different versions of the future. The Trent family and their friends will guide us through a key theme in migrant settlement: temporariness, which is further challenging because they are long-term settlers, which is a distinction made in migration literature between these scales of intention. "Long-term," "temporary," and "contract" are used to signify migrants' temporalities in the literature on migration. The Trent family helps us to begin unpacking the contours and content of lifestyle migration. The Trent family also reveals how the shifting political landscape of Hong Kong in transition reverberates through migrant lives. We will join Peter and Mary in their living room sitting on the sofa facing a large sliding window that opens onto their balcony and a view of the intersection of elevated roads below but the noise and dust from the constant stream of traffic below makes opening the window and using the balcony impractical. We pick up their migration story where it began; with a single journey and uncertainty about where it might lead.

Peter and Mary and their two small children arrived in Hong Kong on a steaming hot day in July in the late 1980s after a seventeen-hour flight from London. They arrived through the old airport in Kowloon. The high-rises in this part of Kowloon are shorter, making the navigation of the runway less perilous on the flight deck, and offering passengers sudden, alarming views into the apartments. Sudden sightings of complete strangers were Peter and Mary's first glimpse of Hong Kong. It was also the beginning of what turns into a new life, a long way from Nottingham in Midlands Britain. New lives begin suddenly. This is the nature of migration. Mary explains it.

I suppose that like many people we were struggling. I was at home. We managed; we didn't have a lot of money. And Peter saw this job advertised for a surveyor to go to Hong Kong. And he said, "Shall I apply?" And I don't think I thought very much of it . . . A few months later he got an offer and we just said we were coming. . . . for two and a half years. And we both thought, well, if we don't like it two and a half years is not very long; we'll come back. It seemed a big thing. . . . years ago this place was a lot further away from Britain than it is now. . . . [It was] the only time we traveled business class. We didn't even know there was business class because we'd never done anything like that before . . . We were in a hotel for five weeks when we came. We'd never stayed in a hotel before, so that was quite nice. . . . the Empress . . . Somebody showed us around.

A single decision, that Peter should take the job as a surveyor with the (colonial) Hong Kong Housing Authority, opens onto a life path that takes the family on a journey to the other side of the world. Mary, who is pregnant with their third child (Jess), wheels the buggy round the city filling up those early days with activity and doing her best to get her two small charges out of the hotel during the day while Peter is at work. Mary finds this dense, unfamiliar, urban landscape hard to navigate. It is hot and humid and not particularly child-friendly. She vividly recalls those early days. The story she tells to explain what it felt like is the story of how she fainted from the heat and no one stopped to help her. For Mary this reveals the local Chinese attitude to foreigners and to proffering assistance to others in public places. She is a long way from home, family, and friends, and has not yet made new friends. As the steamy summer gave way to autumn and winter, Mary is thrilled at the contrast with Britain, where it is starting to get cold. Still wandering the streets with her small charges Mary would wander past Jack and buy a poppy for Remembrance Day. The old soldier with his medals and tray of poppies is something familiar from home.

The young family's first two years in Hong Kong were marked by the death of close family members. This brings them home abruptly, briefly, and then back again to their new lives, feeling a bit stunned and with a sense of loss-at-a-distance. Their story is both unique to them and similar to others' stories; ordinary lives recast in migration, an advertisement, an interview, a flight, a new life in a new place. By the time the Trents set off for Hong Kong the British Government had reached a settlement with China for its return. This period of late colonial migration is less certain for those whose lives it shapes than earlier periods. No one knows when life will become untenable, and have to be recast, suddenly.

An edge of uncertainty settles permanently over the Trents' and their friends' lives. The arrangements returning Hong Kong are in place. A date is set.

Mary and Peter make a life in Hong Kong. They fit in. An apartment on the Kowloon Peninsula, not far from the old airport, comes with the job. This becomes their neighborhood, although they move about within it, as accommodation is constantly reallocated. End-of-contract leave every two and a half years eases them out of the colony and their apartment, and then into another one on their return. These standard conditions of colonial service, with their temporalities of furlough and leave, set the rhythms of migrant life for the Trents and many other British families whose circumstances are cast in similar contractual arrangements. Their three children grow up and roam the city confidently in taxis, meeting up with friends and circulating between the clubs in which their parents have memberships. They participate, like their friends, in various sports games. They move easily back and forth between Hong Kong and Britain for family visits and, later, for university. There is a well-trodden route between Hong Kong's English Schools' Foundation (ESF) and British universities. In the ESF system, which we will tour later on, the Trent children are educated in ethnically mixed classes of highly motivated students, intent on success. Their classmates are children expatriated from a range of Western countries, including professional Indian and Chinese families. They are also educated with a growing number of local Chinese children wanting to learn English even as Chinese schools phased it out after 1997.

The Trents are not in Hong Kong for the jobs or the money, but for the lifestyle these things support. Mary tells us:

> We've got the flats and then the podium downstairs with the swimming pool. The children have a lovely lifestyle, you know. They'd come home and go downstairs to play on their own ... if you wanted a full-time helper you could have one. ... we have good holidays, which we never had in the UK, we never had any spare money. ...
>
> A lot of people [adds Peter] come here to make money and then leave. That's their objective. We've never looked at it like that. Any spare money we have we spend traveling.

Exotic Far Eastern locations are easily accessible from Hong Kong. Thailand, Australia, Vietnam, the Philippines, and other places in the region are the scenes of frequent family holidays. Flexible boundaries are drawn delineating a quality of life that is acceptable, from luxury and being spoilt, which is not acceptable. Being ordinary is important to Peter and Mary. Ordinariness places limits on the kind of life that can be led and strikes a distance with the social relationships they associate with colonial Hong Kong. Ordinariness restricts how much domestic

labor can be contracted out to "helpers." This is the official government term for those who were in the (colonial) past referred to as *ahmers* or maids. Ordinariness also restricts the circumstances in which domestic labor can be reallocated. It is justifiable when women work, but not when they sit by the swimming pool or pursue their hobbies. Connections with the serving class exemplify the social relationships of empire for the Trents and their friends; something they are anxious to reconfigure. Mary says that

> I didn't like that old colonial sort of thing either anyway, it's a bit like the *ahmers* . . .
> they want to call you *madame* and I don't like it, I always say, "Call me Mary," "Call
> me Mary." They like to look up to you . . . I work in a kindergarten . . . [It's] international [and] . . . a mixed bunch. I only work mornings there and then I do private
> tuition because I'm not a teacher, I just read to them and we do games. . . . I didn't
> work when the children were small. . . . It's easy to get jobs here especially if you are
> English because so many have gone. . . . always jobs for native English speakers. . . .
> There are some women who really do have, like they have a driver and they have a full-
> time maid. . . . at clubs playing tennis, meeting for lunch, that sort of thing. . . . on the
> island. . . . Then people like me who try to live quite an ordinary sort of lifestyle.

The year 1997 tested Hong Kong forecasting and decision making. Hong Kong Chinese able to secure citizenship in countries like Canada and Australia left. Many later returned when it seemed like it was business as usual. Mary said, "We just thought, well, we'll stay . . . and if things change dramatically." On the surface things went on as before. For the Trents staying on meant being part of a dwindling British expatriate group. Large numbers of their friends and children's friends left in 1997. Those who remained then trickled out of Hong Kong, reconfiguring their plans. Friends made among new arrivals were more temporary as migrant stays were shortened by new kinds of contracts. Staying meant watching others go. The loss of friendships has heightened meaning in the absence of extended family.

For Mary, staying on meant the loss of neighborhood camaraderie:

> If you look at where we live now there's hardly any expatriates. . . . Now there's just us
> and Bill [the policeman who lives downstairs]. . . . From where we live there used to
> be two school bus–loads of kids going off to school. . . . Now you . . . I started going to
> work. . . I became occupied in a different way.

It brought changes in Peter's work:

I was probably at the end of when they were employing expatriates. In my department there are 15,000 people. Which, I am one of twelve or thirteen expatriates now, so there's not many left. Even when I started there were only thirty. And then come, '96 they said, "We are not going to renew your contract unless you meet a number of conditions." One was naturalize as a Hong Kong resident, which was no problem, form filling and paying money. The second was learning a level of Cantonese, which I did although it doesn't bring you up to a working level . . . No [free] flights [back to Britain]. There was no flat [to go with the job]. It was still a contract at that time . . . Then shortly after that they gave me the option of a permanent job. . . . To be honest one of the reasons [for staying], family aside, is that you wouldn't fit in [in Britain].

Was it Peter securing a permanent job, or recognition that Hong Kong was the only home their children knew, that unravels some of the temporariness in their lives? Mary says:

So he's now on a permanent salaried job . . . Every two years we used to wonder . . . You were never sure you . . . so you were living temporarily . . . You know, should we buy that. . . . started to buy bits [of furniture] we really then decided this was home. . . it's their [the children's] home.

Staying on after 1997 meant fitting in slightly differently, as Peter suggests. It meant making more of an effort. This suited Peter and Mary. Their lives went on much as before, but at a more comfortable distance from the social relations of empire, as Peter explains.

Before 1997 when it was a British colony there was this definite gap—not respect, but almost false sense of, respect isn't the word. But now I have to fall in with what everybody else wants . . . People's English is good, and they know I've made an effort to learn Cantonese.

When we joined [the local club] it was an armed services club and there was an almost total colonial mentality then. I used to cringe sometimes . . . Now it's a much better mix and the atmosphere is much more relaxed . . . more locals. Yeah, that's the way it's going to go.

Staying on placed more local Chinese people in their social scene. But it did not make deep connections. These too remained on the surface as Mary suggests.

I can't say I have a lot of local friends, but I am quite friendly with people where we live. . . . Lots of my friends are mixed couples. . . . majority of the teachers are English. . . . they [the Chinese] are very nice people but different to us. . . . local children tend to spend a lot of time studying. . . . lots of homework. . . . they don't do a lot of sporting activities because of workload . . . you have to have an interview to get into kindergarten and you have lots of homework. . . . they don't hold doors . . . it's just their culture, really . . . I can't honestly say we've got lots of local friends. . . . they tend to use the club in a different way. You don't see them sitting by the pool [but at family dinners]. . . . they play tennis a lot and they've got lawn bowling and you do see some of them swimming. . . . this place has really changed a lot . . . I've never experienced [witnessed] any racial prejudice or anything.

Along with work the club is important in their exposure to Chinese people. But rather than expand their social networks in Chinese directions it seems to reseal selective cultural privacies. We will tour the club later and take a closer look.

Day-trip to Shenzhen

Staying, going, and temporary living are topics of conversation on Mary's cross-border shopping trip to Shenzhen with her friend Nellie. Shopping in the Shenzhen Special Economic Zone (SEZ) is an occasional day-trip for the two women. Twenty years ago Shenzhen was a quiet village surrounded by a rice paddy. It is now a motor of China's economic growth. SEZs are capsules of accelerated growth resulting from direct foreign investment, partitioned from China's centrally planned economy by a degree of autonomy. Shenzhen is the largest and most successful SEZ. It sustains massive factory production of a wide range of products aimed at export. It attracts uncounted millions of rural migrant factory workers and is constantly being extended. Being the world's factory provides plenty of opportunities for local retail. This is why the women visit. Things are cheaper in Shenzhen than in Hong Kong. The women have clothes, curtains, and other items made there by skilled tailors. Thriftiness is a part of ordinariness as far as Nellie, a no-nonsense British northerner, is concerned.

The women meet at the mainline KCR station in Kowloon. The train to Lo Wu on the mainland boarder takes about forty minutes. On the train with them are a couple of other expat shoppers as well as local Chinese traders. Traders have extra-large shopping carts and wheeled suitcases they will bring back fully loaded with discounted goods they will sell in Hong Kong's markets. A handful of

affluent mainland Chinese shoppers are heading back in the opposite direction, into China, laden with designer carrier bags from expensive stores in the central district of Hong Kong Island. At Lo Wu the women move quickly through the checkpoints showing their Hong Kong permanent residents cards.

They move slowly through the stalls and shops in the five-story mall attached to the station that makes shopping from Hong Kong easier. The rest of Shenzhen is more difficult to negotiate, especially in English, and the women can get what they need in this mall at the station. Nelly is picking up the curtains she commissioned last week from a tailor. They will go with the sofa she and her husband bought only last week. After twenty years in Hong Kong they finally buy a sofa of their own, only eighteen months ahead of Norman's retirement. The two women share the joke and the understanding of migration upon which it is based.

Nelly and Norman came to Hong Kong when they were thirty years old to "do something a bit daring." She was a civil servant working for the UK Government Department of Health and Social Security and Norman was an architect. Norman's job is more easily transported, and he secured their move with a two-and-a-half-year contract. Moving apartments every two and a half years between rental properties supplied and furnished (until 1997) by the (colonial) authorities gave them a sense of temporariness. Their children, aged fifteen, nine, and four, settled into school and applied a brake on any plans their parents might have formulated for onward or return mobility. As one child completed a significant stage of their education, the next would be at another crucial stage, making it difficult to move. Not quite managing to leave they ended up staying: temporarily. There are other factors making life temporary, too. Norman and Nelly disagree about the future. She thinks she would like to stay in Hong Kong but knows they can't afford to. She thinks he would like to return to Britain. She only thinks this; it is not something they can discuss. One of their sons lives in Hong Kong. The other lives in Britain. Their daughter lives in Italy. All three see Hong Kong as a place to return. Will that be checked if their parents move back to Britain or on to somewhere else? A crisis looms. Norman retires in eighteen months. They have a new sofa and new curtains and no agreement on where the future might place them. Small decisions are easier to make than big ones. The curtains look very nice, and Nelly is pleased with them.

The two women stop for lunch just outside the mall, in an enormous restaurant that seats five hundred diners on large round tables, served by an army of waiters in bright flowery suits. Lunch is one of two treats in a day that otherwise has a very ordinary purpose in household shopping. They order steaming baskets of dim sum and grapple expertly with them using chopsticks. After a bit more shopping in the mall they head into one of its many grooming salons for the second of the day's treats: a foot massage before taking the train back to Kowloon. Nelly feels still more strongly about ordinariness than Mary. She is, she says, "not a normal expat." She means that she does not spend her day sitting by the pool: the iconic scene of the tropical leisure class. She means that she has "never had a maid" but always done her own housework and childcare. Not being serviced is important to her sense of ordinariness. This is sharpened by a strong moral compass, which stipulates for Nelly the way migrant life ought to be lived: in purposeful activity. Nelly has always had a job and contributed financially to the family. Mindful of the circumstances of other migrants she also worked in Hong Kong's Vietnamese refugee camps, where she met Mary, until they were closed because they were no longer needed.

Tired from their day out the two women once more pass through the border and take the train back to Kowloon.

Inside the Expatriate Bubble

> It's not the best place to have a rabbit. —JANE

The Trent family apartment is neater than when Mary left it. It is one of the days when her part-time domestic helper comes round to clean up. The place is quiet. Peter is not yet back from work and her younger daughter Jess and Jess's friend Jane are home from field hockey practice and comparing homework. Both will sit the British A-level examinations that guard university entrance next year.

Jess is not staying on. She was born in Hong Kong, and this is the only life she knows. Jess is an expert in the fabrication of migrant minority identities. This is something she does rather than talks; but when challenged she articulates her connections with Britain and Hong Kong like this. "England" (as she calls it) is the place she is "from" and Hong Kong is the "place where she lives." Her parents organized her connection with Britain until she was old enough to take over. The place she is from is a place she visits once a year for family holidays, staying with her British grandparents and moving around other family members. Her connections are sorted by age: she is closer to her cousins than anyone else. As she gets older her time in Britain is organized around them and their social networks and activities. It is also organized around others from her school visiting their families in Britain. Networks of Hong Kong migrants and local British teenagers converge. Jess's network gradually detaches from her parents'. She now makes her own connections only using theirs as a starting point. This is how she spends her summers. These connections will develop in new ways when she moves to Britain for three years to attend university.

Jess is more anxious in Britain around girls with whom she shares a "culture" but not a country, and where she does not have to account for herself as she does in Hong Kong. In Britain Jess is just one of the crowds. And yet she says,

> in England I feel quite uncomfortable sometimes . . . it's hard to explain, I think it is because they are the same culture and they've got a reputation for being really hard.

The British girls' make-up, clothes, and social activities are subtly different; and among teenagers subtle differences are important. The wrong cut of jeans can lead to social humiliation. She is nervous traveling around Britain alone and often travels with friends from Hong Kong. Their geographies are concentrated in the South. She says it is difficult to travel around Britain because of the "rubbish transport." She has complaints too about the weather and admits that summers spent in Britain are sometimes "boring." Being "from Britain" is a way of accounting for herself from the vantage point of how she is seen in Hong Kong. She is visibly not Chinese, so who and what is she? "English" is her answer to this question.

The place where she lives is more comfortable than the place she is from. She navigates it confidently by bus, underground, train, and taxi. She moves easily between school, sports fixtures, and field hockey training at the Kowloon Cricket Club, and the night clubs, cinemas, and bars she visits on the weekend with her friends. Jess and her network trade on their parents' social club memberships, circulating around the places where they can add their food and drinks to the family tab. Jess feels safer as a visible minority in Hong Kong than she does in Britain where she melts into the social landscape.

> I mean we've had nights out where we've stayed for the whole night, we've walked around and there's no one that comes up and approaches you. We've sat and like watched the sun rise. The clubs are quite good, they're quite expensive . . . I think being like a Westerner [in Hong Kong]; you stand out, people don't dare approach us, they sort of stick to their side . . . I think that's what I love about it. It's so easy. And safe.

Her comfort is a comfort of separation. On the streets, at school, in clubs, her circumstances are the same. She wears her minority status on her body like a large badge. She is used to standing out and prefers it.

Jess's social network is primarily generated through school. Through school she experiences her version of her parents' experience of staying on. Jane speaks for both of them:

> In my form class [grade] I'm the only white person. In our whole year of one hundred fifty there's like, ten white people . . . There used to be fifty-fifty until it got handed over to China then lots of people left . . . I wish there was more Westerners. It's a bit not lonely, but you wish there were, do you . . . more of your own people you . . .

Jess agrees. "I don't even have any Indians in my class. It's just me, and the Chinese, really." Jane adds an important distinction between local Chinese students and those whose migrant genealogies incorporate Western countries.

> Not local people . . . Canadian Chinese, Australian Chinese . . . Or they are fully Chinese but have lived there and got that passport. One of our best friends is Canadian Chinese. She's fully Chinese but if you ask where she's from she says Canada.

The girls' relationship to Chineseness is complicated by this distinction and the possibilities of closeness and distance it offers. This is repeated in the adult world in differentiating ABCs (American-born Chinese) and BBCs (British-born Chinese) from Chinese. In the drawing of microcosmic social boundaries migrant status overrides origins and ethnicity. This makes Indians closer than the majority local Chinese students. Western migrant status draws tighter boundaries and, when it comes down to it, whiteness and "Englishness" draw the tightest social group of all. Jess explains how their small, cohesive, international expatriate network operates. She is using the term "English" to include those of mixed British origins too.

> We have mainly, say, ten close friends and they're mainly English [She qualifies]. I mean we've got Egyptian, half-Egyptian half-English, [and] one [half]-Chinese girl. And then there's, say, like whites like us. And then there's the Indians that all sit together. But we do all mix. We went to a party and everyone was there, its just that we're not SO close to them. Everyone mixes. . . . Everyone's really good friends, quite an international society . . . Because I've been there so long, I walk along the corridor and get about ten "hellos". . . I just feel like this is where I belong sort of thing . . . In England no one knows me.

Jess is aware that they lead parallel lives in minimal contact with local Chinese teenagers.

We're in our own little bubble here, you know: an international community of us Westerners. You know the odd Chinese person . . . we go to our international school . . . and that's it, whereas there is a whole other life in Hong Kong which is very different from ours.

Reflecting on how the local Chinese view them from outside of the bubble, Jess says,

you . . . they don't think very much of us . . . I mean, like, you sit down [on the bus or the underground] and no one will sit next to you . . . I think they may think we're a bit loud . . . [And when it comes to buying clothes], you can't find the sizes you . . . [When the girls ask for big sizes in shops] They point and laugh at you . . . The local people especially are so different from us.

Jess expresses their relationship to local Chineseness as distant. "Just, I mean, I don't really know any . . . I mean, there's no interaction really."

Life inside the expatriate lifestyle bubble is comfortable if lonely. Internal networks are drawn to prioritize particular forms of similarity and difference. But there are clear routes out. The girls talk about living in other Southeast Asian locations as well as Australia but not Britain. They expect to live as adults as they have been shown—transnationally. They think of China as a very different place from Hong Kong, and, drawing further connections and disconnections around Chineseness they except Shanghai from this assessment. Like their parents they draw connections between cities that might be places to migrate and in so doing exclude their hinterlands. The girls work on differences recognized by their parents. But their lives and Hong Kong connections are quite differently drawn. So they take the differences their parents observe to different places. Like their parents they have "here and there" conversations that compare the merits of life in different locations. They are able to list the advantages and disadvantages of life in Hong Kong. And they agree that it's not the best place to have a rabbit!

Fabricating the City

Cities are "mobilized by flesh and stone interaction."[1] Hong Kong's architects, surveyors, builders, city planners, in concert with its seven million bodies, fabricate the city. The professionals have a disproportionate influence. Peter is a building surveyor with the Hong Kong Housing Authority. Aside from the

Government of Singapore, the Hong Kong Housing Authority is the biggest provider of public housing in the world.

In 1954 the Urban Council Emergency Committee recommended that the government become directly involved in setting up a fund to build multistory resettlement buildings to rehouse those hit by the fire in 1953. This fire had spread through the city and left many people living on the streets and in squatter settlements. A long-term solution was considered more cost-effective than providing regular emergency relief for the victims of fire and typhoons. For many local people this was a first step toward a better life, and much of the atmosphere of village life was preserved in these functional concrete blocks. Despite these efforts, by 1963 there were still 600,000 squatters, double the number of a decade earlier. This was partly due to increases in the population through migration: the arrival of refugees from China and Vietnam. This led to renewed efforts to house the population following new policy initiatives in 1964, which led to the building of high-rise developments housing 50,000 to 100,000 people.[2] The extent of building involved in these schemes has dramatically altered the landscape of Kowloon. It has also produced new towns in the New Territories between Kowloon and the border with mainland China. Many housing developments form self-contained communities with schools, medical facilities, shops, restaurants, and basketball courts.

This was the vast enterprise that Peter entered in the late 1980s when he decided that he'd had enough of building schools for Nottinghamshire City Council in Midlands Britain. He sits at his desk in his modern, open-plan office in Kowloon. His car is parked in the office parking garage below the building.

> We have a lot of regional offices as well, and I've been up there, but I've been here for the last seven years. I think actually my days are numbered, because you are only supposed to actually stay in a post for four years. It's a requirement [that] you move around. Why they haven't moved me, I don't know. To be honest it's been more of an issue since the handover . . . I'm senior maintenance surveyor . . . Setting standards for the housing blocks . . . but it's evolved into something quite different . . . where we have a problem with noncompliance with regulations . . . all sorts, anything really that no one else wants to tackle, anything that becomes an issue, asbestos, all sorts of things, which is very interesting but can be a pain because you get a lot of questions from government.

Although he has a permanent contract, Peter is worried that he hasn't been rotated between different offices recently. Rotation is customary. He suspects that he has been "parked" to serve his time to compulsory retirement at fifty-five. He is parked in "compliance." He is in charge of making sure tenants comply with the regulations governing dense high-rise living conditions. Regulations stipulate how laundry may be hung out of windows; the fixing of air conditioners no one wants to fall out of a fiftieth-story window. This is not how he wants to spend his time. Peter would like to end his working life in Hong Kong with a more significant contribution.

Peter goes out on site visits. He is accompanied by local Chinese workers from the same office. They smooth his path and interpret when necessary. They are benevolent minders who manage his movement from site to site. They mediate his interaction with the managers of the sites he visits. He is respectfully and carefully handled. Things are explained to him. He visits blocks built between the 1950s to the 1970s not far from his office in the southern part of the Kowloon Peninsula on foot. These are low-rise cement buildings with simple amenities, exposed piping, and electrical cables. Apartments are neat and compact, 33 square meters now housing three people, and not, as in the past, six. Bunks for sleeping, hanging space, a small kitchen area; a toilet containing a shower area: tenants put up internal partitions to suit their individual living-space needs. These are pleasant places with doors that open onto wide corridors to filter the breeze in the absence of air conditioning. Neighbors chat or play mahjong in each other's apartments, meet in the corridors, or congregate downstairs at the simple café that operates from a large outdoor wok. Or they meet while buying fish and vegetables from the market stalls in the ground-level area outside the apartments. The older blocks sustain high levels of social interaction.

Later Peter uses his car to visit some apartment buildings to the north. These are more modern, built only two years ago. Forty-two stories high, they contain seven hundred apartments per block, housing three thousand people in a single estate. Entrance halls are clean and bright and tiled; apartments are compact. They have marble floors and nicely finished paintwork, in contrast to the rough, unfinished look of the older cement blocks. These apartments have air conditioners, so front doors are kept closed and neighbors can no longer look in. Some doors have security grilles to discourage intruders. The informal communal life of the older blocks has given way to more formal communal life supported by theaters, basketball courts, supermarkets, and marble. Marble is the surface of modernity and social improvement.

Peter feels sidelined in an operation that is being phased out. In the new scheme of things the Hong Kong Housing Authority is undergoing a seven-year process of privatization and will be run more directly in the interests of property developers.

Subsidized ownership and private participation schemes were dropped when rents and land values began to fall in the economic downturn of the late 1990s, exacerbated by the outbreak of SARS (severe acute respiratory syndrome). This move was to avoid public housing schemes competing with rents in the private sector and the powerful interests of property developers. It came with the new political arrangements supervised by Beijing. Peter used to feel he made a difference. Now he feels like an underemployed part of a discontinued regime.

Suddenly he is given a "real job" in Shatin. He's thrilled, back on the circuit perhaps, moving every four years. He feels useful again. He puts in a request to do six months' Chinese-language immersion in China so he can get to grips with the communication gap between him and his work and local life. He hangs large Chinese characters around the walls of his office and works on learning them everyday. His request is turned down. Limits are placed on Peter fitting in. Foreigners and old colonials are managed rather than integrated into the new regime. Peter is not part of Hong Kong's future: his personal future lies elsewhere. He is granted a temporary place in the new order and is kept in it by the forces that shape his life in Hong Kong. A bit disheartened, he heads home for dinner. Mary is back from teaching, and they make dinner together rather than eat at the club.

Moving On

Anticipation of departure is part of the substance of everyday life and fitting in. Departure calculations are complicated. They are about job prospects and the quality of life and enjoyment of a place. They also involve interpretation of the broader political climate. Abrupt and prolonged periods of unemployment can lead to a recasting of connections to a place. Getting bored and wanting to be somewhere else is not uncommon. Migrants know they can move on; it is one of their skills. Like other migrants the Trent family continuously evaluates the political climate of Hong Kong, anticipating its impact on personal life and the optimum time to move on. As Peter says,

> You have to be prepared to change . . . If you are not, you should go . . . there have been a few decisions you wouldn't have got away with in a democracy . . . Beijing's in charge . . . Two or three incidents where they have put their foot down and said, right, this is what you're going to do . . . There are some injustices . . . [Critical press coverage is not encouraged.]

Peter is referring to the decision taken in Beijing to remove the right of abode in Hong Kong for mainland Chinese children with a Hong Kong parent. He is also referring to press freedom and the fact that some reporters have lost their jobs. Differences between life in Hong Kong and China are drawn around issues like the right of abode and the right to religious expression, which is limited in China. The Falun Gong, for example, is illegal in China but not in Hong Kong. Muslims have problems in China, but not in Hong Kong. People like Peter and Mary who have decided to stay accept these changes as part of broader regime change and their impact on daily life. The Anti-Subversion and Security Bill[3] provided another test case of the fragile political boundaries negotiated in British withdrawal between the two regimes. Under Hong Kong's constitution the Hong Kong SAR is required to pass security laws banning treason, sedition, subversion, and the theft of state secrets. These are issues to which the post–9/11 climate of anxiety adds urgency. The protest against the Anti-Subversion Security Bill, spearheaded by the Civil Human Rights Front, wants to delay the implementation of article 23 until after 2007 when universal suffrage is introduced. This would provide a check against Beijing using article 23 to suppress political freedom and free speech. Peter and Mary and their friends don't feel strongly about universal suffrage. It didn't exist when Hong Kong was a colony either. But they join in the chorus of protest against Hong Kong's political leader, the chief executive, Bei-

jing's man, for a whole string of political blunders that affect everyone's future. This is felt more keenly by the majority of Hong Kong Chinese without foreign passports, who have no escape route if things work out badly.

These transitional political upheavals make Peter, Mary, and their friends nervous. They provide reminders that they live on a shifting political landscape in the orbit of mainland China. Their time in Hong Kong could end abruptly. There must be a plan to leave on short notice. Peter and Mary's sense of temporariness, now that he has a permanent contract of employment, resides in the shifting political conditions in which the Chinese government deals with its citizens and, by extension, its migrants. If Beijing is willing to revoke its former right of abode commitments, will it still pay the pensions of long-term resident-immigrants like Peter? He would lose substantially by failing to identify the right moment to leave.

Staying on means being permanently ready to leave, so that the anticipation of departure is also a way of staying, a way of dwelling: a feature of migrant life.

The prospect of moving on is implicit in everyday conversation. It is behind every calculation and mundane purchase. Peter and Mary cope with this by insisting that they don't plan far ahead; that they live in the moment. Even so, Peter's job carries a nonnegotiable retirement date, and the gap in a privatizing public service he has occupied for many years is closing. Aside from political calculations this raises the issue of what they will do when Peter retires in six or seven years. They own a house in the UK, they rent in Hong Kong, but they have not lived in the UK since the late eighties. Although Peter declares that "my heart's in Croxton in Leicestershire, where I was brought up," he has reservations about returning. These are about fitting in, ironically the skill he has learned living in Hong Kong. Mary does not share his ambivalent commitment: "I'm not going there. . . . I'd rather go to Australia. . . . Just go for a few years and just see whether we like it. . . . Our children all like sport . . . and there's a lot of opportunities." A different form of partial citizenship is available to them there, as Peter explains:

> If you apply before you are fifty and you have a certain amount of liquid assets you can go as a retiree. But you can't work; you can't own property unless it's new, and you can't use public services . . . libraries, health and education . . . That's my understanding.

In the next few years the Trent family—individually or in small groups—will be back at the airport for their final departure from Hong Kong, declaring an end to the lives they have made there. It is unlikely that they will go back to Britain. They are considering taking a route that is increasingly well trodden by expats: from Hong Kong to Shanghai. Here they would freelance, filling the demand for English, retrained as English teachers. Meanwhile, their son is finishing his university course in Britain and heading for a teacher-training course in Perth, Australia. Jess will join her elder sister at university in Britain. Family life is reformulated and moved to new locations.

THE ENGLISH BUSINESS

The Schools and Language Game

The English business elaborates its own lines of separation. Business brought the British to Hong Kong and then English became a business. It served British migrants for whom it provided an alternative to the uncomfortable proximities that might have been forged with the local Chinese population through their language. The English business is not just about language, it is about the business of being English in migration. Being able to operate in English, not having to learn Cantonese, is a privilege and a form of separation. Jess and Jane's description above of the "expat bubble" suggests a vibrant linguistic/cultural/bodily separation is still maintained. Being able to use English as a language of daily operation generates the expat bubble. The English Schools Foundation (ESF) is significant in maintaining lines of separation and the colonial language in postcolonial times.

The teaching of English in Chinese schools ended with the empire in 1997. This simply generated a new demand from Chinese parents concerned about their children's employment prospects and the SAR's global competitive edge. The English language and British education are booming businesses in postcolonial Hong Kong. Institutional support for this comes from the state and private school system and the operation of the British Council. The British Council broker access to British universities through a web of education fairs promoting the UK education "product" as a global currency that can be cashed in transnational labor markets. English is rebranded as the language of international business success.[1] It is now tied to Hong Kong's survival as a viable city of international commerce in competition with Beijing and Shanghai. The colonial stain on British qualifications has similarly been rebranded as an "international" gold standard in negotiating access to British and other leading world university brands: the educational equivalent of wearing Gucci. The new (postcolonial) relationship between Britain, Hong Kong, and China includes the transfer of funds paid by Chinese students as fees to British universities, a significant source of funding for UK higher education. The English business has modern (postcolonial) inscriptions.

Our tour moves on to the western end of Hong Kong Island. From the Trents' flat in Kowloon the underground Mass Transit Railway (MRT) from Jordan Station on Kowloon's main artery, Nathan Road, connects the Kowloon Peninsula with Hong Kong Island at Sheung Wan. From there buses wind southwest to Pokfulam, traversing the low green mountains to the east, which take up the middle of Central Island, to the West Island School. This is a modern block-like structure

that feels a long way (although it isn't) from the dense urban bustle of the central district. The school is part of the ESF system and a good place to pierce the expat bubble described by Jess and Jane. It also opens onto a new segment of migrant lives, employed in the English business as teachers.

The reproduction of the British education system at a distance from Britain and high teachers' wages[2] makes ESF schools attractive to (adventurous or disillusioned) British and other English-speaking—Australian, New Zealander, American, and Canadian—teachers. Zoë and Daniel are two of these teachers. The West Island School enabled them to transfer to the same job in a different place, in a different set of work and social conditions, and for higher wages. The English business allowed them to trade old jobs and lives in London for new ones in Hong Kong without having to retrain or learn a new language or a new education system. Their stories reveal further layers in the meaning of lifestyle migration offered by the Trents and their friends. Zoë and Daniel expose a tension between work and leisure, as well as ambivalence to Hong Kong and Britain as (personally) significant but disturbing places.

Zoë and Daniel prioritized leaving Britain over positively choosing Hong Kong. Their story exposes the limited knowledge with which migrants migrate. It describes what migration scholars describe as "push factors" not usually attributed to Western migrants. They display migrations' disconnections, something poorly understood among scholars who prioritize connections.[3] Their stories slow down the flow of activity in which decisions with far-reaching consequences are made. Like the other stories yet to be told, their connections with Hong Kong reveals a spectrum of relationships with Chineseness. First we will tour the ESF system and its place in Hong Kong's education landscape.

The British education system in Hong Kong is instituted through the ESF and the British-oriented International Schools. It is as highly stratified as the Chinese system in which it sits. It differentiates among British and English-speaking migrants; and sifts Chinese applicants for their ability to operate in English within British educational culture. Potentially a key mechanism of migrant-local Chinese interaction, it protects British migrants from the most challenging (cultural/linguistic) aspects of migration and provides a source of employment for British and other English-speaking teachers.

At the top of this system are the British-oriented International Schools. These were set up in the late 1960s to serve the upper echelons of the colonial and business class and local Chinese of comparable status, income, and transnational inclination. Kelletts School is a good example. It takes pupils between the ages of three and ten, when children can be offshored in British boarding schools. English language is the medium of instruction. The curriculum is British and British OFSTED inspections—providing standard indicators of educational achievement and comparability across schools—are routinely applied. Fees are high,[4] and no child is accepted without a capital contribution (called a debenture) in addition to the fees. Priority in the allocation of school places is given to corporate debentures over those raised by individuals. Places at International Schools, like overseas boarding school fees, are part of the "package" of corporate employment benefits of the global elite.

Money is not the only social filter. Kelletts School announces itself as serving "the English speaking community of Hong Kong" describing the parents of its pupils as "high-achieving expatriates." This filters the local Chinese elite for its diaspora returning from Western countries where they have been educated in English. International schools are key to the interaction between this elite Chinese diaspora and English-speaking (British, American, Canadian, Australian) migrants.

The next tier down in this educational hierarchy is the ESF[5] system, also set up in the sixties (1967) to provide a "modern liberal education"[6] for children of middle-ranking colonial functionaries and business people. It follows the British national curriculum at all levels; the students sit British (GCSE, GNVQ, and A-level) examinations in addition to the International Baccalaureate; and educational standards are assured through OFSTED inspections. The language curriculum also now includes Mandarin, but not the local Chinese language, Cantonese. There is new emphasis post-1997 on the Hong Kong and Southeast Asia[7] context, content, and value system. This implies British quality with a local accent. The ESF system announces that it welcomes "students of all nations who can be educated through the English language": a less severe social (ethnic) filter than the international schools apply. This new spirit of inclusion is also pragmatic. The departure of the colonial class in 1997 produced a student deficit. The ESF system has its own Chinesization process in parallel with other institutions. Consequently 70 percent of ESF students are now local Chinese. The majority expatriate groups originate from the Indian subcontinent with the British a tiny (protected) minority, as Jess and Jane report.

The ESF system still prioritizes "English-speaking children for whom no other suitable educational facilities are available." This allows reconfigured colonials and global operatives outside of the mainstream corporate system to continue to operate in English only. While anticipating bilingual Chinese students eager for an English-language (British) education (with a local accent), the ESF system simultaneously protects an English-language minority from the consequences of its minority status. These circumstances give the "ability to operate effectively in English" entry requirement a new meaning. It is now a focus for contention between the ESF system and Chinese parents eager for entry. As compulsory teaching of English in Chinese state schools ended, so the demand for an ESF education among Chinese parents, mindful of its global benefits and able to pay the fees,[8] increased. The ESF system is also an attractive option because its fee structure is government-subsidized to the tune of HK$299 million (29 percent of the ESF budget).[9] Until these subsidies are phased out, the ESF system is attractively priced. The ESF system maintains British qualifications as a gold standard, guaranteeing entry to universities all over the world. Ninety-five percent of ESF students go on to university,[10] including "the best international higher education" at Oxford, Cambridge, Harvard and Yale.

The ESF system offers an alternative for some students to the Chinese system. This is equally highly stratified, with aptitude testing producing a three-band secondary system leading to the Hong Kong Certificate of Education Examinations (HKCEE, GCSE equivalent) and Hong Kong Advanced Level Education (HKALE, A-level equivalent). In mapping the free, highly stratified, state-funded Chinese system, the International Schools, and the ESF system onto the local social and economic landscape it is important to note that the average income in Hong Kong[11] makes all but free, state education inaccessible to most of the population.

Trading Places

Now we shift from the macrocontours of the Hong Kong education landscape to a microlevel at the West Island School. Here the deafening noise of the bell signals a change of lessons and a thousand pupils—the Trents' younger daughter and her friends among them—converge on the stairwell from many directions. The friction created between bodies causes a human logjam. Daniel and his big Australian colleague Matt, the physical education (PE) teacher, are circumstantially trapped into "stair duty." They ease the flow of uniformly dressed adolescent bodies in transit to the next lesson by pushing the pupils coming downstairs into a more rapid flow, and holding back those who must go upstairs until their passage becomes clearer. It's the same routine every day. There are too many bodies in too little space with a limited window of opportunity for moving from one place (and subject) to the next. Many of the Chinese state-run schools have dealt with their swelling student population by time-sharing the building. The early shift, complete with its own head, teachers, and administration, operates from 6:00 am until midday when the late shift takes over. Daniel has been up since 4:30 this morning working on his lesson plans for the day, having spent his evening as "parents evening" and is in no mood for crowd control.

Although it is only four years since Daniel's first day in Hong Kong, his arrival feels like a lifetime ago. Migration is a steep learning curve. Daniel had sat on the floor of their yet-to-be-furnished (1100 square foot) apartment in Aberdeen on the southwest side of Hong Kong Island not far from the school. This is a location favored by ESF teachers with a certain level of benefits package. With a view of Lamma and outlying Islands shimmering in the South China Sea, Daniel, who was jobless and more than slightly cast adrift, is excited at the prospect of new beginnings. Zoë is out all day teaching modern languages and, no sooner has Daniel begun to wonder what to do with so much free time than Zoë learns that the school needs a part-time psychology teacher and Daniel lands the job. Combining this with a second part-time job teaching sociology in another ESF school not too far away Daniel juggles two jobs, eventually ending up with a full-time job in the same school as Zoë. A more consolidated existence opens up for the couple and provides the structure for their new life as migrants.

The string of events that led to Daniel sitting on the floor of their apartment gazing into the future and the South China Sea were precipitous and catalyzed by Zoë's career. Young, lively, and at an early stage in her career, Zoë was teaching in a tough inner London school where an eruption of student violence had culminated in a murder. Modern languages are never an easy call in British inner-city schools. For the pupils of this school, whose lives were marked by multiple levels of social difficulty, education was not a high priority. This makes teaching a difficult, frustrating, and sometimes dangerous job. Daniel, who in his early fifties is two decades older than Zoë, was teaching part-time in a London further education college. Ironically given his skills in stair duty, he was feeling as though his job was mainly about "crowd control" rather than teaching and learning. Add to this mix of job frustration and poor pay, high mortgage payments, and the negative equity in their house. As Daniel put it, "desperate circumstances require desperate measures." Their circumstances propelled the couple toward a vaguely formed version of another life they could live in some other place: "abroad." With this Zoë began to apply for jobs in places where modern language teachers were needed—Africa and the Middle and the Far East. Neither had given much thought to her applications for Hong Kong or Singapore. Not having visited either place they had only a hazy idea of what life would be like.

Until the phone rang in London at 5:00 am one spring morning. The head-mistress of the West Island School was on the line with a job offer for Zoë. She would give her fifteen minutes to consider her offer and then call back. Knowing nothing about life in Hong Kong or the value of the Hong Kong dollar attached to Zoë salary offer, the couple made a cup of tea and considered the prospect of a radically remodeled future. After Zoë had accepted the job they converted her new salary into British pounds and discovered it was twice as much as she was earning in London, even on the local contract which she had been offered. The expatriate deals of the past had long since been withdrawn. This was the route by which Daniel had ended up on the floor of an empty apartment and then on the stairs on crowd control. This is the migration route called "anywhere but here" referred to by migration scholars under the ubiquitous category of "push factors."

Released from crowd duty as the crush of bodies on the stairs subsides, Daniel closes the door of his classroom and launches into his A-level sociology lesson on Max Weber. A respectful hush in which he still delights falls over the classroom. The students respectfully begin taking notes. At the same time Zoë begins her GCSE Spanish lesson. The entire class hands in their homework. Theirs is a long intense day. Both teach nine forty-five-minute periods a day and forty-five peri-ods a week. This leaves little time for preparation and no time for socializing in the staff room. This is usually empty apart from teachers passing through to grab a coffee or to use the photocopier on their way to class. The work ethic is equally strong among teachers and students. Appearing to have free time during school hours is not consistent with the work culture of the school. There are Saturday classes too during exam re-sit time. Last year Zoë and Daniel did seventeen Satur-day classes, so their weekends were often short and their leisure intense, making holidays all the more significant and longed for.

As Zoë collects the homework, she is able to draw a mental picture of each of the student's parents because she met them all just the night before at parents' night. The students' eagerness for success is matched by their parents' ambition on their behalf in a society where education is seen as a key to later success and, sometimes, a route out of Hong Kong to opportunities beyond. Although teach-ers are not high up the social scale in a place where a person's worth is measured by their salary, they are nevertheless respected because of the importance attached to education as a route to social mobility. Students' motivation is calibrated to the uncertainties of Hong Kong and the place of education in reducing uncertainties at a personal level. Education is an individual way of owning and tackling uncer-

71

tainty. Through the power of parental involvement, monitoring and complaint, students have a louder voice than the students Zoë and Daniel taught in London. They are also prepared to use it to criticize teachers who don't put 100 percent into the job.

Because exam results are the bottom line in educational success they are subjected to minute "forensic examination"—as Daniel puts it—every year, right down to the decimal point. This is important for the two-thirds of teachers like Zoë and Daniel with performance-related contracts. Teachers joke about the blue envelope that can arrive in staffroom mail slots in the spring, terminating their contracts for poor examination results. Not every contract is renewed: and toward the end of a two-year contract period can be a tense time for teachers. All of these things make the job quite different from the way it operates in Britain. Subtle differences add up, although basic similarities between the British and Hong Kong systems are the key to Zoë and Daniel's employability. But like everything else in Hong Kong, the ESF system operates on a shifting landscape, and teachers like Zoë and Daniel experience this in their daily work in the classroom. Teaching students whose first language is Chinese and who speak and write English as a second language is much more challenging than teaching native English speakers. This makes it more difficult to maintain the school's exam pass profile and, by extension, contract teachers' jobs. Chinesization presses against migrant employment.

The school day progresses and Daniel moves on to teaching social stratification to his year thirteen A-level sociology class while Zoë is teaching French to year seven. Daniel is fascinated by the students' lack of interest in social inequalities. They see these as a natural or inevitable outcome of personal success and failure. In a highly competitive society the industrious and deserving succeed. Sociology is never a popular option anyway. Not only are its capacities in social critique unappreciated, it doesn't lead to an obvious job. Daniel is looking forward to a night in with Zoë. Then he remembers that Thursday is *Coronation Street* club night. A video of the week's episodes of this British TV soap opera is airmailed to Hong Kong by Sandy, the biology teacher's mother. Six of the West Island School's teachers will gather at their place to watch it: one of their rituals.

Zoë and Daniel only go out once or twice a week during the term. Most of their social activities involve other teachers from the same school with contractually similar conditions of employment. Strange how that works, that closing in of the world, Daniel thinks as he dashes for the taxi stand outside the school. This is where he meets Zoë and competes with the students for taxis. There is a close correspondence between teachers' ages, length of time in Hong Kong, type of contract, work conditions, and disposable income. These factors effectively stratify those who do the same job.

Daniel is acutely aware of this as he stops to chat to Tom. Tom is in the parking lot rummaging through the back of his car looking for his golf clubs. He is the careers and deputy head teacher, and his wife, Jenny, teaches English. They have been in Hong Kong since the 1970s. In fact they met, married, and brought up their children in Hong Kong. Their daughter is now part of a different expatriate scene in Singapore, and their son has stayed on in Britain after university. Tom and Jenny, like others of a similar vintage, had their contracts overhauled in 1984 when it was acknowledged that Hong Kong would be returned to China. Mindful of the difficulties this might cause in attracting and retaining teachers, the colonial administration awarded fabulous conditions of employment to teachers. Tom, Jenny, and a handful of others got a particularly good deal, which no one has subsequently had the political courage to remove. They are not on performance contracts, and while they care about the exam results, their contracts will not be terminated on account of them. In terms of work stress, income, and lifestyle they live a more sheltered and affluent life than teachers like Zoë and Daniel. They still "go on leave" in the colonial manner of things, rather than "on holiday"

like Daniel and Zoë. Tom and Jenny's life is much more about leisure. Tom travels all over the world with the rugby team he coaches. Their social life consists of parties, dinners, and nights out from the ESF ghetto of subsidized accommodation that Daniel, Zoë, and the others cannot afford. Tom and Jenny own a house in France and an apartment in Sydney. They contemplate an active (globally organized) retirement moving between houses. Zoë and Daniel have a scaled-down version of the same plan with less property. Daniel wishes Tom good luck with his golf game and drifts on to the taxi stand where Zoë is anxious to get home.

The slow taxi journey through the rush hour traffic prompts the feelings they share about Hong Kong: "It's a concrete jungle, it's a dump." It's a dump that can be blotted out if you can afford to live in the "gweilo" economy (*gweilo*, or ghost, a local word for white people, is often used by expatriates to refer to themselves) and use the hotels and restaurants. But if you are the kind of people that like to go out for a walk and enjoy the environment, Zoë thinks Hong Kong is a difficult place to live. She dislikes breathing in traffic fumes and fighting the heat and humidity. Zoë and Daniel both like walking but don't see Hong Kong as a good place to walk, although it has extensive green spaces locals and other expatriates use. The shops don't have a full enough range of vegetarian food for them, either. Their Jewishness, too, is neither visible nor acknowledged.

It is both difficult and easy to be Jewish in Hong Kong. Being indistinguishable to the local eye from other foreigners is also a form of erasure. At least getting a taxi had been easy on this particular evening. Once last week they'd been given what they interpreted as colonial-styled preference when the taxi driver threw a local woman out of his taxi and offered it to them instead. They both still cringe with embarrassment at the thought of it.

They don't want special treatment, yet fitting in is problematic too. Locally they live through restricted routes between their apartment, the apartments of other teachers, and the school. Meanwhile their global routes take in new vacation spots at every opportunity. They live at a distance from local people. Travel by taxi restricts exposure; something their socializing patterns repeat. No one will sit beside them when they do take the bus. They can't follow programs on the TV or the radio or eavesdrop on others' conversations in public places. As Daniel says, they are not part of

the rhythm of life, you have to find it where you are and my only regret is that I can't find it with the local population. We could live here fifty years and never really move in Chinese circles. It's a missed opportunity. But you can't find a rhythm. The expat community has its own rhythm and, you know, accept it. You can't impose the English lifestyle over here.

Linguistic exclusion is worse for Zoë. As a linguist she is used to thinking about herself as fitting in through language.

> There's a separation between the expatriate community and the Chinese community which I found really strange when I came here . . . Before I came here I thought everybody in the school would speak Cantonese and I went out and bought my Cantonese language materials ready to do the course. And when I got here I found people had lived here seventeen years and twenty-one years and didn't know how to speak Cantonese . . . there's no socializing to speak of, and it would be very unusual. . . . [Noting political differences between Britain and Hong Kong she continues] If I want to protest with a banner I can. If I want to protest with thirty people I can't. . . . Does that matter to me because I am earning all this extra money? To be brutally honest, no. . . . I've never not been able to do the things I want to.

Zoë and Daniel don't just live in this separate world. Their work in the English business is part of its very production and the (restricted) relationship with Chineseness that comes with it. Having your native language accommodated as a migrant is both a privilege and a disability. It incorporates migrants in limited terms as it holds them in a special place. Their version of lifestyle migration is work-centered, and their leisure is also circumscribed by work, confined to half-term breaks and end or term vacations. In these ways, their relationship with Hong Kong resembles a child's relationship with a boarding school. They must leave in order to have periods of nonwork life. They are not alone in this. The 6:30 flight to Paris or to Vietnam (or wherever) on the day school ends is "the ESF flight." It is full of teachers and kids departing on vacation: "right off the starting blocks." Zoë says, "We count up the weeks and the months." They count up the years too: five or ten more years of working life until they can afford to live in their house in France. This version of lifestyle migration is job- and income-centered on trudging through the present towards a better, more leisured future in a place they'd prefer to live. Lifestyle migration is sometimes work-style migration. Hong Kong is a node of income generation, tolerated rather than enjoyed, in which a small sustainable life is carved out of myriad possibilities. Migrants sometimes think big (prepared to operate on a global canvas) and yet live small.

OLD CHINA HANDS

Riding the Waves

Our tour moves on to another segment of British migrants and to another part of town, to an island called Lamma, some thirty minutes by boat from Hong Kong Island. John and Lyn are old China hands: experienced migrants in this region, long-term residents, without plans to move on, who think of themselves as Hong Kong belongers. This is displayed in their relationships with other migrants, whom they think about in terms of length of stay and depth of familiarity with Hong Kong. It is also displayed in their troubled relationship with Britain, which rules it out as a place of return. Being an old China hand involves a level of competence in managing life locally. John and Lyn's version of lifestyle migration involves a different configuration of work and leisure from Zoë and Daniel's. Their relationship with Chineseness reveals a different approach to living locally, and a particular version of Chineseness.

Lyn and John shift uncomfortably on the hard plastic seats of the 7:30 ferry from their home on the island of Lamma[1] to work in Hong Kong Island's Wanchai district, slightly to the east of the corporate cluster composing the central district. The boat, which has an upstairs and a downstairs deck, is packed, like the other ten that leave between 6:30 and 9:30 am, transporting the people of Lamma to work. This also explains why the island feels so empty during weekdays. With a strong wind on this particular morning the boat is rolling a bit, but John, Lyn, and the other passengers hardly notice; their journey being a routine part of a five-and-a-half-day week. As the boat tosses its way across the sea to Wanchai's pier number 4, John ploughs on with his military history book. The familiarities and frictions of long-term relationships make conversation between the couple unnecessary.

A thoughtful and serious man in his middle forties, John's view of the world is developed through reading—not just military but colonial histories, too. He speaks with deliberation, revealing capacities he isn't required to use at work, which he didn't indulge in his self-interrupted college education, and for which he struggles to find an outlet. Lyn—thirty-nine—is pretty and feisty, and launches herself sporadically at things like learning Mandarin and studying law. Dressed like John in corporate casuals, she devours the South China Morning Post, noting how many people in the news she's met at one function or another, something that wouldn't happen in Britain.

The couple met at an expat party six months after Lyn had arrived. She hated the place and planned to return to Britain. John had been in Hong Kong a year and loved it. Lyn did too once she'd got used to it and made friends. She achieved

these things more comfortably from the vantage point of her relationship with John than alone. As the boat docks at pier 4 they part and each negotiates the crowded streets of Wanchai to their respective offices.

We'll follow John from the ferry. We won't edit out his walking because it is part of the story: part of the (ethnicized/racialized) choreographies woven by bodies on the streets. It is part of the "chorus of idle foot steps"[2] of which he has a heightened awareness. He knows expats who can't deal comfortably, as he can, with the proximities of the streets, the closeness of bodies in a crowded space. Such people transmit their apprehension to those around them, who feel its delicate reverberations and retaliate with an apprehension of their own. The silent dialogues between bodies on the street form a significant, but unnoticed, layer of multiracial coexistence in postcolonial life. John is at ease with his minority status among the Chinese bodies composing the energy of the streets. He understands that this is where the practicalities of ethnicized coexistence are played out. Knowing this he walks easily: an old China hand.

Following John we enter one of the thousands of twelve-or-so-story commercial buildings lining the main arterial routes of Wanchai. Each commercial building contains the offices of multiple businesses—scaled-down versions of those occupying the corporate central district—sharing space and cutting overhead. They have small neat marble-floored entranceways and elevators. Each has a concierge and there are mail slots for each company: shipping, insurance, small business; the backbone of Hong Kong commercial enterprise. These businesses are respectable and solid, not fancy, not trying to create an impression of wealth, not part of the architectural spectacle of the corporate center. The commercial buildings on the streets are interspersed with retail outlets of various kinds, selling ordinary things like stationary, newspapers, snacks, and coffee. There are market stalls with fruit and flowers, dumplings being fried in big metal drum containers in the spaces between and in front of the buildings. This is a dense and interesting residential/commercial neighborhood. It is cluttered with life and varied commercial activity, in contrast to the pristine uncluttered marble and stone character of the central district. Central's corporate commercial activities are not worn on the surface like Wanchai's, but are subtly concealed. The streets are densely packed with traffic and people doing business as John weaves his way to his office building, greets the concierge and takes the elevator to the eighth floor.

Frances, the Chinese woman who makes coffee, answers the phone and perform other routine tasks, helps John clear some of the paperwork from his desk and brings him coffee. He lights the first of many cigarettes that will leave the office in a fug of smoke. He shares office space with Hamish, who we will meet

later in our tour on boys' night out. John also works with two younger men, who crack jokes betraying the daily familiarities of men sharing office space. Each has a desk and a filing cabinet from which a separate business is run. They operate as a fledgling network of support in times of difficulty. Frances is sometimes late and sometimes takes long lunch breaks. They get exasperated at having to answer the phone while she is away. They admonish, flirt, and patronize, but they couldn't operate without her Cantonese and other support. She has adopted an English name at work in place of her Chinese name so that the men can pronounce it.

John's work is structured by his hobbies. He dabbles in a bit of manufacture, some import and export, and he is trying to set up a car racing business. Racing is the love of his life, along with his vintage car collection he is having shipped from Britain soon. Ironically, he lives on an island without roads. His circumstances are precarious with periods of unemployment, but overall he manages to ride the turbulent tides of Hong Kong's economic landscape, navigating a small niche through expatriate contacts. As long as Lyn manages to find work they stay afloat. Only once, a few months ago, they were both cast adrift at the same time, and had difficulty making their monthly mortgage payment. We leave John in a gathering cloud of smoke frowning at his mail.

Managing Dis/location

Following Lyn from the Lamma ferry we end up in a larger, plusher, Wanchai office, extending over the entire tenth floor of a building with a receptionist at a
desk just inside the main office door. Lyn's niche is less self-generated than John's.
She is employed by a firm handling the relocation of expat personnel on short
contracts, on behalf of the big corporate enterprises that employ them. She eases
the circulation of contract labor into Hong Kong, dealing with partners (usually
wives) and children and solving the practical problems of dislocation. As our tour
takes us to her office she is on the phone organizing to take a man on a house
search before his wife and kids arrive and have to live in his hotel. She's good with
the woman who has just arrived, who is too scared to leave her flat, who doesn't
think she can find her kids' school again this afternoon, and who is in complete
dislocation meltdown. She helps new migrants open bank accounts, shows them
how to use public transport, finds them a plumber when the drain blocks and,
generally, eases the negotiation of the unfamiliar. In servicing others' migration
she consolidates a sense of herself as an experienced migrant with Hong Kong
competence: an old China hand.

Lyn slams the phone down after a brief discussion with a commanding woman
with a posh upper-class British accent who wants an electrician NOW. This
woman can command Lyn to get her an electrician because her husband is important at the bank, and the bank is one of Lyn's big clients. "Filth," she mutters
to her assistant, Jen, a thin pale-faced British girl who has only been in Hong
Kong three months and looks permanently miserable. "Think they're better than
they are"; "failed in London, try Hong Kong"; "Filth"; "They wouldn't do this
well in Britain." Some of her clients are very nice but frankly some of them are
rather spoiled. "There's a worldwide recession. Get real. But it doesn't touch these
people." These people are padded against economic fluctuations by other options,
other postings, and anyway they do OK at home, too, in Britain, Australia, the
United States, despite Lyn's assessment of them. "Expats" has a specific meaning
for Lyn. It means people with packages of benefits and other forms of corporate
sponsorship she and John do not have. John and Lyn have a tenuous relationship
with global capital and a strandedness that comes from their reluctance to return
to Britain. Their reluctance comes from their lack of resources and disinclination,
despite the accumulation of minor irritations and short periods of unemployment, to move on to new locations. Although they talk mobile, John and Lyn are
actually rather stuck in Hong Kong. Or, rather, it would take a more dramatic shift
in personal and political circumstances to move them on elsewhere.

Lyn's circumstances are as precarious as John's. A few years ago her firm landed Nortel as a client with a big contract to relocate their employees arriving in Hong Kong. A couple of year's later Nortel pulls out, and 7,000 people worldwide, who live on the servicing fringes of the corporate center, lose their jobs. Although she is annoyed with the plummy woman on the phone, Lyn's thrilled to get this job because she was recently unemployed for several months after being fired from the last relocation company she worked for. This left her spending many lonely days on the island while everyone else left for work. She knows about "face,"[3] but finds it difficult not to say what she thinks. "With Chinese management it's all 'face' and I'm not a yes person." Her refusal to fit in—and her unfavorable assessment of Chinese social relationships—limits her options to companies with expatriate management and workplace culture. Another problem is the sensitivity of the relocation industry to the prevailing business climate, which rolls up and down on these shores. A third problem is the Chineseization of business culture gathering pace since 1997 and what Lyn describes as its "gweilos out" policy. The gap in the labor market for those who can't operate in Cantonese or Mandarin is closing. She doesn't speak Cantonese and, while she understands some of what is said around her, it isn't enough: "Today you cannot get a job. If you're not Chinese-speaking, forget it. . . . 'Get out, we don't want any gweilos in our offices.'" In Lyn's view this is a mistake, as down the road Hong Kong will pay for this in a loss of international business and status. The phone rings again and Lyn rushes off to meet a new arrival, a young woman with a small child and whose husband is never home, at their flat for grocery shopping. And so in this way Lyn gets through the day until she meets John at the ferry for the trip back to Lamma: the most eagerly anticipated part of the day. Work isn't particularly interesting but it provides access to a Hong Kong life(style), which they both enjoy and are prepared to switch jobs to maintain.

Island Life

It's 7:30 pm, and John and Lyn sit next to each other in tired silence on the ferry's top deck for the journey home. When the return ferry pulls into Lamma Island at the end of a long work day that routinely extends to 8 p.m., its work-weary passengers are in Yung Shue Wan Village. There are no roads, only concrete pathways along which people walk and bicycle. This gives Lamma a striking tranquility compared to the noise and frantic busyness of the rest of Hong Kong. This quality first drew John to the island in the days before he'd met Lyn. John's sense

of the island settles around this bit of waterfront. The fishermen's wooden huts on stilts at the water's edge in the typhoon shelter; the quaint old junks with their shoreline residents; and the Tin Hau Buddhist Temple to the goddess of the sea and fishing folk provide an old (colonial) Hong Kong aesthetic John is attracted to. An elderly friend who helped him start his Hong Kong business said this was how the rest of Hong Kong had looked when he arrived in the fifties, and John likes it this way. He stops and exchanges greetings in Hakka with the fishermen standing at the village end of the pier. He enjoys this ritual although his conversation is limited.

The couple walk on past the fish shop with buckets of fresh shrimp outside and other evidence of the fishermen's daily labors, past a Chinese restaurant with tables outside under an awning and some gift shops selling knickknacks. As they move from the shoreline into the village old Hong Kong gives way to a different aesthetic. Yung Shue Wan's outside bars and restaurants provide a Mediterranean holiday resort feel in what is, for John and Lyn, a landscape of everyday life. Producing the mundane in the exotic heat of tropical landscape reconfigures work and leisure. The frisson this produces lies at the heart of lifestyle migration. A number of expatriates from the ferry are settling into a drink or a meal

in the gap between work and home. John and Lyn choose a table in the court-yard of their favorite bar. Once an opium den and much later a hippy café, it is now a sports bar with a big flat-screen television showing the big British foot-ball matches. The waterfront and the area around the café with its cluster of fish shops and knickknack shops could easily be a holiday village in coastal Greece or Spain. The climate, too, suggests this. Life can be a beach. The vacation is the tem-plate for the good life, even if you have to work all day to pay for it.

The social alchemy of the island unfolds around them. There are no official es-timates of the population of the island because it forms a part of a bigger admin-istrative region, but unofficial estimates vary between 8,000 and 10,000. This is a substantial growth from the early 1990s when it was estimated at only 4,000. John thinks that a quarter of the island's population is expat, and given its small size, this is a significant concentration of migrants. British couples in their late twenties and early thirties with babies in buggies and tribes of tangle-haired chil-dren pause as they walk past the bar and exchange greetings and bits of island news. These are the people Lyn refers to when she says that Lamma is more "re-alistic" with no filth and no wealthy expats on corporate packages, only, "people like ourselves without pretension." Housing is modest and cheap compared with other Hong Kong locations.[4] Lamma is alternative. Its expats are not those of

the corporate center. They have alternative interests, as the island's Web site, advertising New Age workshops on subjects like dreams and images, suggests. Its "laid-back" lifestyle reports itself as an alternative to the frenetic pace and money-making ethos of (other parts of) Hong Kong. Lamma's hint of alternative values is not fully articulated. Its alternative reputation was once bolstered by backpackers en route to and from Australia who would take temporary employment before resuming their travels.[5]

For the local Chinese, Lamma is a vacation spot. They visit in search of hiking/camping breaks from their usual routines. Alternative versions of Chineseness provide the local color expatriates are attracted to as well as their supply of housing. Hakka "villagers" who have established traditional rights to the land through their long-term use of it commonly build three-story buildings. They will live in one apartment and sell or rent the other two. The Hakka fisherman whose son recently died of cancer—in the course of which expatriate sympathy was extended increasing the usual levels of interaction—walks past the bar and pauses to speak to John. John unpacks Chineseness into some of its (ethnicized) components and elaborates his understanding of Cantonese-Hakka relationships. In this he considers expats to be interlocutors. "The Chinese community can be sometimes thought standoffish. Whereas the expat community thought, "What the hell, he's

a good lad." At public events as well as these in more private moments, Hakka, expatriate, and Cantonese islanders interact over elements of public culture. These include maypole dancing, sampan racing, dragon boat racing, the Tin Hau Festival, and the Chinese opera. It appears from the (English-language) island Web site they also share an interest in dog rescue.

The group at John and Lyn's table has grown to six. Another British expatriate couple is attending to their children with treats and trips to the playground. The other couple is childless, like John and Lyn. Drinking is an established part of expat island culture. Tribes of small blond children speaking English with names like Phoebe and Emily play along the waterfront. Leaving the group at the table the couple walks to their flat in a low-rise—three-story—building past crops and vegetables tended by Hakka farmers in the silence of the island and their relationship.

"Britain Saddens Me"

Later that evening John decides to tell Lyn about the e-mail message from his sister he'd picked up at work. John, Lyn, and John's sister maintain a dialogue

in which the relative merits of British and Hong Kong life are continually evaluated. After looking at the local secondary schools in the British county of Berkshire John's sister has put her son into a private school. She'll struggle with the fees. John understands. He says, "Britain saddens me." John and Lyn have many conversations on this theme. Their Britain is London marked by the "idiocy" of 1980s' local government with trendy schemes supporting multiculturalism and lesbians. It is, as far as they are concerned, falling into an abyss of decline and incivility.[6] When pressed on what's wrong with Britain John refers to "dumbing-down," "standards," the "lack of discipline," and the need to roll back the "forty-odd years of social engineering" that would be necessary to tempt him to consider returning. John is disturbed by what he sees as the "slow breakdown in society" in law and order and the stark division between the public and the police. Lyn's Britain is one in which she felt "tied back" by the nine-to-five routine and another night in front of the TV in a discordant first marriage. This life lacked the resources and excitement Hong Kong provides in higher disposable income and glittering night life. John and Lyn have worked these comparative themes around the material provided by their experiences. John's sister provides continuous evidence that their assessment is correct. They will never move back to Britain. They visit infrequently for big family occasions, weddings, funerals, eightieth birthday

91

parties. Last time they were visiting an aggressive young woman shoved a pram into Lyn's leg. A motorist swore at them. The incivilities of British streets are unbearable. John says, "Britain is the only place I've been badly beaten up, for no reason at all." As in relationships, some people need to fall out of love in order to justify leaving. Lyn misses clay pigeon shooting and country pubs.

It was not the smallness of her life in East London, but its disintegration when her husband left, that precipitated Lyn's move to Hong Kong. She wanted to start a new life in a new place. Expatriate Hong Kong has a close relationship with divorce in expat mythology. It either precipitates it or provides a new start following it. John first came to Hong Kong on holiday because his girlfriend was here and because his engineering business in Britain folded under the weight of the bureaucracies he thinks strangle entrepreneurial culture. He sees Hong Kong as a place where people "make it happen" in the back alleys, with no start-up costs and with sheer hard work. His holiday turned into the rest of his life. They were married in Hong Kong with friends and family members who could attend and with Jack, the old soldier, standing in as father figure and best man for John.

The couple's shared displeasure in Britain and determination not to return places a question mark over their future. It rules out Britain in the event of sudden departure. Their irritation with the political climate and ineptitude in the governing classes, whether in relation to Britain or Hong Kong, is well developed. Their list of things wrong with the postcolonial administration of Hong Kong grows in the years following 1997. They are concerned about what they saw as poor political judgment by the Legislative Council, LEGCO, and the chief executive. Of particular concern is Hong Kong's loss of influence in relation to Beijing and Shanghai. These cities appear to be overtaking Hong Kong, threatening its global-city status, transforming it into "just another southern Chinese city." These things matter more to some people than others. John and Lyn need to have faith in the competence of their political ruling class. It is this class that sets the context in which enterprise, opportunity, and lifestyle can properly flourish. These concerns and their views about Britain reveal their version of lifestyle migration.

Lifestyle Migration

John is a fierce social critic. He expects things to operate in line with his personal convenience and life opportunities. His life and his requirements are the vantage point from which the world is judged. He is able to comparison-shop in other countries and other lifestyles and make choices. He is a knit-your-own world global citizen, and his actions are a form of globally organized individualism. John belongs, not in a country, but in a set of circumstances that promote, or at least do not impede, the things he wants to have and do. He regards these things as entitlements. While British multiracialism gets in his way and annoys him; living as an ethnic minority brings many of the things he wants in life. What John wants from his life is about forms of private pleasure that come from living a certain way. He seeks a political and social context that supports these entitlements. Ironically—given his right-wing libertarian political views on democracy and fears of social disintegration—he finds his version of the good life in a postcolonial bubble inside a SAR in the People's Republic of China.

Lifestyle migrants weave together bits of what they need or demand in life from different places. Thy use this bricolage to think about belonging as the satisfaction of needs. Lifestyle migrants do not need to move. They seek a change of place in order to upgrade their circumstances. Need is problematic. Even refugees do not need to move. Many stay and suffer the consequences in persecution and execution. But the concept of need has a different valency in their lives, which are organized by more basic forms of survival. All forms of migration ultimately bleed into each other, and trying to differentiate them cleanly is pointless. If the term "diaspora" were used to refer to the circumstances of white British people like John and Lyn—which it isn't[7]—then their circumstances could be described as a diaspora of privilege. John grew up in New Zealand between the ages of five and seventeen. Then his family returned to Britain. He has lived in Hong Kong since 1990 and sees it as "my home. I have no particular desire to go back to Britain at all." His migration was not corporate nor was it part of the apparatus of Empire. It was, however, facilitated by empire's routes and the privileges concerning entry that this afforded British migrants.

The Baby

In the same bar a year later Lyn sits on a Saturday morning with their adopted child looking relaxed and happy. The tension and disappointment of her previous interactions with John has disappeared. The bureaucratic wheels of the adoption system worked with surprising speed making them parents, suddenly, the way everyone becomes a parent. Their microworld has changed forever. Lyn no longer sits in the bar on the way back from work. In fact she doesn't travel with John anymore. She leaves work earlier so that she is at home to spend time with

their son before he goes to bed. While Lyn is at work the baby is cared for by Nana, their maid from Sri Lanka. The women timeshare the space of the 700-square-foot apartment, shrinking under the sheer volume of baby paraphernalia. They also timeshare the baby in carefully choreographed intimacies.

The baby is Hong Kong (not mainland) Chinese. He came from an orphanage, aged six months, with a "memory book." This detailed his body weight at birth and other landmarks: the first time he did things like sit up and smile. These are things a mother would know; the mother who is conspicuously absent from the book. John and Lyn have made a photo album of the baby's arrival and the days following in which they entered the steep learning curve of parenting. They beam happily out of the photographs. The baby is presented to them by the orphanage as Chinese but Lyn is speculative. She unravels Chineseness in a different way from John in his assessment of the Hakka. She thinks that the mother is Chinese but that the father is an older white man. These imagined intimacies arising from postempire proximities parallel their assessment of Lamma as a surviving slice of "old Hong Kong." They make their lives around this material. She submits the baby's small face as evidence. "He doesn't look very Chinese."

An unanticipated layer of intimate complexity is added to their relationship with Chineseness. This involved their superficial affinity with the older Hakka

residents of the island. It involved their participation with other expatriates in local Chinese festivals. It involved their work relationships with Chinese subordinates and bosses demanding submission and "face" Lyn found so hard. It involved the closing cultural and workspace gap narrowed by Chineseization. It now involved their son with his British (and ambiguous) Chineseness: a long-term intimate relationship. Matrices of (racialized and ethnicized) difference are incorporated into these new intimacies. These operate between Lyn and John and the baby becoming theirs. They operate between the three of them and the baby's absent biological parents. They operate between Lyn and Nana, and between Nana and the baby she is employed to care for. Lyn and John will work on the Chinese (genetic) material presented by the baby, making him British in their own way. They have shown their willingness to claim him as theirs in challenging the depth of his Chineseness. Adept at working with the Chinese human fabric of the streets, they turn to a piece of it they have appropriated and nurture in their home. They will work on these new relationships in the same way they have elaborated their versions of postcolonial Britain and Hong Kong.

The relationship between Nana and Lyn includes modernized elements of colonial life. Lyn pays well and is respectful of Nana's circumstances. But their relationship involves differences in social and material circumstances magnified

in migration. If we were to follow Nana home we would walk up the hill on the island to a tiny crowded flat she shares with other Sri Lankan domestic helpers. This maximizes the income that can be sent home to Sri Lanka. Nana is a migrant, but not like Lyn. She has moved from Sri Lanka to upgrade her circumstances. But her departure, arrival, and settlement conditions make her a different kind of migrant.

> I need the money. I have my parents with me. I have one sister. She is studying. So
> I am the one who must take care of them. So I need the money, because my mother
> had a heart attack. So she has a battery, I have to change the battery after three years,
> maybe.... So ... I don't know.

Nana is a serving-class migrant. Her visa and her conditions of stay depend on her sustaining an employee relationship with women like Lyn. She lives precariously. These themes will be more fully explored in later in our tour when we meet Filipino domestic helpers.

John and Lyn's connection with Hong Kong as old China hands is subtly mediated through their private lifestyle requirements. These take priority over their other connections, like their affection for the island, its landscape and its Hakka

fishermen, and their expatriate friends. These connections will be reconfigured if things don't work out. They can move to another country. They list Singapore and New Zealand as possibilities. Their curious nostalgia for the landscapes and intimacies of empire are not the result of colonial genealogies or because they are recycled colonial personnel like the Trents. Their migration operated the conduits of empire without being part of it. They articulate a different kind of ordinariness from Mary Trent and live in a different version of the expat bubble. The old China hand is a narrowing niche.

WORKING GLOBAL SYSTEMS

Corporate Lives/Wives

Now we are in elegant Shouson Hill, a tranquil neighborhood with detached low villas in ample bougainvillea-splattered grounds. This quiet space is separated from the noise and high-rise commotion of the city by the low green mountains that run through the center of Hong Kong Island. Nestling into the aside of Hong Kong Island, views from Shooson Hill to the south are blocked by the green mountains. To the north are the Kowloon Peninsula, the New Territories, and the Chinese mainland. The South China Sea, with its archipelago of small islands shimmering in the distance, resembles a traditional Chinese painting. In this quiet neighborhood with the luxury of low-rise space, gardeners tend and water tropical plants and flowers.

American Chuck and his British wife Amanda sit at the breakfast table reading the newspapers in their large dinning room, among highly polished wood floors and well-kept furniture. Furniture, artifacts, and polish contain social commentaries. Social being is entwined with objects that collude in social self-creation. The objects with which Chuck and Amanda's life is entwined announce tasteful affluence and the skill of those who know how to consume objects properly.[1] Clothes, too, are intimately entangled with social being and comportment[2] of which they are both producer and product. In their late fifties, and elegantly dressed, they speak softly to each other in measured educated tones. Touchingly devoted to each other, Amanda, for whom this is a second marriage, gets up when Chuck comes into the room and offers to fetch him whatever it is he needs. Early morning light floods the three-story house, adding to the glow of polished wood. This, along with the breakfast, is the work of their Filipino maid, who remains unobtrusively ready to serve as they stare in disbelief at the newspapers. Not having to maintain floors, furniture, artifacts, and meals through their own labor, but through the labor of others create particular kinds of lives.

It is the morning of September 12, 2001. Chuck and Amanda are scouring the *South China Morning Post* and the *International Herald Tribune* trying to understand as the story still unfolds: 9/11 is a Hong Kong story too. The destruction of the World Trade Centre wiped out Chuck's company's office. It signaled a new world order of heightened anxieties aroused by sudden attack, by enemies that are difficult to distinguish and loosely orchestrated without settled place or face. Parallel, discordant, interconnected global networks sustain and grate against each other. Jihadic warriors strike at the heart of what appears to be the only remaining empire. Chuck had watched the TV coverage over and over; numb with incomprehension as his colleagues fall spectacularly from the skies.

Amanda drives Chuck to work in their Jaguar through the tunnel that cuts through the low green mountains to Central. There Chuck works in one of the more spectacular office towers. He trades US dollars in China and the Asia Pacific countries; a small cog in the mainstream global system. He could easily take a taxi but likes her to drive him. They talk on the way, checking in with the others' activities, thoughts, and plans. This is a routine established in their five years in Hong Kong, which will soon come to an end. Having spent his entire working life commuting to Manhattan from the New York suburbs, the Hong Kong posting offered Chuck a change of scene in a familiar (job) context. "I am sort of doing the same things that I was doing in New York but in a different format so it's been fun." Hong Kong is a low-risk move inside the firm where he has worked since he left law school thirty years ago. His passage to Hong Kong is eased by generous relocation benefits and other practical details processed by Amanda, making use of Lyn's expertise. From the vantage point of his well-padded cocoon Chuck is able to decide: "I just wanted to do something different."

As Amanda drives away to her bridge game Chuck walks into the shiny marble foyer of his office building. He describes his work:

> Mostly financial work with capital-raising activities. Companies out here want to access the US markets, [to] sell stock or bonds or borrow from the US. A kind of cross-border thing I would be involved in, . . . for US companies, investing in China . . . There are all sorts of permutations. . . . For me basically being a US lawyer I am looking for activity here that would be targeting the US. So that was in short supply last year. . . . First six months of this year we didn't see much activity. The issues out here are: do companies want dollars? Do they want exposure to the dollar for various reasons? . . . The lesson of '97[3] is to be very cautious in terms of accessing foreign [versus local] currencies because you have to pay them back.

The economic motor of corporate life has been running a little slowly since the 1997 downturn in the Asia Pacific economies. But this doesn't impact on Chuck's life in any important sense. His job, pay, and social and work conditions remain the same. It is life, if not business, as usual inside this mainstream sector of global corporate enterprise. It rides out just this kind of cyclical fluctuation. Chuck's conditions of employment are protected. Hong Kong life is accessible to him. He can operate in English and trade on the professional expertise he accumulated in New York. "The patterns of life here were established by the British, it's Chinese, but if it's something else it's British." This makes Hong Kong an easy place to live. Its intersections with Britain, the United States, and China make it an easily negotiated, globally connected, city. At least it does so at the surface level at which Chuck operates. His relationship with Chineseness runs along the surface of major corporate threads of professional social networks, places, and activities. In terms of the categories used by migration scholars, Chuck is a temporary, elite, transnational migrant.

Amanda's life is subtly different. She has had greater mobility and depth of expatriate experience in places with distinctive relationships to empire. Now a corporate wife in Hong Kong, she reconfigures her life as a corporate wife in the New York suburbs. She draws on her life in Australia with her first husband. And she draws on her childhood in British-administered India. Amanda is a serial expatriate; her routes etched by empire. She gave up her own job, nursing, over twenty years ago when her children were born. Since then it had not been "necessary" to work. With grown children in the United States, she is always ready to return at short notice to sort out a crisis. Meanwhile she throws herself into bridge, golf, shopping, charity work, being a patron of the arts, enjoying teas, dinner, lunches, and being involved in Chuck's commitments. This produces a subtly different relationship with Chineseness from Chuck's. Hers operates through other women and is organized around leisure and interests rather than work. The substance of this life is explored more fully later when our tour takes in the Ladies who Lunch. Hers is a temporary and affluent form of lifestyle migration for women whose relationship with employment operates indirectly through a partner.

> . . . the obligatory aspects of the spouse are quite significant here. Socially, and I would also say emotionally, to be there for the working spouse, . . . He does like me, and needs me, . . . to be available to go on his business trips even though I don't know what they are talking about. That doesn't matter, to dilute some dreadfully boring, yet again Chinese dinner or meeting or cocktail party, or something, or just to ease the burden of the hotel room afterwards . . . So to just go along to all these tedious things because it helps prop him up, because that's also part of the role of being here, and because you are in it as a partnership together . . . he doing his and, I have girlfriends in England, successful lawyer, doctor, whatever. . . . and they have their careers quite independent of their husbands. I mean they socialize at weekends with their group of friends. . . . But here you need that extra degree of support because you are so far away. I guess that's an excuse . . . They work long hours so you need to be involved if you are going to see very much of them . . . And then there's golf.

Amanda eases Chuck's exposure to the beyond-work side of elite Chinese corporate life. She provides support services and distraction, carving a niche for herself in a work-centered life in which she plays a supporting role.

The Hong Kong social and economic climate has started to improve again, after the impact of SARS. This decimated the local tourist and service industry and left Chuck, Amanda, and their friends feeling a "bit claustrophobic" from the travel restrictions and the fear of public association spreading the disease. This kept people like them at home, rather than in the bars and restaurants in the evenings. They are inconvenienced by forces decimating the lives and fortunes of others. Rather than seeing Hong Kong as a point of access to other exciting places to visit, they see it as small and confining. Chuck's assessment of it as a workplace is repeated at the level of leisure. They are not interested in travel. "I think it's very repetitive here because the [financial] markets are quite small compared to New York or London." They have made Hong Kong small through their activities, their movements, their ways of being in and thinking about the world, and their scale of priorities. Chuck and Amanda will return to New York's suburbs soon, to a bigger place with more people and places to (meaningfully) connect with. This is their center of gravity. It is the place where people and things matter. Their migration to Hong Kong is highly protected and temporary. It failed to deliver the quality of new lifestyle experiences they anticipated in moving there as temporary migrants.

The United States and the Matrix of Global Dominance

Lives are always part of bigger (social, political, and economic) schemes and processes. The problem is how to conceptualize the forms to which they accumulate: the connections between macro- and micro-processes making lives and circumstances. Chuck is a legal cog in a bridge between the United States, and China. The game they play involves Chinese industrial/economic development and the investment and profit opportunities this creates. This is a game played in American dollars.

> One thing that has changed during our stay, initially there was this great fear of China, it was kept at arms' length and now there is this embrace of China. The way the place sees itself and what's in its future has changed probably . . . We have offices in China and we do things regionally from Korea and we've been as far as India for different things, mostly China is the focus.

Hong Kong is "a unique 'between place'"[4] in the economic and technical geographies of mainstream globalization. The United States is poised to take "full economic advantage"[5] of doing business with China as it expands its market system. Hong Kong is more than a bridge of British familiarity into Chinese markets and investment opportunities for the United States. With two-way trade totaling over US$25 billion a year, Hong Kong is the United States' fifteenth trading partner. The United States is making over US$21 billions worth of direct investment in China.[6] In 2001 the US trade surplus with Hong Kong was US$23.3 billion. Hong Kong is expected to remain an important platform for US business operating in this region.[7] US companies with significant offices in Hong Kong include Citibank, Hewlett Packard, Disney, Motorola and Marriott.[8]

Chuck and Amanda become part of the US–Asia Pacific global scene as he scrutinizes the legal paperwork on cross-boarder currency dealings. At a macrolevel the global geographies of work and money-making form the substance and the framework of people's lives. Approximately 50,000 Americans live and work in Hong Kong.[9] Volumes and sources of migration, flows of money and goods, and the lives people lead are closely interconnected.

Bilateral arrangements between the United States and Hong Kong are part of a bigger system with a power geometry skewed toward the United States ever since the 1950s. This intensified with the collapse of the Soviet Union and the Eastern Block countries in the last years of the twentieth century. US economic strength in the Asia Pacific region is replicated elsewhere. It dominates the key international agencies created to regulate the postwar landscape in which nations interact economically. The World Trade Organization (WTO), the International Monetary Fund (IMF), and the World Bank (WB)[10]—key supernational institutions of global governance—are US-dominated. Add to this economic dominance over world trade,[11] the terms on which developing countries can contract loans and service their population's needs, and US military strength. The United States has intervened in twenty other countries since the end of the Second World War to protect its interests.[12] Condoleezza Rice, chief advisor on security during the Bush (junior) Administration, assured the world that the US armed forces are ready to defend US *vital interests* and *world stability*.[13] These two objectives are connected, in combat and noncombat missions. Militarily and economically there is one superpower.

A lively debate ensues about whether or not US military, economic and cultural dominance make an empire.[14] What might "empire" mean in postcolonial times? European empires of the eighteenth and nineteenth centuries used military conquest and long-term occupation to secure economic dominance. US dominance, on the other hand, is secured through corporations seeking economic superiority and trade advantage. It is secured through diffuse political and cultural influence. It is not secured by occupation and microgovernance. There are no competing global forces that begin to match the United States; it is *the* dominant world force and as a result other nations position themselves in relation to it. The arrangements they make and the bargains they strike acknowledge US dominance with support or opposition. Recent European foreign policy, in British enthusiasm for American military projects and French truculence, confirm this. US corporations form a central axis running through the shifting matrix constituting globalization. No other nation, conglomerate of nations, or their corporations can match this influence. In practice other players on the mainstream global scene consolidate US global influence through their participation in global networks they dominate.

British (imperial) decline and US (global) ascendance intersect in Hong Kong. Chuck acknowledged that Britain established systems that made it possible for him and his colleagues to operate and prosper. Here we see one of many of the intersections between empire and globalization. The postcolonial shift in influence reformulated Britain's stake in Hong Kong but did not eliminate it. There are still one thousand companies in Hong Kong with British involvement through direct control, investment, or management. British corporations are well represented in key sectors such as trading, finance, insurance, retailing, and other service sectors too.[15] In 2002 there were eighty British companies with regional headquarters in Hong Kong, and 167 companies with regional offices. The usual suspects—Standard Chartered Bank, Nat West, Barclays, Prudential, British Airways, British Steel, and Pilkington—are all there.[16] After Japan, Hong Kong is Britain's biggest trading partner in the Asia Pacific region.[17]

Old (imperial) forms of global enterprise have been transformed. They become part of new systems, and their operatives adapt. Commercial interests and colonial governance always lived cheek by jowl and colonial governance in Hong Kong has new inscriptions. The executive director of the British Chamber of Commerce in Hong Kong, Brigadier Christopher Hammerbeck, is actually the former deputy commander of the British Forces in Hong Kong.[18] The operatives of one global system sometimes transfer to another. Colonial officials have transferable skills and are recycled wearing new briefs. Global tectonic plates have shifted, and Chuck and Amanda are part of an expanding global matrix of US influence. They are strongly interconnected with empire's mutations.

"Choosers and Losers"

Our tour moves on to lives and parts of the city that extend beyond globalization's mainstream[19] to other, intersecting, global conduits. We will now tour some of these conduits and pathways that pass through Hong Kong. Meet Jake. Jake is a young British migrant who quit corporate life to operate beneath its radar as an independent broker, dealing with smaller opportunities overlooked by key corporate operators on the global scene.

> Choose your lifestyle, chose the people you know, choose the guys you decide to let into your fold . . . choose everything. I get to choose. But most people don't get to choose . . . because they don't have the confidence to choose. . . . It's always about choosing. Everything about your culture . . . It's about choosers and losers and when you get guys that don't know what to do, . . the tramps in the subways in London, they have chosen to do that and nine times out of ten in my personal experience, they have chosen more aggressively than the vast majority of people . . . You confront somebody with the option, and you say, "Wherever you are in your life right now with your house and your kids and your wife . . . you chose all that shit, all of that you chose," and they go, "Oh I didn't choose that, that was, like, foisted on me." And if you try to make

them take responsibility for what they've chosen they don't like it. . . . and the guys that are happy with the choices they've made are generally the guys that have taken it the next step, the guys that have chosen because its something outside of their box. And they are the guys that are enjoying life. . . . They don't know what's around the corner; they don't know what's coming next. . . .

Say you did an audit. How much are you worth?. . . Sell your house, sell your car, dump your boyfriend, dump your kids. How much can you come away with in cash? And what would you do with it? . . . it's a benchmark . . . . if you cash in everything you've got, everything, dump every responsibility that you've got: every relationship, every asset, loyalty, cash it in . . . I'm not talking about emotional cash it in; I'm talking about money. . . . I'm not saying do it. I'm saying know your choices. I'm saying given all the other stuff that you've got, all the relationships and all the money and all that shit, add a dollar value to those and [ask] would I do anything different than I did? . . . What would I do? I'm doing the Hong Kong thing.

To meet the man behind this philosophy we would have to find a gap in his schedule or follow him around town. His day begins not with breakfast but with breakfast meetings. It continues late into the night when it fades into "drinks." This is a more informal kind of meeting. It's best to meet him at the bar that is only an elevator ride from his office in the Bank of America Tower in Central. This saves "wasting time." Jake's life is about work. This is not intended to suggest he doesn't know how to enjoy himself; in fact he is rather a good dancer. In his thirties, smart, and attractive, Jake is a career expatriate from an Anglo-Jewish refugee background. He arrived in Hong Kong from Kuala Lumpur and is planning to move on to Switzerland when Hong Kong no longer delivers the kinds of choices that make money. The money isn't important; it's a way of keeping score of personal business success. His version of lifestyle migration is subtly different from the Trents, John, Lyn, Zoë, and Daniel; and has an edge of precariousness Chuck wouldn't tolerate.

Jake arrived in Hong Kong the same year as Chuck (1998), the year after Hong Kong was returned to China, hoping to be a part of a future that drew a line under the (colonial) past. His migration career had started humbly enough. He was deposited (ancestrally speaking) in East London when it was still Jewish, if only just, by the mid-twentieth-century tides of migrants escaping the Final Solution. He moved with the upward and outward flow of social mobility to Cambridgeshire with his parents' improving circumstances.

Not that Jake relied on family to make his way in the world. Starting on the foreign currency counter at the National Westminster Bank, he worked his way

through university and into IT when the job in Kuala Lumpur caught his attention. Exchanging a small flat in the British Midlands for a new lifestyle, his spacious Kuala Lumpur apartment with a pool and expatriate package of benefits, served as his introduction to expatriate corporate life. Head-hunted in his late twenties as a rising young executive, he was recruited to work in Hong Kong for an American-based multinational finance company providing advice on a range of financial strategies and transactions: choices. A boutique investment banking firm, this was a company that paid particular attention to the opportunities afforded by others' bankruptcy.

Jake goes along with this for a while but can't help noticing the equally lucrative but smaller-scale business opportunities bypassed by big inflexible financial organizations with rigid lending policies and bureaucratic structures. Nor can he help thinking about what life would be like without bosses breathing down his neck and being held to a specified job description: More choices. Certain that there is money to be made; he quits the corporate mainstream after only two years in Hong Kong and strikes out on his own. He creates a loose network of temporary business partners that are reconfigured with every deal: a whole new world of choice.

These arrangements suit Jake's philosophy of life. Good and bad choices levering opportunity and loss forms this philosophy's center. It involves a particular approach to the place of the individual in society: "It's all about me! That's it, it's a philosophy. Yes it is. It's like; do not try to imagine that what you are doing is for the greater good." But not everyone is capable of effective self-interest. The world is divided into those who are able to navigate their way by making intelligent choices—"choosers"—and those who are not—"losers." Making fine judgments about people and situations—living his own philosophy of life—Jake weaves his street-smart entrepreneurial acumen through the places and circumstances in Hong Kong where money is made. Hong Kong is composed of opportunities; opportunities to do well and opportunities to do badly. Opportunities not felt quite as keenly inside the corporate cocoon by suits like Chuck. Choosers are able to spot an opportunity, calculate the risks, exploit the situation, and know exactly when to get out before an opportunity turns into a liability. Losers come in many varieties of feebleness, including those who develop loyalties to their moneymaking ideas, their business partners, or their network of associates and contacts. Losers lack the flexibility to switch contacts, ideas, and moneymaking schemes.

As in dancing, timing and flexibility are crucial when it comes to combining activities and keeping your options open; knowing when to make a new move

into something else; and knowing how to turn time into money. Choosers have a well-honed instinct for these things.

> To be honest if I lose one deal, because I was on the phone to somebody else orga
> nizing a £300 a month contract and that deal is US$10 million and my percent is a
> US$100,000, then that's a mistake. So I should be always making a call on where
> I should be spending my time and where the opportunities are, rather than just
> tunnel vision. Doing what you do, it's about being able to make the choice to do the
> other thing.

Jake doesn't waste time in attending business functions or "chewing the fat" with business associates on the phone. He only calls if he has something relevant to say; information to ask for or pass on or something to arrange. Flexibility involves being "an entrepreneur with lots of fingers in lots of pies" rather than being a "restaurant guy" or a "manufacturing guy." Choosers are adept at multitasking and managing multiple interests. They are not specialists with loyalties. They are good at "going where the money is." Jake does a bit of headhunting, bringing new people into Hong Kong to work where he sees a gap in local ex-

113

pertise. He notices new arrivals need accommodation and puts them in contact with a housing agency. This starts to pay him for referrals. Someone has an idea for a business and doesn't know who to approach for start-up capital. He introduces them to people he knows with money to invest and takes a fee. He does the same connecting highly specialized IT—customer relations management and software management—people with big organizations who want to buy their services: flexibly, of course.

With business partners he has bought a chalet in a ski resort in France. He will hire this out to the "financial community" who want to buy executive retreats and places for team-building activities without wracking up bills in five-star hotels. This is an especially attractive option when margins need trimming and people are being laid off. He brings in his friend from university who once ran the student ski club to run it for him. He trades in risk. Sometimes these are big risks. He buys up senior life insurance policies in the United States from those who want to cash in their life insurance before they die, and are prepared to do it at a discounted rate. He takes over their policies, paying the premiums and becomes the policy beneficiary. Bundling these policies together he levers them into an investment opportunity at guaranteed interest rates and invites people to invest. This generates fees, commission, and interest. It is all very lucrative. This is a US enterprise, and he is able to broker its extension into Asia where he has local financial knowledge and contacts on the ground. Many of Jake's connections are with US companies trading in Hong Kong or through Hong Kong with China or other countries in the Pacific Rim. This is run-on business from the mainstream corporate system.

As a hobby he raises start-up capital for projects he particularly likes—new bars and clubs—but which don't make him much money: "Just for fun!" Jake "goes with the flow," working on ten different things in a work day. He connects people to other people—he brokers his connections—and money flows in his and his associates' direction, the Hong Kong way. "Don't waste any time at all on anything that you can't make money on. Unless it's for fun, and there is a for-fun element." When times are difficult for corporations with big overheads, opportunities are created for those who are small and flexible, and Jake is in a position to take advantage of bankruptcies and others' misfortunes. Bad times are also good times, for someone.

Timing, flexibility, and business multitasking leave little time for other things in Jake's life. Being connected is what makes his world work. He knows who is doing what and anticipates their requirements. He has (expat) "friends" in every major institution. He meets them for a drink and work takes a slightly different form. What looks like leisure is actually work. All social encounters are potentially business encounters; and this makes for a work-centered life. It composes his social circle from his work requirements. Even at a party he will be doing business. But he draws boundaries. At parties with "friends" he won't actually "do business," only remind people that there is "business to be done" and that he will be calling them later.

On Friday nights work fades into having fun. Jake and a group of young men who operate on the work/leisure associate/friend boundary meet up for a drink. By mid-evening they are joined by wives and partners in the crowded, stylish, trendy restaurants and bars of Lang Kwai Fong frequented by young affluent expats. This is conveniently adjacent to Central, the center of the work day. They dance and drink well into the night. Working and playing hard go together in their world.

Jake works a six-and-a-half-day week. Keeping Saturdays for "people work" rather than "paperwork," he distinguishing types of work that more closely resemble leisure in their activities and their social relationships. Only on a Sunday afternoon does he take time off completely, with his equally work-centered "lady wife." Marie gives private music lessons at an attractively high hourly rate. An "Isle of Wight girl," as Jake describes her, highlighting the social distance she has traveled to Hong Kong, she finds work (money) difficult to turn down. They walk the dog, ride out to the New Territories on their motorbike and eat Sunday lunch together in an English sort of way in an effort to catch up on each other's life.

Their flat in Discovery Bay on the western (airport) island of Lantau stands empty most of the time. In a work-centered society it is hard to make the effort required to maintain social interaction of any sort beyond that which has a business utility. Jake's best friend in Hong Kong lives ten minutes away and yet he hasn't seen him in six weeks. He has never been invited into a neighbor's flat. One of their friends tries to hold a birthday party for a spouse. Few friends turn up. They have other commitments and demands on their limited time for non-work or marginal-to-work activity. Jake and Marie have no children, and it is difficult to see how they would find the time to have them or to care for them. Family life in Hong Kong has a particular character where men rarely see partners and children and where partners transfer childcare onto maids.

The intensity of work in Jake's life makes him a subtly different kind of lifestyle migrant from the others. His highly constrained relationship with Chineseness is prosecuted through work and schemes for making money. His social network is overwhelmingly expatriate and early thirties. He will know exactly when to leave Hong Kong. He will leave when it fails to deliver the kinds of money-making opportunities that make it a place to live. Although he likes it well enough, this is the bottom line in his connection.

Chungking Mansions

Walk from Chuck and Jake's work world in the central district of Hong Kong Island to the waterfront built on reclaimed land. Board the old Star Ferry. Cross the narrow strip of water to Kowloon. Look back toward Central as you sail and watch the corporate buildings converge into a cluster as your perspective on the landmass shifts. In ten minutes we will be on the quayside in Kowloon facing the Peninsula Hotel. This is a capsule of elegant Englishness. Listen to the string quartet while you eat high tea served on proper china. Make your way along Nathan Road. You are in Tsim Sha Tsui. In marked contrast to the corporate center's glass and steel monuments a distinctive, more subtly announced parallel world of (Indian subcontinent) global entrepreneurial activity in manufacturing, retailing, and shipping composes the built and commercial landscape here.

Hidden among this hive of enterprise is Chungking Mansions. Once a place of Chinese entrepreneurial activity, popularly connected to the world of the Triad gangs in the film *Chungking Express,* Chungking Mansions now forms part of a complex multilayered migrant world in the Tsim Sha Tsui district of Kowloon at the west end of Nathan Road. Chungking's layers, lives, and networks are unraveled in this section in a series of interconnected stories centered on the characters that operate through its stalls and hallways. Buildings and neighborhood are tightly bound up with people, their networks, and the local and global neighborhoods across which their feet have cut intersecting pathways. Buildings are a convenient, if limited—architectural—manifestation of lives. We can think of them as concrete expressions of routines, networks, pathways, and journeys. Chungking Mansions is the entranceway to a global matrix that is very different from the glittering towers of corporate Central. We will step inside this word and see where it leads us.

Chuck and Jake operate in parallel[20] global enterprises distinguished by their scale of operation, the character of the networks, the products through which they operate, and the mix of local/distant operations in play at any particular moment. The pathways running through Chungking Mansions reveal other global conduits of money-generating activities, risks, and rewards. Some of these conduits open onto others that we will visit subsequently. The global pathways running through Chungking Mansions work like this. They connect a distinctively

Indian (in the subcontinental sense) part of the city on the west end of Nathan Road, with factories in China's special economic zones, and market outlets on the Indian subcontinent and in Africa. The "Indian" character of this part of Nathan Road is marked by Indian-owned and -run jewelers, silk shops, electrical goods outlets, and tailors.

By Hong Kong standards Chungking Mansions is an old (opened in 1964), low-rise (seventeen-story) building housing a labyrinth of market stalls and small shops trading in electrical goods, mobile telephones, luggage, African artifacts, clothing, and snacks. It is dominated by small shopkeepers of Indian-subcontinental origin, many of them long settled in Hong Kong. It is a cheaper, shabbier version of the malls in Central and offers its wares to a different clientele. In the entranceway—commanding the most expensive pitches in a building where a modest rent is more than US$3,000 a month—are the money transfer and exchanging facilities. These broker flow of goods and money guarded by Plexiglas screens. On top of this layer of ("Indian") commercial activity with clearly marked-out rented pitches is another, more fluid layer of human and (invisible) commodity fabric. West and Central African traders[21] (predominantly Nigerian and Ghanaian), without offices, working out of briefcases, connect by mobile phones to a loose network of customers and suppliers broker deals. The

117

African's manufacturing contacts are in China too. They are gradually taking the African market from the "Indian" traders to forge their own networks across Africa.

As day turns to night the Indian stall- and shop-owners close up. African bodies, voices, and music expand to fill the spaces between shops and stalls. Chungking Mansions, which is open twenty-four hours a day, takes on a louder, more kinetic character. Flexible, mobile operatives (predominantly men) with dress codes ranging from traditional robes and cotton trousers to jeans and T-shirts, take over. The building vibrates day and night with these ethnically marked commercial activities and performances. Beneath this the building looks shabby and dilapidated although a renovation plan is in process, which will bring central air conditioning and the marble favored by Chinese business to its dingy surfaces. Shabbiness conceals its significance. While dabbling in a surface of retail sales, Chungking traders buy and sell goods by the ship container load. Unofficial estimates suggest it turns over a million (US) dollars a day, all in small-scale activity. On the upper floors shabby turns to squalid. Via creaky unreliable lifts with closed-circuit television cameras, and beyond the retail/wholesales floors, are fledgling Indian restaurants and hostels that offer cheap accommodation to backpackers and newly arrived migrant workers and traders. These are referred to as "businessmen." These service enterprises trade off the other forms of trading on the floors below. Restaurants start off here as members-only clubs, which are cheaper to license and have lower overhead costs. These often move on to better locations where they can charge higher prices.

Manju makes his way to Chungking Mansions and the tiny overpacked electrical store that he shares with his partners, Hamid and Hamid's brother, who lives in Newcastle in northern Britain. The bus journey from Manju's flat in the New Territories that he shares with his wife and three mostly grown-up children takes forty-five minutes. In his midsixties with a wizened face and gaps where he used to have teeth, Manju, who is under pressure from his wife to work less, shuffles more slowly now along Nathan Road from the bus stop. Although his wife does not work outside of the home, both of his daughters are working and one is a nurse. Only his youngest—his only son—is still in school, and Manju needs to earn money for his education. Anyway, what would he do with himself all day if not the work that is ingrained in his body? He walks into the building as the shutters are being lifted, revealing the tiny highly stocked shops behind them. All along the corridor, stalls are being opened up, and goods set out with an air of expectation. Manju lifts up the metal shutter and goes into the shop to put on the kettle before Hamid arrives. Various other traders originating from the Indian subcontinent—all men—drift in and out of the shop to offer Manju their Eid festival greetings—Ramadan had finished only the day before.

Well-known and respected, Manju is considered something of a pioneer, having arrived from East Pakistan—which became Bangladesh in his absence—in the mid-1960s. At this time there were few migrants in Hong Kong from the subcontinent, save those serving in colonial enterprises as police and soldiers. He'd arrived knowing no one and got himself a job as a mechanic with a Chinese company. This was how he'd learned Chinese. He goes back to Bangladesh occasionally, mostly on business. His immediate family is settled in Hong Kong and every year there are fewer people to visit back home.

Dark-haired and still youthful at forty, Hamid arrives fresh from morning prayers at the mosque and starts making phone calls to one of the factories in China where they buy their tape recorders. Well-connected to Chinese production and its system of brokers and fluent in Cantonese, Hamid finds this side of the business easier than Manju does. Hamid has also lived most of his life in Hong Kong. His childhood was shaped by the military apparatus of empire. He arrived when he was two with his family, returning to Pakistan when he was ten years old to attend school. He came back to Hong Kong as a teenager. Hamid's father was in the Pakistani Army, stationed in Hong Kong from 1937, under British command. Imprisoned in the war by the Japanese like Jack, he had reached the rank of major by the time he was demobilized. The major found postwar employment in the Royal Hong Kong Police Force as a superintendent. He was in charge of 350 other Pakistanis by the time Hamid was born; he stayed in Hong Kong until his need for a bigger house than he could afford, and his desire to live near his daughters, won out over the pull of Hong Kong family connections. He returned to Pakistan, visiting Hong Kong only occasionally to see Hamid. Although Hamid's three sisters still live in Pakistan and he visits from time to time, he and his family are Hong Kong belongers. With his wife and five children he has made a life in Hong Kong and, if suddenly he had to move—Pakistani migrants also have departure plans in the event of the deterioration of the Hong Kong business climate—he is more likely to reconfigure his business dealings with his brother in Newcastle (Britain) than return to Pakistan.

Manju and Hamid's business is still recovering from the drop in trading following the SARS outbreak in 2002. Things have been more tense and tenuous than usual and both are aware that one bad business decision could bankrupt them. Their business dealings are finely balanced on trust in others' integrity. As one of their friends put it when he dropped by their shop, "If you don't trust you cannot move, you cannot run. You cannot move one step. . . . a risk of life. This is

also gamble. You think a lot first. This is a style of business." Hamid's multilingualism—in addition to fluent English and Cantonese he speaks Urdu and Bengali—makes it possible for the two men to act as interlocutors between Chinese manufacturers and customers. Their customers live throughout the Indian subcontinent, especially Bangladesh where Manju has contacts, as well as in Nigeria, Senegal, Togo, Mali, Congo, and Madagascar. Hamid says:

> Actually we do the export . . . Yes, because the Africa people if they order there sometimes they order something different [than the] Chinese people [send], also when they are loading they cannot come to see everything, it's too expensive and also the money problem. If they pay all the money [for the] container at least one month [ahead] they don't know what is inside. When they open maybe there is nothing.

Manju and Hamid's customers trust them to supply the kinds of technology no longer used in other places—FM radios, microphones, tape recorders—from factories in China. Ninety percent of the Indian Chamber of Commerce members in Hong Kong are Hong Kong–based, family-run businesses just like theirs.[22] Even the Indian multinationals in Hong Kong are small- and medium-sized businesses. In the bigger scheme of things trade between India and Hong Kong is highly significant and works in India's favor. Hong Kong is also India's, as well as Pakistan's and Bangladesh's, entry point into the commercial possibilities offered by China.[23] This is a different set of opportunities from the ones negotiated by Chuck, possibilities based on obsolescent technologies. Manju and Hamid's skills as linguists, negotiators, and traders—human skills brokering profitable cooper-

ation—are important resources. They are trusted to check for quality and verify container contents so that their African and Indian customers are not cheated by manufacturers. As Hamid says, "We buy small quantities . . sometimes we buy from [Chinese] middlemen." They are able to negotiate good prices on behalf of their customers. Like Jake, they are flexible enough to supply what people want to buy, including toys, clothes, and gift items. Unlike Jake (and Chuck), who can only negotiate in one language, they are multilingual. Their networks are less ethnically and culturally homogenous too. Manju and Hamid are on intimate terms with Chinese manufacturers and middlemen. They work through trust in personal integrity and, sometimes, this brings social invitations.

Only last week Manju, Hamid, and their friends were invited to a wedding by one of the managers of the battery factory they deal with in Shenzhen, just over the boarder in mainland China. They were particularly touched that their Chinese hosts had been mindful that it was Ramadan and timed the wedding feast to coincide with the end of their holiday fast. They had been served special food in place of pork and soft drinks instead of alcohol. They were introduced to all the relatives of the bride and groom and photographed. Their relationship with Chineseness has a personal quality on which they all depend for their livelihood. As in mainstream global enterprise this works around the fusion of business and social occasions but, most importantly, and distinctively from the mainstream, on the trust on which modest fortunes hang. In these distinctive global networks Hamid and Manju operate as interlocutors between China, Africa, and the Indian subcontinent. It is both riskier and more precarious than the mainstream.

Central Kowloon Mosque

The mosque is connected with Chungking Mansions by the feet and bodies that tread a pathway from the mansions to the mosque's elaborate door. Like Chungking Mansions and the corporate center, the mosque too is part of a global network. It is one of the capsules that life in Chungking Mansions lead us to and hence is part of our tour. Because it is the first Friday after Eid, and because he wants to speak to the chief imam about his son attending weekly classes on the Koran, Manju leaves Hamid to make phone calls about a consignment of radios that haven't arrived from China, and crosses Nathan Road to the mosque for evening prayers.

The Central Kowloon Mosque is rapidly filling with evening worshippers as Manju approaches, pulling his cap out of his pocket and heading for the bathing area to begin his ritual ablutions and prayers. The mosque's loudspeakers start the call to prayer as he enters. Its tones drown in the roar of traffic and the voices of the bodies shuffling rapidly along Nathan Road. The mosque is linked with other mosques in Hong Kong and on the Chinese mainland. Some Chinese mosques have difficulty sustaining the same kinds of local organization as those in Hong Kong. Restricted to acts of religious worship, their integral social and community functions are hard to sustain. Mainland China struggles with the forms of civil society that accompany its new economic structures. The Chief Imam for Hong Kong is Chinese and services are run in Chinese as well as other languages. Money and religious functionaries circulate from Saudi Arabia and the Indian subcontinent; a global matrix based on spirituality rather than commerce is formed. Personnel circulate. The chief imam in the Kowloon Central Mosque was once a chaplain in the Pakistani Air Force. Money circulates. The money needed to boost local contributions and expand the mosque in 1987 from its tiny colonial form—when it served the religious needs of Muslim soldiers under British command from 1895—came from Saudi Arabia. The global conduits of the mosque run along their own routes and the same routes as commerce with different outcomes.

Every time he visits the mosque Manju sees people he doesn't recognize. There are new migrants from Pakistan, Bangladesh, India, and increasingly, from northern Nigeria, Somalia, and other Muslim African countries and regions. As the British colonial class decamped in 1997, new migrants arrived from other directions. They arrived from other postcolonial territories, once formed through subordinate relationships to empire. Thus (postcolonial) Hong Kong's relationship with empire is reconfigured through migration, as well as through other means.

The mosque-attending Muslim population of Hong Kong, including the Chinese Muslims, is more than 18,000, which equals the remaining British presence. Yet the mosque manages to absorb its congregation through a massive operation providing refreshments at the closing of the Ramadan fast every night for a month. It distributes support to the poor; runs supplementary Koran classes, Arabic classes, and conversions.

More than a thousand bodies on this Friday following Eid are packed into all three tiers of the mosque, and Manju struggles to find a place to stand. The Anglican Church on the opposite side of Nathan Road, although vibrant and popular, can only dream of congregations on this scale. Manju finds a place in one of the many long lines of men and from years of habit his body falls into the rhythmic kneeling motions connected with the prayers chanted by the Imam. The bodily rhythms of daily work in the Chunking Mansions are briefly transcended. It's all over in ten minutes, and he joins the queue outside the imam's office to ask about the Koran classes for young people he wants his son to join. When he finally gets into his office, past the administrator who is fielding calls on his mobile phone, the imam is seated behind a large impressive dark wood desk, checking his e-mail. The imam is a serious Koranic scholar who deals kindly and sympathetically with what he sees as his largely working-class congregation. Manju feels a bit awkward

in his company, although the imam always asks after his family and is pleased to hear that Manju's son will come to classes. Manju leaves, slowly crossing back over the road to the shop with a sense that things are as they should be.

Indian Food

Hamid has sorted out the missing consignment of radios by the time Manju gets back and so the two men leave the shop to the boy who comes to help them. They take the creaking lift to the eighth floor to the unpromising-looking grimy door of the Khyber Pass Mess Club. The sign on the door says Members Only, but this is a technical, licensing requirement as anyone can become a member. The two men sit at one of the half-dozen trestle tables beneath a notice board that contains a glowing review of the restaurant published in the *South China Morning Post*. Above the cash register is a framed six-by-four inch color photograph of the Khyber Pass after which the restaurant is named. This is the mountain pass that connects Pakistan with Afghanistan, and the photo is taken from the Pakistan side looking through the Khyber Gate into Afghanistan. The Khyber Pass was also where the revenge firing on British occupying troops in the 1930 Afghan wars took place. But no one in the restaurant would tell you this. The restaurant owner, Mr. Iqbal, "borrowed" the name from a friend who had an import/export company named Khyber because this is where he grew up. Khyber is historically a route for trade, migration, invasion, conquest, and retreating colonial powers. For Mr. Iqbal, his friends, and ancestors it is the route out of Pakistan. Mr. Iqbal senior passed through it to serve in the Royal Hong Kong Police. He subsequently married a Chinese woman and stayed for the rest of his life. The current Mr. Iqbal is the mixed-heritage product of this migration and its emotional entanglements.

The restaurant is noisy and full of diners, Indian and African traders, and a party of Chinese twenty-somethings—the source of most of the noise—celebrating a birthday. The waiters move quickly, serving their noisy diners steaming plates of Indian food. Manju and Hamid decide to move to an adjoining room where Mr. Iqbal himself sits reading quietly in a part of the restaurant reserved for (more strictly Muslim) customers who don't want to sit among people drinking alcohol. It is after ten o'clock when the men return from dinner to close the shop for the night and make their way home. Like Jake and other entrepreneurs, they barely take any time off. Life is work and work is life.

Although the Khyber Pass is a modest, fledgling business hidden in the back of an unannounced building, Indian food, like pizza, is a local business with global reach. Mr. Iqbal has plans to open two more restaurants in other parts of Hong Kong once he recovers from the dramatic drop in business that accompanied the SARS outbreak. This would have crippled him financially but for the modest overhead at his Chungking Mansions location. Hong Kong has a growing number of Indian restaurants and these are important to its self-image as a world-tourist destination. Some of these expensive and glamorous; others are more modest. They cater to a significant part of British dining taste; they service the food preferences of a sizeable migrant population from the subcontinent; and they cater to a growing fashion in Chinese dining. Many successful Indian restaurants started modestly in places like Chungking Mansions, in greenhouses that propagate restaurant businesses.

This is how Ram's boss started, and now he owns a small chain of five restaurants spread across the city employing sixty people. Ram manages one of these restaurants in an upscale mall in Shatin in the New Territories. His boss is an Indian success story, and so is Ram. He and his wife operate at the upper end of a global serving class, differentiated from domestic workers by wages, conditions of work, and migration circumstances. Recruited by his boss in Bombay, where he was working in a hotel, Ram had been on the lookout for advancement through overseas employment. He was thinking of moving to Kuwait when he was headhunted and offered a job in Hong Kong as a waiter. Being only twenty-one and without dependants, he took it. His boss arranged his travel and visa and Ram, a slender, well-dressed young man, soon progressed from waiter to manager. Lunchtime and evenings, six days a week, he now stands outside the restaurant beside a tall lectern. On this stands a menu and list of reservations. Dressed in a black suit he meets and greets, guiding diners to their tables.

The restaurant has modern upscale décor and a cooking area that opens onto the restaurant through a glass panel. Here diners can observe three men working quickly and constantly. One fries curries, another, a specialist tandoori chef, makes bread, throwing it against the brick side of the oven. A third washes up and prepares meat and vegetables. Their workspace is hot and small. The men in the kitchen were recruited in India like Ram and they share a small apartment in Hung Hom on the eastern end of the Kowloon waterfront. This is a cheaper part of town because it is near the mortuary and, inconveniently, not serviced by the subway. The restaurant has a largely Chinese clientele, but British and other expatriates are also well represented—given their numbers—among the diners.

Like the men in Chungking Mansions, Ram works from midmorning until late at night with a couple of hours off in the day between the end of the lunch shift

and the beginning of dinner. This is barely enough time to get home as the bus takes forty-five minutes each way so he spends his break in Shatin, lengthening the workday. The dreary routine nature of his life is apparent in the heavy voice in which he complains to his wife: "I wake up and go to work. And come back." Despite Ram's success there is a sense of struggle and monotony about the young couple's lives. They couldn't manage without his wife's wage, and there is a baby on the way. They will have to pay someone, a neighbor or friend, for childcare. Ram says:

> You really try to squeeze some time for yourself and family: same thing. Here, they have to [work hard], otherwise it's very difficult here. . . . accommodation is very expensive so if one person is earning and if there are two or three back home, it won't work out. Husband and wife both have to work and they both have to share expenses. Normally everybody faces the struggle when there are two, it's not like other countries, when you have children there are other people to look after them, mother or somebody else. It is very difficult here. You have to hire a maid here so the rent and the salary of the maid are equal to one person's salary. Well previously I never had plans like this. Now I think Hong Kong is just a workplace, for anybody, not only me. If someone wants to earn money Hong Kong is OK. If you want to make, if you want to spend your life here, I think this is not the place. You see. . . . it's just mechanical. . . . You wake up early in the morning, you do nothing else. There is not much greenery, there is greenery, there are parks, but not much like other countries like India, maybe England. It's not natural. So I think I feel held up. It's like you do things, every day the same things, you repeat it every day. I think it goes on for months and months. Nothing new, nothing new. You see the same people, you do the same things every day, every day of your life. Maybe because Hong Kong is a small place, I think that's what I mean, yes.

The young couple is bored and isolated, sharing with other (British) migrants the sense that Hong Kong is a good place to *work* but no place to *live*. They share with Chuck and Amanda the experience of it as small and confining, although the conditions of Ram and his wife's confinement are quite different from Chuck and Amanda's.

Ram's wife, Raminder, minds this more than Ram, although she knew when she married him three years earlier that they would live in Hong Kong. She knew she would know no one to start with except for him. First excited about leaving Mangalore and living in a new country, she soon learned that Hong Kong is not hospitable for migrant workers from India. She learned that life was both difficult and expensive. Accustomed to the noisy nosiness of south Indian neighborhood

and family, Raminder barely knows her neighbors and hasn't been invited into any apartment in their densely populated building. Her mostly Chinese neighbors pass her wordlessly on the stairs and firmly close their doors against the possibility of interaction. Even the minority of Indian neighbors behave in the same privatized way although without the hostility of her Chinese neighbors. Indian neighbors go out to work and back through their gated front doors without looking or speaking. Raminder is sure that this is quite unlike the way they would have lived in India, where everyone is just too involved in the affairs of others.

Small and vivacious Raminder is hungry for company and, while she knows a couple of other South Indian women, they live too far away for her to visit. So she relies on her waitress job in the coffee shop at the United Services Recreation Club, not far from where they live near the mosque. She is especially close to two other waitresses. These women are Nepalese and descended from men who served in Hong Kong Ghurkha regiments, disbanded in 1997 with the rest of the colonial military apparatus. They are practically locals. She chats to the club members, too, of course. She is very popular with the members like Mary Trent, who we visited earlier, because she speaks good English and because she is especially good at her job. The club was supposed to be a stopgap for Raminder as she is well educated and from a professional Mangalore family. But her qualifications do not easily transfer. And it is additionally difficult to get the job she wants, working with handicapped children, until her Cantonese is more fluent. She doesn't get to practice it much at the club, where she is prized for the fluency of her English.

When she finishes work at the club at 5:00 pm Raminder wanders along the fish and flower market in Mong Kok. This is the densely populated and poorer part of Kowloon on the north end of Nathan Road. She wanders into Ikea. Aimlessly extending her tour against the prospect of returning to an empty flat, she goes night window shopping with the crowds, mentally compiling a list of the presents she will take back to Mangalore on her next visit. Visits to India provide the timeframe in which she thinks about her life. She can't wait to "go home." Ram doesn't get home from the restaurant until midnight, and he will be tired. She feels especially lonely when they fight, which they do regularly, over how things are done in the apartment. She wonders what it will be like when the baby arrives.

Many global pathways intersect in Hong Kong. Its tangle of loosely connected bodies, enterprises, activities, moneymaking schemes, friend, and business networks, faith, and food are cast in journeys around, in, and out of the city in many directions.

LIFE AT THE TOP

The Peak

> I will not describe its cliques, its boundless hospitalities, its extravagances in living, its quarrels, its gaieties, its picnics, balls, regattas, races, dinner parties, amateur theatricals, afternoon teas, and all its other modes of creating a whirl that passes for pleasure or occupation.[1]

Our tour retraces its passage along Nathan Road from Chungking Mansions to the Kowloon waterfront and back across Victoria Harbor on the Star Ferry. Approaching Hong Kong Island, the tangled corporate cluster of high-rise offices begin to separate into distinctive buildings and architectural styles. Above and behind them is the precipitous green mountain called the Peak. The best way to scale the Peak is on the Peak Tram funicular favored by tourists. It will whisk you rapidly above the building level of the island, and then over a dense tangle of tropical trees and shrubs to the landing station at its summit. The fit might tackle it on foot. There is a steeply winding road, traversed by buses, taxis, and cars, and there are several small pathways to walk on. But by whatever means the Peak is tackled, it is a long climb to the top.

The social topography of Hong Kong once clearly revolved around land elevation. People were distributed over the Peak, Midlevels, and the shoreline, where some lived with the sea, sometimes on Sampans. Things are no longer this clear-cut. But life on the Peak is still life at the top of the social heap, so it still has a special place in the layered social geography of Hong Kong.[2] With elevations of 1,800 feet above sea level and a microclimate that makes it cooler than lower lying regions, the Peak ameliorates the steaminess of tropical life in the same way as the Himalayas did in colonial India. It also provides gracious accommodation and the most exclusive addresses in town. Once called Victoria Peak—Victoria being the colonial name for what is now called the central district—it was strictly reserved for Europeans. This arrangement left the colonial serving class seeking special permission from the governor to serve at Peak elevations. Before the Peak tram was built in the 1890s a visceral colonialism operated in which Chinese "coolies" carried white folk up the Peak in sedan chairs. This resulted in boiling (racialized) resentment that periodically erupted into violence.

Spatial arrangement and separation of bodies was the cornerstone of colonial governance. In the nineteenth century the Chinese residents of Hong Kong were organized into territorial units of 1,000 households, watched over by local agents appointed by magistrates. There were curfews, curfew passes, residential permits, lodgers' permits, and employer certification.[3] Extensive policing and public floggings patrolled and enforced the spatial organization of the colonial social fabric.

These social processes generated the social geographies of the Peak. But in post-colonial Hong Kong the (ethnic) social relationships of altitude are reconfigured and the Peak is firmly under (wealthy) Chinese occupation.

Stephanie doesn't live on the Peak although many of her friends do. She will guide this part of our tour. We will *walk* Stephanie's day in the city and meet her social network. We will eavesdrop on her conversations with other women. These are women (including Amanda) whose lives are not shaped by formal paid employment or unmediated domestic responsibility but by a matrix of other priorities in what are unmistakably privileged expatriate women's lives. As well as propelling the body forward, walking is a way of negotiating space. It is a way of organizing social space, and it is a way of organizing time in a proper life. It is important to live a proper life and, without the scaffolding of employment, this takes thought and effort. Stephanie's walking group takes time to organize, but it assembles a sterling group of likeminded, interesting women in a context in which creating your own social world is an indispensable life skill.

The walk starts straight after breakfast. Robust-looking women in shorts and walking boots congregate in the Tai Pan Country Park to tackle Violet Hill. They walk over the Peak and down the southeastern side of the island. This takes more than two hours and provides stunning views over the South China Sea on the way. Surprisingly, 60 percent of Hong Kong is country park. The seam between country and city—concrete and grass—is puckered by the sheer abruptness with which one turns into the other in the place where the walk starts by the reservoir. The walk is about energy, effort, vitality, and talk among women who are available during the day.

As the women walk Stephanie tells the story of her recent experience in a play in Oxford (UK). Her daughter was one of the student-actors and when a fellow actor drops out, someone has to play the mother at short notice. Stephanie is adept at stepping in and doing what needs to be done. Her story is about her trepidation, her family's support, and her success; all modestly claimed. The significance of the story is not immediately evident. Acting for Stephanie is the path not taken. After "just" studying French, English, and psychology at Durham University in the sixties, Stephanie opts for the "safer option" of becoming a secretary rather than an actress. She first works in Paris in a merchant bank. Later in the UK she works in a law firm where she meets and marries Bartholomew. She slips seamlessly into a supporting role. While Bartholomew scaled the corporate ladder Stephanie looked after two children. A woman who gets on with things with minimal fuss, she can organize a move to Hong Kong or Tokyo at short notice. She can drive her husband to work in the center of Tokyo on their first day

and find her way home again to an apartment she barely knows. Stephanie can hit the ground running. She can find a house, furnish it, and assemble makeshift toys while the packing crates arrive. Her efforts leave her husband free to focus on work.

Twenty-five years ago they'd arrived in Hong Kong and Bartholomew made his way to the top, a vantage point from which he no longer feels the need to socialize, even with his wife. "He's exhausted every avenue with me, so that's it. Cul-de-sac," she says cheerfully. Bartholomew reads military history over dinner unless the children are around, which they aren't much anymore. Stephanie is free to fly to Britain and perform in a play, and this is both reward and acknowledgement of her contribution. The walking group is amused by the story and impressed with her courage. In the parking garage at the end of the walk they disperse into their separate daily activities: bridge, shopping, golf, charity work, chores, mahjong.

Stephanie heads home. She had intended to go to mass before Ellen arrived for morning coffee but she is running a bit late. Home is plush red carpet and highly polished wood. Stephanie lives in a beautiful, spacious house maintained by others under her direction. To furnish a house is to practice bricolage; assembling what is available to create a particular atmosphere.[4] What is available to Stephanie is elegant and expensive-looking, like the rest of the material composing her life. A squatter village she thinks picturesque lies in full view outside through the window. She is not disturbed by proximities drawn through social polarities. In the coastal area around Aberdeen fabulous houses like Stephanie's share a sea view with "boat people" who live on Sampans and tiny junks. She makes and serves the cappuccino. Her maid has yet to master the machine. What kind of relationship might rural Filipino hands form with a machine that services intricate taste and style in coffee? Relationships formed with material and mechanical objects provide insightful minisocial commentaries.

Ellen arrives in an enormous black four-wheel-drive vehicle she leaves in the forecourt in front of the gated house. She is groomed in a manner suggesting time and effort spent on the details of jewelry and nail polish, facials, and massage. Stephanie is impatient with such things although her trim skirt and blouse are impeccable. Tim, Stephanie's nineteen-year-old, is commanded to make an appearance in the living room and wisely obeys. Ellen hasn't seen him for some time so he explains that he is going to Scotland's Edinburgh University next year to read history. This is his "gap year," so he is doing a ski instructor's course in Quebec. He'll return in time for the big rugby Sevens match before setting off for Southeast Asia and on to Australia. His gap year is much like his friends'. For now

Tim is working at one of the big banks in the city, a position he secured through a school friend's father, who is the CEO. This experience will add to his employability after he graduates from university. "They've made me assistant marketing manager . . . the lowest of the low . . . I prefer to call myself the coffee boy." He presents his business card to Ellen in a humble and self-mocking way: "They got me about a thousand . . . It's a good idea to keep one of all the business cards you ever have so you can frame them and you can see where you started and where you finish up." Like Stephanie, Ellen doesn't have a job. She does a "bit of reflexology," some charity work, and belongs to a Christian group. She used to run marathons with her husband who works in clothing retail until she injured her knee. "I'm not a businesswoman," she says in a tone that doesn't reveal whether this counts as social success or not.

Ladies Who Lunch

Following coffee with Ellen, Stephanie has a ladies lunch to attend at the Aberdeen Yacht Club. As she sits through the traffic from her house down the mountain to the Aberdeen shoreline, she has time to reflect that her day is slightly too packed with arrangements and appointments.

The yacht club is luxurious. Public as well as private places assemble important social messages about those for whom they are intended, encoded in the atmosphere composed through furniture, artifacts, and decor. She brushes past the gingerbread house; four feet square and made entirely from confectionary. At the entrance to the playroom Filipino nannies guard small charges climbing elaborate structures or playing on the computers. She passes down a stairway being decorated with cream ribbons and flowers leading to a ballroom where tables are being set out elaborately, immaculately. They are in honor of a Chinese couple who are celebrating twenty-five years of marriage with the help of two hundred guests that evening.

Out on the terrace the ladies—Celia and Julia—are waiting at a table in a shady spot with a view taking in the harbor and the pool. Celia and Stephanie are fifty. Julia is in her early forties. The lunch date is a long-standing one. Even with time available in the day it is difficult to find time to get together given other commitments. Their friendships too are long-standing and the women have many things in common. This includes children, now mainly grown, apart from one of Julia's who is only ten years old. Julia's older children by a previous marriage, are

at university. The women also share a long-term (quarter-century) relationship with Hong Kong, which they anticipate extending into the future. These women are long-term residents who have made arrangements to stay on.

Their commitment to Hong Kong takes the form of a Chinese (second) husband (in the case of Julia) and real estate. Celia and Stephanie's husbands have taken advantage of what turns out to be a temporary drop in housing prices to buy property. Their first conversation drifts onto this topic. Stephanie and Bartholomew have bought an apartment not far from their house on the south side of the island. It has impressive communal facilities but they are not planning to live in it. They prefer their rented house, which Bartholomew's company pays for. The apartment is an investment, a hedge against future spiraling prices and, perhaps, a place to live once they are only two and Bartholomew's company no longer pays the rent. Celia and her lawyer husband have bought a flat in an old colonial building on the Peak, in the newly converted Jardines[5] mess. The other women tease her and threaten not to visit. This jibe distances them from the (iconic) colonial past of the Peak and Jardines. It also acknowledges new territorial loyalties drawn between the south side of the island and the Peak. They consider these places to be occupied by different kinds of (wealthy) expatriates. Empire hovers beneath the surface of the conversation. Julia is keen to rebrand Hong Kong as an international place: "A lot of the colonial types who used to live here don't live here anymore." Julia thinks this is definitely an improvement.

Tim's arrival reminds the women of the many ways in which daily life in Hong Kong and its bigger schemes of transnational connection are organized around children. With little to do that day, his mother's invitation to lunch is irresistible. Tim's gap year brought to an end an established routine of connection with Britain, which Stephanie refers to as the "expat housewife package." It works like this. Until children are ten years of age they go to Kelletts, the international school featured earlier in our tour. The humid summers involve the flight of the "memsabs to the hills," as Stephanie puts it. In her case this meant spending time with family and friends in Britain. She remembers this as time spent in perpetual motion from one place (obligation) to another, packing and unpacking. Bartholomew, back in Hong Kong working, would only join them for two weeks' vacation; servicing the British connections is a highly gendered business. An alternate version of this plan involved setting up a base somewhere in the UK in a rented or borrowed house for the summer and letting friends and family do the traveling instead. Once children are in (British) boarding schools the pattern shifts. Parents (usually mothers) visit at half term, so trips to Britain are shorter and more frequent. Children are reluctant to spend school holidays in Britain; they are instead

anxious to get back to Hong Kong and meet up with their friends, who have also returned from other boarding schools. These close-knit social circles of friends are quite different from the ESF crowd who spend their summers in Britain. Summer in Hong Kong is party time for the boarding school crowd, and their return initiates a frenetic round of junk trips and other leisure activities, supervised by mothers.

Now this phase in their lives is over and Stephanie is unsure how connections with Britain will be organized in the future. She and Bartholomew both have elderly parents who constitute a fragile connection with perplexing and difficult obligations. Celia's life in Hong Kong, and her connection with Britain, was organized in a similar way to Bartholomew and Stephanie's. But now her youngest child is at university in Britain and her son decided to stay on after graduation. Celia lives at a distance from those in her family she is closest to. Julia too confirms her British connections on behalf of her (older) children. "We've kept a home too all the way through." This is despite the fact that her second husband is Chinese, and her mixed-race ten-year-old is schooled locally in Chinese. Her connection with both places is radically different from that of her two friends.

Connections with Britain are geographically located around shifting key fam-

ily relationships and versions of British life. Home ownership, in either place, constitutes a solid commitment. Ellen—who wasn't invited to lunch—returned to Britain annually throughout her now grown-up children's childhood. The entire family would go to the rural north of Britain. Here they would stay in a rented farm cottage in close connection with the land, farming, and animals. They would stay near, but not actually with, her family. Ellen's example underscores an important point about connections with Britain. These temporary forms of British life connected with Hong Kong are intricately staged and come in many versions. Ellen's version of a "proper" British life involves animals and rural landscape as well as family connection and provides a counterpoint to a thoroughly urban existence in Hong Kong.

Children, works of Hong Kong–British identity-in-the-making, provide the catalysts for these productions of Britishness. It is through them that British–Hong Kong connections are worked. A version of British life and family is selected and arranged for them in time-limited ways. This is the material children are offered with which to fabricate their Britishness from the vantage point of Hong Kong. Through patterns of housing tenure, schools, children's commitments, and journeys of differing kinds between Hong Kong and Britain each woman—and this is the work of women—created connections to both places. They also create ways of being more permanently at home in Hong Kong where they expect to continue to reside.

Lunch is light and leafy, the way women eat. Drinks are strictly nonalcoholic. The conversation switches to work and the activities replacing it. Julia teases Tim for his lack of stamina. When she was younger she would arrive home from clubbing just in time to get a couple of hours' sleep, and then get up and go to work. Tim is struggling, being new at combining work and nightlife.

Julia no longer works full-time since she got married. She has always had "little jobs." She means that while she makes a contribution to the family budget she does not have to support herself on the income derived from it. Her current little job involves accounting in firms where she has contacts. She doesn't have to search for work. Work finds her and she does it to help out. She relishes the structure to her day and the company this provides, especially as it doesn't take up her whole day. "I work part-time . . . I play tennis. We had a golden retriever until last week and it died . . . I work for a little head-hunting company doing accounts." A dog is both an activity and a practical way of composing a relationship with the world.

Celia's relationship with work is more troubled:

> I was a working girl. I worked for a publishing company as an audio person . . . I did all the editing at home [to fit in with childcare when her children were in schools in Hong Kong] on the computer. I was at the BBC before I came here . . . I was a studio manager . . . I have to admit when I first came to Hong Kong I was not terribly happy because I was brought kicking and screaming. I had to give up my job to come and I was *not* happy. From having had a job I was person in my own right I became Michael's wife and I found that very tough. . . . and then I became James's mummy.

Her self-mocking tone reveals a knowing capitulation in the family enterprise of child care and supporting her husband's job. This urge to work has passed with time and age and Celia has become "a real tennis *tai tai*, which I swore I would never do. I would never live on the Peak, I would never be a tennis *tai tai*." Julia supplies another image of inauthentic life, adding: "I would never sit by the pool all day." Celia joins in this collective marking of a proper life: "Actually I still haven't sat by the pool all day. I would never be one of those ladies who lunched."

Stephanie, who left paid employment when she got married, joins in the joking and self-mocking.

I put my nail polish on, take it off and put it on again . . . I am the only expatriate women you will ever meet in Hong Kong who has never had a manicure, a pedicure, or a massage. . . . I am proud of myself. I am NOT a tai tai. A *tai tai* is a Chinese word for number one wife, . . . most important wife. The best, the goodest.

She goes on to expresses respect for women who get paid for their work. Her work is neither recognized nor rewarded with payment. The women contrast their situations with Chinese women of similar social standing. They work. For them work is a vital ingredient in a proper life. The conversation switches abruptly to whether Hong Kong supermarkets match up to the British quality-chain Waitrose.

After lunch Stephanie departs for Central with Tim in tow to run errands en route to the charity organization she supervises. *"Josan, josan,"* she cheerily greets the underground parking attendant under an impressive office tower, dismissing Tim's accusation that she is being patronizing. Greeting is a minimal form of social contact, and Tim is feeling reflexive about the fact that his family lives in Hong Kong without speaking Chinese and has little contact with Chinese people. He knows a couple of Chinese boys but only because they went to the same British boarding school as he.[6] The difference between his and Jess's expat bubble is class. Unable to resist the temptation to organize Tim's errands, Stephanie takes him to the best place to get his shoes repaired. Being in charge of the unremarkable is an unbounded remit. She heads for Saint Joseph's Cathedral shop to buy Christmas cards for those in her social circle for whom Christmas has a religious significance. Like visiting Britain, sending Christmas cards puts the work in net-*work*. It is part of living at a distance from family and keeping up with equally mobile friends, scattered all over the world, even if it is only once a year. Each December Stephanie sends out a computer-written family letter detailing key activities and achievements over the year. She also writes two hundred cards all with personal messages that acknowledge the circumstances of each recipient. Her alphabetical filing system of the cards received the previous year provides an archive and the memory for the next.

Threading her way through Midlevels below the Peak Stephanie arrives at the modern office block in Central that houses the advice bureau she runs. As Stephanie arrives, a female Australian volunteer is advising a woman by telephone on where to get a pressure cooker repaired. Pamphlets displayed around the office provide information on how to get a divorce and how to employ foreign domestic helpers. These staples of expatriate life offer a lifeline to new migrants and those whose familiarity with the city is limited by language, curiosity, or cross-cultural skill. The advice bureau is funded by the Jockey Club of Hong Kong and other wealthy sponsors. It deploys experienced migrants, like Stephanie, in the dissemination of essential migration knowledge. Stephanie deals with her e-mail and sets off again.

We will walk with Stephanie to her afternoon tea appointment. This walk takes us through Midlevels and her encounter with the Chineseness of the streets. She admires Ladder Street arranged along stone steps for its market stalls. She walks along Wellington Street.

> There's always a lot of deliveries going on. There's a lovely butcher's here [a pig's head hangs outside]. There's a locksmith's here and all these little tap shops. . . . and this funny old shop. It's kind of stationary and it's kind of inks. A market street. . . . fresh fish. . . . I get my fruit here.

This area makes her feel, in a comfortable way, that she lives in a Chinese city. She interacts with shopkeepers keepers happily on a "*Josan, josan*" level. She says, "People like me live in a bit of a cultural vacuum. We don't interact a lot with local Chinese and that's OK with them, and I guess it's OK with us." She sums up her relationship with Chineseness as the distant admiration of the aesthetics of (certain) public spaces in the city, rather than as close personal ties. In this commotion of Chinese bodies and commerce she admires, Stephanie bumps into two other British expatriate women she knows well. They are similar in social standing to Stephanie and equally well groomed. At each encounter the women stop and spend some time comparing Christmas plans. Some of their social circle stays in Hong Kong for Christmas. Others head off on holiday or back to visit family in Britain. Stephanie's family likes to stay in Hong Kong and enjoy a casual, al fresco Christmas on the beach with close expat friends.

Tea?

Amanda is waiting at a table with a crisp white tablecloth and expensive china as Stephanie arrives for tea at Helena May. Tea is an old-fashioned, light British meal of sandwiches, tea, and cakes, taken in late afternoon. Archaic and anachronistic, its elite version has an icon status as "English" and this combination of factors also mark it as "colonial." Tea is exported round the (postcolonial) world, packaged as a tourist attraction and available in places like the Raffles Hotel in Singapore. Helena May has another set of colonial associations, named after the wife of the governor of the colony between 1912 and 1919, Sir Henry May.

Helena May is an elegant turn-of-the-century building nestling amongst Central's tower blocks. One of few surviving colonial building in the area, it evokes a "sense of nostalgia."[7] Helena May was a staging post in the accommodation needs of professional women seeking employment opportunities in Hong Kong, and missionaries on their way to China, a strategy in the feminization of empire. It was envisaged that "well-managed accommodation"[8] offered a safeguard against women ending up in hotels of "dubious reputation" when more respectable hotels were "beyond the means of the average working woman."[9] Behind the setting up of Helena May was a concern about prostitution and the dangers posed by the "ruffians and robbers who have come down from Canton."[10] This is reference to Chinese migration following the collapse of the Ch'ing Dynasty and establishment of the Chinese republic (1911). Helena May was intended as a safe and affordable temporary place for migrant women to stay in the colony.

A racialized filtering mechanism for respectability (class) and Europeanness, the Helena May organization grew out of the YWCA. By 1898 the YWCA was managed by missionaries concerned with the "welfare of women and girls in Hong Kong"[11] and made no attempt to cater specifically for European women. Helena May grew out of a demand to separate European and Chinese women.

The WMCA provided for the accommodation and recreational needs of Chinese women, and Helena May focused on Europeans. Today securing the involvement of Chinese women in Helena May is considered a vital part of its postcolonial development. This has proved difficult. Helena May's racial separation of women remains an obstacle in the memories and calculations of Chinese women who might consider joining.

Colonial filigree under the table and white napkins on top; Helena May has intellectual leanings. It boasts a fine library and runs discussion groups. It is a place for social gatherings controlled by women and still has a small number of rooms rented out to women arriving or passing through Hong Kong on business.

A young woman on her way to look at clothing factories in China was in residence at the time of Amanda and Stephanie's tea. Amanda reflects, gesturing at Stephanie that

> Madam and madam are not finding our way [like these girls] because that is found for us, isn't it? I could not be the lady here without my maid. Because who is making my bed, who is cleaning my toilet and buying the food for dinner tonight? And cooking it? Not me. I can do this stuff, but I am not doing it here, because there is no need and we employ people. And, this is going to sound like Lady Bountiful, but that is what I want to be as well as sit in cafés.

The two women acknowledge that maids service their lifestyle. Boundaries are drawn around what tasks women (in their position) should keep control of and what they might relinquish to maids. Their boundaries are different from Mary's and Nelly's. Stephanie wanted to be "hands on" with the care of her children, although she was glad for the babysitting that gave her free time. She has always done her own cooking, but not the washing, ironing, or cleaning. For Amanda on the other hand:

> My decision is that I have relinquished everything. . . . In Australia I did everything. That's being an expat without the frills. That's what you do. . . . The other thing you do as an expat is that you play golf, bridge, mahjong in the afternoons. Or learn things.

The relationship between mistress and maid frames the context and content of daily life. These women's lives can be about interests, hobbies, and social activities, while their maids attend to the practical fabric of domestic work. The relationship between mistress and maid is logged in the circulation of material objects. Maids play a significant role in the recycling of used clothes and other unwanted items. Amanda's castoffs are dispatched to the Philippines, to new owners, distributed through her maid's social networks. Stephanie's maid hoards unwanted items in her room. This is bursting with stuff Stephanie no longer needs and a source of tension between them. Maids free their mistresses for new consumption by providing a conduit of redistribution with the moral purpose of helping the less well-off. These little-investigated circuits of global redistribution expose deep social inequalities. How do these used items enter Philippine village lives? In what new purposes and social arrangements do they become entangled?

Mistress-maid relations are also modern configurations with colonial resonance. As Amanda, who was born in British India, says,

> I've been an expatriate all my life. . . . My father was a jute merchant for a French company and had been in India before the [Second World] War. . . . one of those young men with no hope in England. His father wanted to get rid of him, but it was very useful, England had colonies. I mean, what else? So he went out there and did alright for himself. And the war started and that's why he joined the army as a Ghurka. . . . He never spoke [about the war]. The only thing I know is that while he was in Burma his batman [army servant] came to live with us in Madras and was our guard outside our compound every night. My father sent for him, and he came. And I don't know what happened, but my father looked after him until he died, he lived in a hut where the servants lived, slept on a string bed. And he went back every year to Nepal and he sent someone to take his place for a month while he went back. And he was in full puttees. . . . I can still see him.

This reveals the expectations that once formed and still form the substance of Amanda's life. This was structured by the service she and her parents thought normal. This version of normal is ingrained in the architecture of social life. Having an indirect, managerial relationship to the work of running a house and rearing children is normal in this world. Social relationships based on command are normalized. "My father sent for him, and he came." Command is based on a sense of entitlement to service. When the family servant returns to Nepal another is dispatched to fill in. Life continues for those who issue commands. Serving lives and bodies are shuffled and this involves them in making new accommodations. This version of normativity involves a mental "upstairs/downstairs" attitude in which some lives are entitled to be sustained by others. It also creates conduits of obligation—in generosity and kindness—that acknowledge this social architecture.

Amanda's life and her sense of self were forged in these circumstances. They are ingrained in her habits and movements, in her thinking, in her social relationships, and in her sense of who she is and how she might operate in the world. In circumstances where service continues to be a feature of normal everyday life, postcolonial being and doing is subtly inflected with the past. Colonial productions of white Britishness persist, unevenly, subtly and modernized, in these regimes of service. Stephanie has no colonial genealogy but draws selectively on service relationships in casting her life. Mary is wary and hesitant in her use of service. And Nelly will have nothing to do with it. There are many versions of gendered whiteness.

The two women say goodbye. Stephanie goes home to make dinner for Tim, Bartholomew, and herself. Amanda goes home to see what her maid has produced for her dinner with Chuck. Although they are not employed, they work, as in the meaning of work as activities of production. They work in producing the networks and activities sustaining a proper life on behalf of themselves and their families. They produce elaborate material infrastructures in housing, decoration, and furnishing. They produce regimes of self and family maintenance in clothes, grooming, and exercise. They run households, in a managerial capacity, to particular standards of child and daily life production. They produce the right kinds of social networks and activities on behalf of their children and working spouses. They produce and service their migrant family relationships with the appropriate aspects of British life. These things accumulate to bigger things. Social structure is produced in routine, mundane, everyday actions.[12] Anyway, Stephanie could run a small country.

SERVICE

Serving-Class Migrants

Service compresses multiple meanings and social locations. Lyn operates in a relocation-industry service relationship to Amanda and Chuck, and Indian waiters serve their customers. But these are temporary arrangements around specific transactions, rather than life-entangled, enduring processes. Lyn and the Indian waiters point to a place where the migration categories we are working with— lifestyle and serving-class migration—bleed into each other. Life is always messier than the social categories we impose to order and analyze it. We now unravel the world of Filipino maids. Maids are a clearer case of serving-class migration than waiters. Service is deeply entangled in their lives. It defines their entry conditions and the terms of their settlement. It defines the social architecture in which they operate. In the official immigration and labor policies of the SAR government they are refereed to as "domestic helpers." Our tour remains in the same neighborhood: around the Peak and its southern flanks, around the Shooson Hill neighborhood with the ladies who lunch. Here we shift to a parallel world of intimate social proximities. Stephanie and Amanda acknowledge these in producing the daily lives of expatriate women like themselves. They are equally central in the daily lives of Chinese women of varying circumstances.

Domestic helpers in Hong Kong live within diverse social and material circumstances. The government-established income threshold required to allow households to employ foreign domestic labor is KH$15,000 (approximately US$ 3,000) a year. Slightly above the average wage, this threshold puts the services of domestic helpers within the reach of a large proportion of ordinary Chinese households. It releases women to work[1] without the additional burden of domestic labor and childcare. Before 1970 most maids in Hong Kong were poor local or mainland Chinese. Today few Chinese people seek this type of work because they are able to earn more in other occupations.

Foreign domestic workers are now predominantly women migrants from the Philippines.[2] They are also the most highly politically organized. Their popularity, from 1970, was fuelled by their ability to operate in English, as a result of a long-standing subordinate relationship with the United States.[3] But maids also come from Sri Lanka (like Lyn's maid), Thailand, Nepal, and Indonesia. The term "maid" has become synonymous with women migrants from these countries. These source countries share low-wage economies, economic difficulties, and high levels of unemployment and their nationhood was forged in subordinate relationships with European empires.

Maids, as Stephanie puts it, are "important to the smooth running of things . . . It's easy to take them for granted because they are so unobtrusive." Maids service others' lives and obligations in a delicate symbiosis. Symbiosis is a highly adapted, specialized relationship in which the participants provides the material and emotional conditions of the others' existence. This is not a mutually beneficial balance. The substance of maids' lives is intimately entangled in subordinate relationships within the households employing them. These take small and trivial forms in everyday transactions that accumulate to more substantial social differences. Beyond the domestic spaces of their employment, maids establish distinctive relationships with places in the city and routes connecting them. Their use of space and rhythms of movement distinguish them from other migrants and from locals. So too do the bigger journeys, between Hong Kong and the Philippines, that form the context of their local ones. Through their activities at these different levels of scale, maids make their lives as migrants. Big and small things are connected.

Living inside Others' Lives

Hong Kong immigration legislation requires that migrant domestic helpers live with their employers. Employers live in a variety of circumstances. Some maids have a spacious private room and bathroom. Others sleep on a mat in the corner of the lounge or share a bedroom with the child they are employed to care for. Sharing living space brings intimate entanglement between the lives it produces. Lives are produced through habits and dress; through ways of eating and resting, through mobile habits, through interaction with material objects, through ways of interacting with children and pets, through ways of walking; through social relationships, through the arrangement of living space, and through negotiated boundaries between cleanliness and dirt and public and private activities.[4] Those who share living space negotiate this intimate world of household practice on a daily basis. Maids occupy a central place in the production of everyday life. And they do so across the social distances of subordination and ethic and cultural difference. Living inside others' lives, maids deal with the underside of hygiene and laundry habits, emotional states, and tangled familiarities. What is this like? How does it work from the maid's perspective?

Janine can reflect on twenty-one years' experience as a maid in Hong Kong. She will be our guide in these matters. Janine works for Celia, who is still at her

ladies' lunch when Janine arrives and lets herself into the spacious apartment in Shouson Hill that Celia shares with her husband. Janine gathers up laundry so that she can get the washing machine going before she starts cleaning. Her movement around the apartment—dusting, washing things, polishing floors, picking up objects, and returning them to their place—is energetic and practiced. It approximately reproduces an earlier set of movements in another house for her "morning lady." Her morning lady has a job so they meet rarely. Instructions are left in a note and things run smoothly in an anonymous sort of way. This extra morning work provides the money Janine and her boyfriend need for the mortgage on their tiny new flat in Tsuen Wan. She dusts the framed photograph of the family home in the UK county of Hertfordshire. The house is substantial, detached, and nicely situated in its own grounds, and Janine understands it is important in sustaining the family's routes, roots, and British–Hong Kong identities. This is a part of their lives that is mysterious to her yet she knows their life in Hong Kong intimately. She lived in the apartment with them for many years before moving in with her boyfriend.

It is early evening before the apartment looks beautiful with everything cleaned and put away, with the washing and ironing done and neatly arranged in the linen closet. Celia arrives back from her ladies lunch via a shopping trip. The two women hug and exchange news. As Celia's husband Mark is not expected home for dinner she invites Janine to stay to eat the dinner Janine will cook. Chatting, they work together, moving round each other in the small kitchen. Normally they would eat together only on special occasions, like Christmas, or when the children return from England. The activity of cooking and the conversation between the women reveals how Janine lives inside this family over nine years. Celia takes a close interest in Janine's well-being and the decisions she makes about her life. She offers advice as she would counsel an older and semi-independent daughter,[5] although Janine is forty years old and has a long-term relationship. Celia sees Janine life as a project that can be improved through intelligent decision making. This demands the kind of subtle and discreet guidance Celia is practiced at providing as an experienced mother. In these ways Janine is both family member and staff. Family members might, but don't, perform the domestic tasks she performs. And they certainly wouldn't do so in a financial transaction involving living and (migrant) conditions of stay. In this frame Janine is not family.

Janine and Celia's relationship shapes Celia's life, making her available for lunch and tennis, allowing her to live in a clean and ordered home without cleaning and ordering it herself. It shapes Janine's life in still more fundamental ways. It provides the employment and income on which her Hong Kong visa and permanently temporary rights of residence hang. Janine's permanent temporariness is an official part of her conditions of stay, and this distinguishes her from Mary and Nelly. Although the terms of her visa officially require her to live in, Celia is flexible. Thus Janine has her own home, a live-in relationship and other work, things she has no legal right to. Celia is a "good employer" compared with others Janine has worked for. Good and bad employers are a regular conversational theme between the two women. Janine supplies details of less desirable models of service, family conduct, material conditions, and living space she has experienced.

Janine shows us that living in someone else's life means operating inside their material and emotional landscape. In addition to intimate habits, household objects, and social relationships alluded to earlier, there is also the conduct of family business to think about. Maids live in a dynamic landscape of private family behavior. Much depends on the way families behave and think about themselves, what they think a servant is, and the kinds of relationships they are prepared to form with them. Most maids work for Chinese families and so much depends on the (infinitely variable) conduct of Chinese family business and relationships with social inferiors. Maids' relationships with Chineseness consist of living on terms of intimacy as social inferiors, and this makes them distinctive from the other migrants we are concerned with. Researchers with more systematic data[6] suggest that maids report more traditional, segregated, and hierarchical relationships with Chinese employers. Before there were maids from the Philippines. local traditions of service involved employing poor men as servants, and so Chinese class and gender relations of service involve quite different traditions.

Living inside Chinese lives can involve dramatic shifts in circumstances. Janine explains that they might start out quite humbly, living in modest circumstances, and then suddenly become wealthy. Conversely Chinese families experience dramatic downward social mobility when business ventures fail. This microcosm of shifting circumstances is a personal, scaled-down version of macroeconomic and political changes that impact on everyone. All of this touches the circumstances in which maids work. Household physical space shapes maids' lives too, as Janine suggests.

> During my first contract I worked with a Chinese family, a very simple family with a small flat. . . . Robinson Road Midlevels, . . . And there is no way for me to sleep anywhere. It has only two rooms, small rooms, and one small bathroom and one small kitchen. . . . so I was sleeping in a living room with a folding bed, with just a cover, so they asked me to use a screen. So when you move one way it's going to fall, the folding

bed. So I slept there for two years. But the good thing is [following the move] I have a big room. It's just a room but you can feel it's yours.

Expat migrants are not as vulnerable to dramatic shifts in circumstances and always have the possibility of onward migration as a solution. Apart from service traditions, ways of thinking about servants, and volatile economic conditions, it makes no difference whether the employing family is Chinese or expat.

Securing private space inside the family is no guarantee of privacy and autonomy, as Janine tells us.

> When you're out they're going to check everything. . . . They're minding everything, like your private things. When you buy something and she says to me, oh, why are you buying this, this and that? And then of course, when you are still young you are having makeup, lipstick, and everything and then she will tell me, "Oh, you are not supposed to fix up your face. Because you just came here to work as a domestic helper.". . . they just treat you like, they are paying you, like you are just working with them. You're doing the job and they are paying you. So whatever good things you do with them, that's my experience with my previous employers, whatever you do, they're not thinking that it's a good thing that you're doing for them, they're thinking anyway, "I'm paying you for the job." I tried to finish that contract no matter how bad it is and I learn a lot.

There are other limitations too. Maids' movements and use of public space are often circumscribed. Curfews are common and Janine has experienced these too.

> They're going to tell you, "OK, come back at seven o'clock." You know so if you then come back the time they told you it's either they're going to scold you or they are going to double lock the door. What my experience is, she's going to lock the door. Even I have a key I can't get in because it's double locked. It's like they are not giving you freedom, to live normally . . . . sometimes they won't let you move freely so you feel at home and you won't feel homesick. You feel like you're a stranger in their house. You're a stranger.

This underscores the observation above that maids are treated as adolescents. No other adult use of public space is mediated by the threat of temporary homelessness of the lockout. This adds a further layer to the complexities of maids' belonging.

Living inside any family's life as a maid involves negotiating emotional complexities of family life and conduct. These become particularly transparent in times of difficulty, as Janine suggests.

> It's just like, it's like torture, you know. You can't move and you can't, I mean you're not really free, and I said, "If I say something you're angry". . . . I don't know what to do, just like my mother you know. . . . so I just said, "OK, just talk." And when something dropped from the window, and then she would say, "Oh, you don't care because it's not yours. This is not your house." Oh my God, that's like you feel, very, a stranger and you feel homesick, you know, you're alone and then they're still treating you like that . . . You feel that you are really the slave, you know, you're nothing, something like that.

Maids live inside employing families' material and emotional landscapes without belonging. Their guest status as migrants at the macrolevel is replicated at a microlevel in their position inside employers' families. Their connections with their employing families extend this. Not belonging has other dimensions too. Maids are easily disposable for quite trivial reasons. Sacking a maid has little consequence for employers and potentially dramatic consequences for the maid. If she fails to secure alternate employment quickly she can be returned to the Philippines. Maids have a big investment in things going well.

Aside from the relationships with (mostly female) employers there are also the complexities of relationships with their children. These are often scenes of cultural humiliation and still deeper levels of servitude.

> . . . sometimes you start working with a family and they got children, say, like fourteen years old, ten years old. How can you discipline those children? It should be you as a parent right, and they shouldn't expect me to, "Oh, discipline my children." Because they are very, you know, rude. . . . They are quite spoiled, you know, because they're paying you, so you do everything for them. It's like, OK, you have to put everything on the table, and when they can't get it they say, "Oh, can you get that for me?' No, please. They just really treating you like, oh you're just a helper.

Living in others' lives without belonging also involves unfamiliar domestic routines. Janine, an expert in the practical intimacies of cultural difference, recounts this as she and Celia seamlessly serve the dinner in ways long ago agreed. These involve predinner drinks, knives and forks, napkins, place mats, wine, and water glasses. When Janine first arrived in Hong Kong other people's domestic routines were particularly challenging. Not only were they unfamiliar, domestic routines are ingrained in a place beyond negotiation and explanation. For these reasons employers often have difficulty articulating them in sufficient detail.

> And everything is very strange, just like, things that you're not seeing at home. And then thinking, yeah, and crying all the time: I can't do this I can't manage. I don't know how to do this, iron bedsheets. Shirts, so I called my aunty, I said, "Aunty, I can't do this." And she said, "You're stupid, you are already here, you must do it." So I'm going to ask. . . . And I said, "I don't know how to do this." She shows me how to do it, iron those sheets her way. And then little by little I'm learning. . . but the thing is all the family members would come over for dinner almost every night, you know, thousands of families, you know, you have to cook, you have to do all the laundry and everything . . . . And then again I think I found a job with an Australian family which is quite demanding. And then she expects you to be perfect with everything you do. Everything, everything, and once you do something wrong she say. . . . she's going to tell you, it doesn't suit her. People have different way, of housekeeping and so on, . . . It's like when your preparing food for Chinese you just have to, Ok, bring all the plates, cutleries and the chopsticks and that's all. . . . And soup, you know first, but in a Western family, no. You have to serve wine glasses first or cocktails and bring everything; after that main course, the soup and there's a mat. So there is really a big difference. Yes. When it comes to household, really, Chinese is simpler, but you learn. They are going to teach you the way they want.

Maids operate by tactile learning of routines of intimate life in others' homes. Getting her own home means that Janine no longer has to deal with the challenges of her living-in years. But she shares her home with her boyfriend, and this brings its own demands:

> My boyfriend is Muslim, you know, and he is a bit traditional and when it comes to cooking you must cook perfectly and when it comes to housekeeping arranging things and that you must be careful because he's a bit fussy. If I am just on my own I can do everything. You know, without people who will complain at all, oh, this is this like this.

Compared to former employment, Janine's employment with Celia is relaxed, independent, and personable. It is based on liberal familial-styled relationships that are well intended even if they do freeze Janine in a permanent state of adolescence. There are worse models. Acutely aware of the colonial antecedents in her

relationship with Janine, this is how Celia, a thoroughly modern, kindly memsab, thinks about it:

> I think it's in our upbringing, Brits, to believe that everybody is a human being. And I'm afraid I don't think that's in everybody's upbringing . . . The whole thing about British colonialism as opposed to other types of colonialism generally speaking doing it for the good of the locals, they get it wrong sometimes. And it is an arrogant and a superior sort of thought but also you looked after your staff, because if you looked after your staff they would work better for you. But I know, my mother, used to say, "Of course the trouble is"—there was a full-time maid in her household and she would look at youngsters, not me, mistreating their helpers or whatever and she'd say, "The trouble is they weren't brought up with maids in the house themselves, they don't know how to treat staff."

Proper comportment with staff is a matter of class and breeding. In Hong Kong it also depends on a family's relationship with (particular configurations of) empire. Indian and Chinese employers, of course, have their own relationships with empire and its deep structures of expectation and comportment with their serving classes.

Maids' relationships with the material arrangement and social relationships of domestic space are unique. This forms the fabric of their serving-class status. For the majority who work and live with Chinese families this forges the basis of their connection with Chineseness, one that operates from the inside of Chinese domestic life. Maids' broader relationship with Chineseness is forged in their connection with the city. This too is structured by their relationship with domestic space and the demands placed on their time by the families they serve. Maids' relationship with Chineseness, with the families in which they live, with each other, with the city, and with their families and friends in the Philippines draw a complex matrix. This is composed of emotional and material connections across social and nation-state boundaries.[7] These issues will be explored below.

Sundays in Statue Square

Time dissects space. In the central district of Hong Kong Island there is a place called Statue Square, surrounded by the glass-and-steel-tower operations of the global corporate elite. On Sundays the suits are replaced by their servants and the square fills up from early morning into the dusk by Filipino maids. Sundays

in Statue Square, "holidays" as the maids refer to it, occupy a significant place in the rhythm of the maids' week, as well as in the urban ecology of the city. Statue Square looks like public space. It is, in fact, private, corporate space. This distinction became important in 1992–93 when the retailers operating in Chater Road complained to their landlords about the nuisance of the Sunday Filipino "invasion."[8] The women stood their ground. The Sunday holiday is the only day when they are not on call twenty-four hours. A trip to the square is time away from their live-in workplace, time away from the demands of their employing family, time to eat their own food, which they may not be allowed to cook in their employer's house; time with other Filipino women, and time to speak their own language and tell their stories. Janine no longer goes to the square on Sundays but she went when she was new to Hong Kong, and the square provided an important source of social contact and friendship with other Filipino women as a way of building her new life as a migrant.

Early in the morning the square starts to fill up with women of all ages, from young girls to well-established grandmothers. They all look young dressed in jeans and T-shirts. For some the day begins at the Roman Catholic Church. Gathering at one end of the square, the Catholic women are identifiable by their long and modest dresses as well as their singing and praying. The square is composed through the many activities occurring simultaneously and produces a carnival atmosphere. There are petty forms of commerce involving the making and selling of food, grooming hair and manicuring nails, and trading in toys and clothes stored in large sturdy plastic bags. Letters and photographs are drawn out of designer shopping bags and passed between women arranged in small groups. New arrivals and those of long standing pose for photographers standing in front of the fountain or one of the grand modern buildings. Photographs are to send home to offer a glimpse of life in a glamorous city for those who have stayed in the village.

The array of baggage creates the impression that the women have brought the transportable part of their life with them to the square. They look elegantly and neatly homeless. They are not homeless, but insecurely housed. As immigrant guest workers on two-year contracts they have nowhere else to be away from work. And they live precariously inside others' lives. Ann, who was once a maid but "got out," says maids go to the square because "they don't have a choice because there is no place for them to go. That's just the available place you can go, they go to find a place to relax. . . . . They just sit there and eat and talk." The square is a place to go without depleting their slender financial resources, which the use of public space generally demands.

The women in the square share an implicit understanding of how their lives work. Maids are the first up and the last to go to bed. In between they are on call for domestic duties that include shopping, cooking, cleaning, laundry, child-care, and sometimes, and most unpopular, cleaning the car. Employers are evaluated on the range of duties they require as well as on their treatment of the maid. There are good employers "who treat me like a human being," who "don't hurt me." and there are bad employers who are demanding and cruel to the point of physical injury. Complaint exposes the maid to the prospect of dismissal, unemployment, and return to the Philippines.

Angela sits with her friends and her niece on a rectangle of cloth in the part of the square that is under cover, sharing fish paste sandwiches and iced tea. They know that her father is a farmer and her husband is a carpenter in the Philippines. Her husband earns only 200 pesos a day when there is work, and nothing in the rainy season when there is none. They know that he takes care—after a fashion—of their four children. Angela has been working in Hong Kong for the last seven years so that her children can stay in school and go on to university. A great deal of faith is placed in education as a route to a better life, despite the evidence to the contrary in the graduate unemployment rate which drives these well-qualified women overseas to work. She misses her children very much; it is hard to be without them and her mobile phone is a vital connection to their lives. Her husband is pretty good at looking after them, but she knows women who call the Philippines on a daily basis to check the homework and schoolbags of their children. For some, practical mothering must work at a distance. Only three hours away by plane and yet so far!

The maids' stories are complex in the simplicity of their rich silences. They get up, work, sleep, meet up with their friends on Sundays, they send money to the Philippines. They work for the money so their families can get by. Their lives are lived outside in the square and inside the lives of other people: people with better circumstances and more money than they have. Maids live through learning unfamiliar domestic routines, through life's textures and smells. They handle others' children while their own stay in the Philippines and make do with fathers, aunts, uncles, and grandmothers. They manage this in the service of bigger priorities, like making ends meet and investing in a better future. Cultural details are concrete and practical accomplishments.

Maids' movements are restricted by their domestic routines and the length of the work day. They are limited to the errands they run serving the household and its children, with only Sundays for going to Statue Square or church or to visit an

aunt, a cousin a friend, maybe for a birthday party. Their movements are transnational but on restricted terms. Their local movements are restricted by their (service) relationship with employers[9] and by a lack of funds. In these respects they are unlike other migrants. They are serving-class migrants. Their relationship with Chineseness is intimate, restricted, and subordinate. Their subordination, deeply inscribed in their lives and taken for granted by employers, is contested by these lively and resourceful transmigrant women.[10]

Relationships in the Philippines

The Philippines is a top labor-exporting country, and maids are a significant proportion of this labor. They are exported to 130 different countries, and their domestic responsibilities are redistributed onto rural women who are too poor to migrate.[11] Their remittances are a significantly contribution to Philippine gross national product (GNP).[12] Filipino Maids leave home in order to make ends meet for those who remain and for those who are unable to migrate or who choose not to.[13] On a macroscale their remittances boost Philippine GNP. On a microscale they transform relationships with friends and family. Complex financial and emotional webs are woven in migration. Maids' wages, HK$3,270 a month,[14] are a small sum by Hong Kong standards but a small fortune in the Philippines. Migration reconfigures relationships and social standing. It transformed Janine's relationship with parents, her siblings, and their children, who depend on the money she sends them. But for those who have husbands and children in the Philippines there are further layers of complexity, as Janine explains in relation to a friend of hers.

> At first the husband was working for the family, and then the wife decided that it's not enough, so I should go somewhere and do something to help the family. So, OK, so she went overseas to work and then she started sending money. And then the husband has started to get lazy, because the money is coming every month. And then after that, because the wife is the one supporting the whole family, she started being, like, you know, superior, husband is doing nothing, so husband's pride became, like, useless just like he is stayed at home; she is wearing pants and he is wearing skirt, so he started to find another way to make himself the head of the family, and so that is why husbands have started having an affair with other women, so sometimes it is a wife's fault, you know. She thinks she is the one who can hold everything. The husband is losing his power in the family and the wife doesn't want to accept that she's doing

wrong. . . . .What happens is that husbands ask their wife to go back, and of course they have children to look after and the husband wants the whole family to be united you know, but the question is the wife doesn't want to go back, not really. So the husband will find another wife. Until everything is [too] late; then she will go home and her husband is already with another.

Janine knows maids supporting a husband, their children, a new wife, and her children in the Philippines. Being a key provider of family income brings new responsibilities. It brings new freedoms too from the strictures of Philippine family discipline. Janine explains.

Because they always saying that no, no, so when you want to obtain a party, like dance party or whatever, you ask them and they say, "No, you are not allowed." You know. So when I came to Hong Kong the good thing is I was free. And I can make all decisions for myself. But I never did bad things.

Despite the disciplinary regimes of service Janine describes, she and other maids also experience new forms of freedom in migration. These reconfigure traditional relationships with children, husbands, and others into more distant, financially based, connections. These are removed from daily life and animated by long-distance connection and infrequent visits. Daily life takes place in Hong Kong producing new intimacies and new forms of service in others' families rather than their own. In describing her boyfriend's fussiness over domestic routines Janine hints that these are differences in forms of servitude. Servitude also brings freedom from family relations in the Philippines, and this complicates the business of returning, even for short visits. Celia thinks Janine should go back to the Philippines more often. But Janine experiences time spent in the Philippines as a loss of the autonomy her life in Hong Kong provides. Whenever she steps out in the Philippines a string of family and friends go with her. Being alone, something she is used to in Hong Kong, is not an option.

Lifestyle migrants also reconstitute versions of family in migration. They live permanently temporary lives. But maids' new lives and freedoms are permanently temporary in a different way. Celia's relationship with Hong Kong, for example, is structured by her husband's employment prospects, which are both secure and prosperous. Celia and her family have permanent residence and are not tied to a particular job. Janine's twenty-one years in Hong Kong have not secured permanent residence status. She and the other maids operate on two-year contracts tied to specific jobs, which can be terminated at any point by employers. They are

designed to never accumulate to permanent residence. Maids' relationships with Hong Kong involve a deeper intimacy in the lives of local Chinese families, more restricted access to the city, and limited rights to remain as contract domestic labor.

Routes Out

Routes out of the Hong Kong domestic contract-labor trap are restricted. They involve new intimacies. Anne's story reveals one of these exits. Others are visible in the chapters that treat the tour through boys' night out and on patrol. Anne, who is in her thirties, was a consultant in a manpower agency in the Philippines operating in Qatar and other places. She is a qualified civil engineer but can't find work in the Philippines. This is common; many maids are actually unemployed professionals. Anne's business as a manpower consultant was as precarious as the Philippine economy, and this caused her to move through Southeast Asia attempting to maintain her career. She had a husband and two children, aged thirteen and six, whom she had to leave with her mother, brother, and sister

in the Philippines. When her business failed for the last time Anne's sister helped get her a job in Hong Kong as a maid. It was a big step down.

> [A]nd it was very, very different, very sad. I lost all my freedom, it's different. I live in my employer's house so I have to do things . . . what they want me to do. I think of my children back there in my country. So it's a very, very different kind of life . . . I am working so nobody would take care of them. Life here in Hong Kong is very, very hard. Things are expensive. I pay for my rent of my house, my daily expenses, and [my] salary isn't going to be enough for us here. So they stay in the Philippines, it's just affordable . . . . I always cry at night. We are two Filipinas in the family, . . . And working with another Filipina's different also. . . . I tried to get along with her, but it's very hard to please them . . . . she was my senior. She works with them for a long time . . . So she would tell them [i.e., report her actions to her boss]. I cooked for them. I helped her because the house not very big, three small rooms [and] two helpers. . . . I sleep with [over] the first child I am taking care of [on a bunk] . . . . a baby and a four year old . . . [The room is 10 feet by 8 feet and each maid sleeps over the child they are "in charge" of]. . . .They [her employers and the other, senior, maid reporting to them] just think that they are my boss and I should, I should do what they wanted. They expect me to

clean the car . . . and it makes me cry. And she [her employer] has her mother, she's not staying with us but she come over every day, she just, she just comes without our knowing so she just comes and checks us, what we are doing. And she always tells her daughter what we are doing. There are [too many] . . . in the house, we can't move, it's very difficult, it's hard to breathe. . . . They're nice but the problem with my female boss is that she always listens to her mother. And we are not allowed to cook what we want to eat. So I always go with the mother to the market, she just bought us a $10 fish for the whole day [less than US$2] . . . and then last time she comes unexpectedly during lunch, and we cooked some rice but we don't have anything for that rice, so we just cook noodles, and then when the grandmother saw that she called her daughter, and I don't know what she told her daughter and the daughter rushed back home and she scolded us, she's saying we . . . are wasting her food. From that time we are so afraid to cook for ourselves for the rest of the time.

Again with her sister's help Anne "buys my freedom" by divorcing her Philippine husband and marrying a young Chinese man who needed the money. This secures her a dependent's visa, a way out of the domestic foreign contract-labor trap and a passport to better job opportunities. The immigration department checks out the marriage and can't find anything wrong with it. It looks plausible enough. The young man is nice, and they remain good friends while dissolving the marriage so that the young man can marry his girlfriend. Had he been cruel, Anne could have been exposed to abuse and exploitation. She now works for a relocation company and can afford to rent a very small flat on her own not far from where her sister lives. She still can't afford to bring her children to live with her because she has no one to leave them with while she works.

Other routes out of being a maid include more traditional forms of marriage, relationships with male benefactors, and friendships of various kinds that fade into sexual services. The boundaries between domestic and sexual services have always been porous; so too are the boundaries between different kinds of temporary contract labor from different parts of Southeast Asia. Next, the boys' night out tour explores these forms of intimacy in the lives of (some) British-lifestyle migrants.

BOYS' NIGHT OUT

Night and Day in Wanchai

Our tour remains on Hong Kong Island and becomes a night excursion. Wanchai is where John and Lyn work, just to the east of the central district on the north side of the island, not far from Victoria Harbor and the ferries. But Wanchai during the day and at night are two different places. When John and Lyn walk through it at the beginning and end of the workday, it is densely packed with daytime commerce. Offices like John's form a layer of hidden commercial activities in which goods from manufacturers (in China) are shipped round the world. Other enterprises are more visible at street level. Food and drinks and other goods that service the population's daily existence are available from thousands of small shops and market stalls. The transitional parts of the day, the twilight of sunrise and of sunset, most starkly expose Wanchai's temporal rhythms.

At dusk the offices empty, and the day shift scurries home. Another set of businesses—bars and other places that are not open in the daytime—light up and add to the glow of the night. A new set of workers arrive for the night shift. Among the waiters and barmen, beautiful young women arrive to dance on bars in exotic underwear and serve drinks, or simply to encourage men to dance and buy drinks. Older, more ferocious-looking women perch on stools outside of the bars. They direct the flow of customers in and out, sorting out troublemakers and generally protecting the girls' working conditions. The restaurants and bars put on their garish party clothes and take in a new set of customers. Or they may be the same set with different purposes: out for the evening partying rather than taking a midday break. The market stalls and shops both light up and step back into the nightscape. Other premises and their activities—bars and clubs—associated with a different kind of leisure become more prominent and make up the landscape of the night in Wanchai. The streets are brightly lit in neon, sporting a jumble of signs in English and Cantonese. Buildings that are inconspicuous by day, "love hotels," where rooms, complete with pornographic movies, towels, and condoms, can be rented by the hour, become more prominent in the nightscape.

The human fabric on the sidewalk slows down to a more leisurely lingering pace. It adopts a new countenance and composition. It becomes visibly more male. We will join in and walk along at a leisurely stroll. Western and Chinese popular music combine randomly to produce a soundscape otherwise dominated by the burble of voices, the shuffle of feet, and the slow movement of traffic. Streets and people intertwine in the syncopated rhythms of the night in Wanchai.

As Hamish shuts down his computer and tidies his desk he becomes part of this transformation of Wanchai from day to night. Hamish is an old China hand

of almost twenty years standing, despite his accent, which still betrays his Scottish origins. In his early fifties he is silver-haired and has intense eyes that dart about the room, checking that everything is as it should be for the night. Like the Chungking Mansion traders, Hamish is part of the global circulation of goods that is Hong Kong. He ships things round the world that are too big to be put in containers; mostly big pieces of factories and machinery. He specializes in machines that operate in construction, oil rigs, production platforms, and chemical plants. His current frustration is the control of the Hong Kong container port by a cartel of big shipping interests, which is intent on blocking plans to build a new, bigger port in North Lantau Island near the new airport. This is necessary if Hong Kong is to compete with Shanghai and Singapore in handling the new supersized ships with which it is struggling. The cartel doesn't want to abandon its infrastructural investment in the old port and start again with large capital investment in a new one. But a new port would make it easier for Hamish to ship big equipment and keep Hong Kong in the circuit of key Pacific shipping routes. Shipping is indisputably an "international business."

Hamish and his office mates interpret this as "must operate in English." This absolves them of the need to struggle with Cantonese or Mandarin and is a relief for the US companies that want to arrange shipping through Hong Kong in a language they understand. On a bad day Hamish gets "idiots sending us e-mail in Cantonese." He sends them back with a message in English. Hamish thinks the erosion of English and the eclipse of the port are reasons for Hong Kong's decline. He is inclined to one-man tirades against (commercial) Chineseization even as he enjoys living in a Chinese city. Hamish can swear without once repeating himself for a good five minutes in Cantonese when he is down at the docks with the stevedores. But he has never seriously focused on learning the language. This is despite the efforts of his Malay Chinese wife to teach him and her evident annoyance that he doesn't really try.

Today was a good day for Hamish. There were no annoying Cantonese e-mail messages and he has just landed the Southeast Asia contract for shipping and assembling the Saab showrooms. It's going to be a logistical challenge. But business is thriving despite the problems with the port. And income tax is low so Hamish gets to keep most of what he makes. He's also bidding for a salvage contract for a wreck that sank off Hong Kong. Recovery will be a challenge because it is carrying oil, which will leak out when the ship is raised. His family has been in salvage as well as the military (military careers, being short, allow a second career) since the 1860s. Like other British expatriate migrants, he's in Hong Kong for the lifestyle. He conceptualizes this in terms of comparative costs, calculated item by item, but this masks deeper reasons to migrate. Everything in Hong Kong is "cheaper than Britain" making the things he likes to do—go for a drink, a meal, a show, or take a holiday—accessible. He places a high premium on easy and cheap mobility. He can quote the price of every form of transport, whether it is a local tram ride or a plane trip to Bali or the Philippines, where he can take short, cheap holidays on the beach. His life is a set of calculations. On his balance sheet Hong Kong has "everything that Britain doesn't have."

Deeper layers in the story of how Hamish got to Hong Kong are developed in the conversations he has with John. Hamish's route to Hong Kong was paved with disappointment in Britain. He left in the late eighties for a tangle of reasons that are not all immediately offered. At first he will say that he left Britain because the London borough of Lambeth, where he used to live, gives priority to "black lesbians." In Hong Kong people make their own way rather than live on the "handouts" of municipal equal opportunity. This slight to his sense of social justice—and delving deeper into Hamish's reasons for leaving—was compounded by his being under investigation by the British tax authorities. This came from their mistake in calculating Hamish's business taxes, which in his view and in comparison with Hong Kong, were unduly high to begin with. But these indignities were compounded by a deeper wound, which strikes at the heart of Hamish's sense of himself as a man. Hamish is an old warrior four generations deep. His father fought in the Second World War, his grandfather fought in the First World War, and his great-grandfather fought in the Boer War. In Hamish's calculation these military contributions from his family were betrayed in the Falklands War. This war was a military defeat for the British Empire, in contrast to the pageant marking the end of empire in Hong Kong. In the Falklands War Hamish thinks the military was "taken down" to the point where the British Royal Navy had to hire merchant ships to defend colonially conquered territory. Black lesbians are stacked up against worthier causes like the defense of empire.

Still worse was the injustice that denied Hamish his rightful place in the family roll of military honors. Hamish was also part of Britain's unacknowledged contribution to the Vietnam War. As a pilot taking part in operation Crown Force he flew unmarked planes for the Thai Air Force as "top cover" for their helicopter operations in Vietnam. Since then he has had to "live with your ghosts," without acknowledgment. He leaves Britain disgusted with its military strategies and its social priorities. He moves to a colonial (now postcolonial) place he knows from his soldiering days when it was an R & R break from the Vietnam War. His Malaysian wife of thirty years has been through most of this with him. She telephones just as he is about to leave work, remembering that it's boys' night out and that she won't be able to contact him later. She's abroad on British Council business, and Hamish is feeling less and less married as time passes and she works overseas more often.

John has already left for the ferry to Lamma and his quiet island life as Hamish turns off the lights and takes the lift from his office to the ground floor. It's already 8:00 pm and he's put in a "proper" twelve-hour day. Hamish loves Wanchai. Unusually for a British expatriate, Wanchai is where he lives, in a 1,200 square foot apartment. It is where he works in his shared office with John and the boys, and it is where he plays with other boys. Wanchai has just about everything he needs. He uses other parts of the city only occasionally. Hamish is a Wanchai warrior—the local term for the men who go out to play in Wanchai.

Wanchai Warriors

The night-time activities of Hamish and the other Wanchai warriors expose dialogues of entitlement and service, which are distinct from the ladies who live at the top of the hill on the efforts of their maids. This section is about some Western men's relationships with some "Oriental" women. Myths are (re)shaped by flesh and social practices. This involves a version of Chineseness animated in the Wanchai district at night. Hamish is the organizing force in boys' night out. He is the point of contact with the other men and women we will meet as the night unfolds. His network of Wanchai warriors is open to emotional arrangements and opportunities that do not exist in the same way in Britain. They are forged in the peculiar alchemy of Hong Kong migrant life.[1]

Boys' night out is a routine nocturnal journey round a small part of the city by a small group of men, not an exposé of expatriate male behavior. It reveals circumstances that shape expat male migration in subtle ways that are difficult to calculate and impossible to overlook. The majority of the Filipino maids encountered in our tour of service would not associate with this place at this time and with these men. But through their networks they know women for whom the activity of boys' night out provides opportunities for survival or advancement. Some of the women for whom boys' night out—using this term in a more generic sense—is a source of influence, intimacy, or extra cash, are from the Philippines. Others are from Thailand or Indonesia. They are beautiful, young, and in need of money to support themselves and their families.

Hamish, the old warrior, steps into the warm night air where the jumble of neon signs in Cantonese and English cast an eerie orange-yellow light over the early evening streets. A Wednesday night in Wanchai,[2] boys' night out has its own cartographies. It has its own order of activities. It involves a set of routines. Hamish explains it as an organized foray into the "world of Susie Wong." This is the Orientalist fantasy Western men have about Eastern women promoted by Richard Mason in a novel of the same name (1957) and popularized by the 1960 film starring Nancy Kwan. In this iconic film an American writer falls in love with a prostitute. Along with Madame Butterfly, this "usurped the image of Asian womanhood in the Western imagination."[3] Susie Wong was the result of US economic/military involvement in Indo-China, and later, the Vietnam War. Sexual services thrived as thousands of US military personnel rotated in and out of Hong Kong for rest and recreation between battles.

But the connection between Wanchai, soldiers, and sexual services has a deeper history than late colonial skirmishes in Indo-China. It dates back to the early days of British colonial settlement: "Hong Kong was dominated by armed services and the services they sought."[4] Estimates in 1860 suggest there were 18,000–20,000 prostitutes in what was at that time a garrison town following the conquest of Hong Kong in the Opium Wars. Prostitution at this time was racially and geographically segmented and aimed at equally (racially and ethnically)

segmented client populations.[5] Chinese prostitutes served Chinese clients as well as European soldiers, sailors, and permanent European residents like policemen in Wanchai. European and American prostitutes served middle-class European men in Central. Chinese men were forbidden to hire European prostitutes. Brothels were part of colonial governance. They were inspected, and they paid taxes.[6]

Boys' night out begins at the Old China Hand. This is a pub that wouldn't look out of place in London. It's the sort of pub you would find on the Old Kent Road, where you can get a steak and kidney pie and a pint of beer. It is full of white men aged between their midtwenties and their midfifties. British expatriates of varying migration vintages predominate among a smattering of Australians and Americans. The Union flag is hung around the inside and the menu contains jokes about Britain.

Hamish is greeted at the door by a beautiful and scantily clad Thai woman who is part of the night shift and obviously knows him as a regular; the Old China Hand is on the route between his office and his apartment. They stroke hands in a manner that hovers between sexual and paternalistic. She tells him about her stomach ache and he gently dispenses advice. Her job is to meet and greet, flatter and encourage men into the bar and into buying drinks. Her job is to make them feel recognized and valued. Hamish orders a pint and is called over to examine another British man's business plan. A couple of pints later it's time for dinner, and Hamish and some of the other men he is talking to order meat pies and chips. Hamish makes a call to another bar not far away on his mobile phone.

In minutes Brian from Manchester arrives and joins in. Brian—dyed brown hair, blue suit, late forties, hyperactive, singing along with the music when a tune appeals to him—is one of the expatriate divorce statistics Hamish refers to in his story about what "this place" does to expatriate relationships. Brian's domestic arrangements didn't work out as well as Hamish's. There is strongly implied criticism of the "wrong attitude" on the part of British women migrants who can't manage Hong Kong. Hamish's "Oriental" wife does all the domestic chores without the help of a maid. She "allows" him to go "out with the boys" three times a week, too. Not so Brian's ex. Her main activity, in Brian's version of events, was "lying on the beach all day." Western women are spoiled and lazy. "Oriental" women, on the other hand, are accommodating and understanding. In choosing wives and intimate partners it is important in the boys' world to bear these differences in mind. On the surface Brian and Hamish have produced their own version of Susie Wong in which Southeast Asian women make better wives. But that is the surface. The lived version of Hamish's life with his professional and inde-

pendent Malaysian wife, may well be different from the one he describes on boys' night out. Brian says:

> My daughters were born here. '85 and '87 and the missus just hacked it for four years, sat by the pool every day: coffee mornings, [hot] chocolate mornings. I'm working sixteen hours a day. She went back. I made a mistake. I bought a house for £200,000 in about 1990; one-and-a-half acres, and I said you go back with the two kids, who were four and two, and furnish and decorate it. Stay for three months, have a holiday. The house was finished, brand-new house . . . three months to the day she rang me: I'm not coming back; you've always been an asshole. I want the house, and I want £100,000.

British expatriate women are greedy as well as spoiled. "My fucking ex-wife" would text Brian to "send money" although she lived with her boyfriend in their house "wearing my fucking dressing gown." Brian is not to be outwitted. He defaults on the mortgage, which gets his wife and two daughters evicted by the mortgage lender. He reacquires the house for himself in a costly financial maneuver, and triumphantly gives the girls their room back in what is now his house, at least it is when he is visiting Britain to see his "old mum" and they are able to stay with him. Brian joins in loudly with a Beatles song—"I love music, though"—a prelude to reminiscing about his younger days in Manchester. Hamish decides it's time to move on. On the way out of the Old China Hand he stops to speak with Alan, forties, vacuous-looking, dark hair and dark rimmed glasses. Alan is married to a Thai woman who once worked as a bar-girl selling sexual services. "I fucked her then I married her." His rescue means she is now working at home as a daycare provider. She is fending off demands from numerous relatives in Thailand for money and waiting for Alan to get home from the pub.

Leaving behind the noise of the Old China Hand, Hamish and Brian walk out into the warmth and street sounds of the eerie yellow night and head for Delaney's, the popular Irish pub a five minute walk away. The streets are still more crowded. The demographic more skewed toward white men than two hours earlier. Delaney's is a large open-plan pub, where Hamish and Brian are instantly part of a much bigger circle of expatriate men in suits drinking after work. A drunken Australian in his late thirties lurches over to Hamish with a photo of his daughter—aged eight—to show round the crowd of men. His evident attachment to his daughter has been insufficient to move him homeward and by now someone else must have put her to bed because it's after 10:00 pm. The Irish pub has louder music than the Old China Hand and more Filipino and Thai women in still shorter skirts milling around among the crowd, encouraging men to buy drinks. Hamish greets a number of the women and pursues the same sensuous hand stroking routine as earlier. These women are freelance PR greeters, who get a cut of the profits for getting men to dance and buy drinks. They make their own arrangements to provide sexual services outside the bar if they choose to. There are also women less ambiguously (and visibly) available for hire for sexual services.

So far we have encountered tolerant Southeast Asian wives (like Hamish's). We have met spoiled and lazy expatriate wives (like Brian's ex). We have met mamasans,[7] who may or may not be superannuated sex workers, who sit outside and direct the flow of traffic in and out of the pub or club and weed out unsuitable—drunk and aggressive—customers. We have met PR girls who make the men feel attractive and important while separating them from their cash. And we have encountered women who sell sex more directly. Prostitution in Hong Kong is not illegal; but the things associated with it—like soliciting, trafficking, controlling women for the purposes of prostitution, living off prostitutes' earnings and allowing premises to be used for sexual services—are illegal.[8]

With his canny nose for a bargain, Hamish knows that "working girls" fall into two categories. There are professionals, prostitutes who are "very, very ex-

pensive,"[9] and Filipino or Indonesian maids freelancing on the side.[10] The latter will "fuck your brains out for the price of a gin and tonic." Alternatively they may want to form intimate alliances[11] of various kinds with (Chinese and Western) men of financial substance who can buy them presents or give them small amounts of money.[12] Hamish astutely connects the labor force around what he calls the "girlie bars" and the maids he sees in Statue Square on Sundays in what he dismissively calls the "birdcage" because of its concentration of women chattering. Some of them freelance in a variety of ways in Wanchai. He identifies a spectrum of Southeast Asian female migration circumstances in which "gweilo" men are a resource for accumulating money and opportunities. Intimate relationships with wealthier men supplement low wages. Marriage offers a route out to another kind of life all together, as we will see below. The emotional and the financial are interconnected.[13] It is easy, Hamish says wistfully, for men of his age to fall in love with younger women: especially when they are beautiful. Love, sex, and money form a powerful matrix in the Wanchai night.

Surrounded by beautiful, young, available female bodies, Hamish and the other expatriate men busy themselves talking to each other about schemes for making money. The central theme of their conversation is not far removed from

189

the women's interests, but it is organized differently. They are doing business and making money. These things are also about emotion and intimacy. Jake—"Choosers and Losers"—was supposed to meet up with some men after work and go out for dinner in the more stylish area of Lang Kwai Fong. But he has been stood up. Left in Delaney's, he comes to speak to Hamish. Jake wouldn't normally speak to someone like Hamish, whom he sees as lacking in education and style. But Hamish has been courting Jake because he needs his contacts to raise venture capital to invest in a restaurant. Connecting people is what Jake specializes in, although he sneers he wouldn't normally bother with such small amounts. Hamish dislikes Jake because he's overconcerned with making money. "He's an obnoxious little shit, isn't he? I know exactly who I can trust. I also know who I can use. He wants me because I need the three million. I have to put US$ 3 million together, and he'll get 5 percent of it." Each man takes advantage of periodic absence by the other to voice these opinions to any of the other men within earshot who are prepared to listen.

Although it's after midnight Hamish shows no signs of tiring. He announces that it's time for "walkies." A small posse of men, including Jake, who by this time has nothing better to do, but minus Brian, who wanders off in another direction entirely, detach themselves from Delaney's and plunge once more into the warm night air and bustle of the street. The energy shows no signs of abating; if anything, the sidewalks are still more crowded than earlier. Boy's Night Out has reached the "girlie bar" stage of the evening.[14] In the jumble of neon lights and blare of music a mamasan sits outside surveying the footfall on the pavement and trail of men in and out the club.

The girlie bar looks less like a pub. There is a bar area but the space is dominated by a dance floor where two or three expatriate men dance closely and slowly with Thai[15] women in underwear or short skirts. Hamish positions himself at the bar, again adopting a stroking relationship with the barmaid whom he knows well. Aging for men is different in Britain, he explains, and this is yet another benefit of migration, another entry on the balance sheet of here and there. Oriental women really like older Western men, Hamish thinks, and Hamish and some of his pals feel the same about them. Thai women are especially delicious. Hamish ventures into the geopolitics of intimacy. They will wake a man up "on the hour every hour through the night and sit on his cock." This obviously adds substantially to the log of their advantages. The "working women" in the bar try hard to get Jake and Hamish to dance. They decline, but some of the other men dance in between trips to the bar. There is more drinking and more talk between the men. The conversation still centers on business.

Hamish, as the older man in the group, fills the younger men in on a piece of Hong Kong history. He was a young serviceman stationed on rest and recreation leave between the unacknowledged (Vietnam) battles in which he was a pilot in the late sixties and early seventies:

> There were ballrooms, I mean, proper ballrooms, where you could go and have dancing and if you wanted to dance with somebody you had to buy a book of tickets. And when you went to dance with a girl you gave her a ticket and that was how she got paid, she got paid by the dance, and she also got 50 percent of any drink you bought her.

At that time the girls were not from the Philippines but were local Chinese women or migrants/refugees from China. As employment opportunities for migrant Chinese women were limited, girlie bars and ticket dances provided significant avenues of employment. Hamish still refers to "being out on a pink ticket"—wife at home, men out on the town—it's like "boys in a toy shop," he says. This is one of the things that make Hong Kong a great place for a Western expat man to live. Hamish has options he doesn't have in other locations and other circumstances; options that, moreover, appear not to diminish with age.

Being a "boy in a toy shop" also forces expatriate (and other) men to think about what kinds of relationships they want to have with women. Jake thinks the girlie bars are for "sad old wankers" like Hamish. Jake differentiates himself and his tastes in women from Hamish's. He compares Wanchai unfavorably with other Southeast Asian red-light districts, particularly Singapore, which is "fantastic." He also thinks that red-light districts and available beautiful women are problematic.

> The [European] girls I used to work with in Ernst & Young had a hell of a job getting themselves sorted in relationships because they were strong, independent and in the '90s . . . they won't put up with their boys coming home at 4 o'clock in the morning smashed out their brains, and they wouldn't put up with them going to girlie bars, and they wouldn't put up with them, you know, doing all the things that single Hong Kong boys do when they go out in Hong Kong. Which is fair enough and absolutely right, but the boys have got to make that call. It's their decision. Again, you got to make a choice. So it's generally been a pretty tough market for them, because if a guy here is looking for some attention he can get it from people who don't ask anything from him. It's just—they inundate you with love and affection. The styles, in my personal experience, of Thai/Filipino women are that the man in their relationship is the center of their being, so they do stuff, and they consider it normal to wash and clean and look after them and do everything they say, and some of these guys like that. . . . and some of these girls are not bad-looking either. . . . If you were to take a thousand Western European women, a thousand Thai women and a thousand Filipino women, you add them all together then, the vast the vast majority of the Thai and Filipino women, in terms of being good-looking to your average white European man, would be in the top two-thirds, because it's the novelty factor. If you go through the process of learning that it's not just how flat her tummy is and how small her bottom is, there are issues of culture and humor and. . . . well there certainly are for me. My wife is from the Isle of Wight. But I dabbled there as well before that. But it wasn't very satisfying relationships. And you never really felt committed to it because you knew that you could do whatever you wanted to do and that there was no grief associated with it.

As Jake articulates the architecture of expatriate intimacy, he defines "Oriental" women as easy and pleasing to the point of dissatisfaction. Instant relationships are also disposable relationships with lower social value. Like Hamish's view of "Oriental women," from which Jake demurs, this formulates intimate versions of racial and ethnic hierarchies around social and emotional values. This version of "Oriental women" as pleasing, pliant, and sexually available to Western expatriate men is strongly contested in oral evidence collected from Southeast Asian women forming transnational relationships. These women articulate intelligent, active, decision making around themselves and their lives. Their calculations about relationships reveal subtle intersections between money, social circumstances, and romance that form the substance of human relationships the world over.[16]

By now it's 2:00 am and Jake, having remembered his wife from the Isle of Wight waiting at home, jumps into a taxi. The other men emerge one last time into the eerie glow of the light cast by the neon signs, and Hamish strolls off into the night smiling. There is silent agreement to forego the lap-dancing club. This is the optional crescendo of the evening. It will climax instead where it ended in the girlie bar, although there are still deeper layers to this matrix to pursue. Love, sex, money, lifestyle, survival, and a range of intimate relationships—between partners and families negotiated across ethnicities and culture—are made in webs of global migration and everyday expatriate life in Hong Kong, one encounter at a time.

As darkness turns into dawn the daytime activities and occupants come once more to the fore as the bars and nightclubs close. The love hotels switch off their signs and the revelers of the Wanchai night return home to sleep before work begins again. The Wanchai night fades into the Wanchai day, and different forms of commerce and their entanglements come to the fore.

The "Girlies"

The rolling nocturnal activities of the Wanchai warriors on boys' night out have backstage stories, too. Back at the Old China Hand and across the street at the Waikiki Club things are moving a little slowly, given the hour. The Waikiki is a small space dominated by a bar on which women dance while men sit and drink. Kandy and Amee, who are both from the Philippines,[17] are sitting at the bar in black-knitted mini-skirts and tank tops. Three other girls are dancing on the bar in black stockings, bras, suspender belts, and high-heeled black shoes. They look bored while their bodies move suggestively, automatically, vacantly. They look sad, and the song playing is "This Is the Story of My Life." The mirror behind the bar reveals a scene not intended for public display. It reflects their handbags and the paraphernalia within. Lipstick, mobile phones, and photographs of loved ones reveal the signs of a less exotic life than the one they live on the surface servicing male fantasies of Oriental women. As two American men in their forties arrive and take stools at the bar, Kandy and Amee spring into action. Off come their

193

skirts and tank tops, and they sit close to the men, wearing the same as the women dancing on the bar; hands and tongues all over them. This is the first serious business they have had all night, although things usually pick up later. An aggressive Chinese woman working the bar demands the men buy drinks for the girls as well as themselves. The bill for four drinks is US$100. Both girls are experienced at tempting men to buy sex from them. They stroke, complement, and cajole.

Kandy, who is twenty-three, has worked in sexual services in Philippines since she was fifteen and has only been in Hong Kong five months. Amee, who is twenty-eight, has been working in the trade for eight years and is still slightly dazed from being in Hong Kong only three days. She will send money back to the Philippines to care for her eight-year-old son. The Waikiki is not the top of the market, but it is high end, and both girls have a "manager" who arranges their trips to and from the Philippines. They enter Hong Kong on six-month tourist visas through the "agency." This belongs to the fierce Chinese woman who owns or manages the bar.[18] An elaborate bureaucracy runs these operations hovering on the edge of legitimacy, but tangling with immigration laws.[19] The women rotate in and out of Hong Kong on short "contracts" earning higher wages than maids.[20]

A Filipino woman in her thirties is also sitting at the bar. Officially she works as a "domestic" for the Chinese owner. But she runs the agency, doing domestic work only one week a month, in technical compliance with immigration regulations, which deny her other avenues of employment. Amee, who is making some progress with her American, takes her turn dancing on the bar. She directs all her attention to him, revealing further bits of her body in an effort to secure a deal. In the end there is no deal. The Americans, thinking better of it, leave after only two drinks with a very large bill. The girls resume their bored posture. It's still early. There will be other business, there always is, the later it gets and the more alcohol is consumed.

Beautiful women with slender bodies and circumstances but with imagination and ingenuity, detach themselves from Southeast Asian villages and set off abroad to make ends meet for those who stay behind. The opportunities of Wanchai at night, even if they are not acted upon, are part of what is possible. A range of intimacies are proffered as a means of survival. These range from marriage to passing encounters transacted with money. These things are as much a part of global social inequalities as having a maid and the time for hobbies. Everything is connected, somehow, in the flow composing human life. The trick is to slow it down long enough to take a look.

CLUBBING

Club Scenes

"The club" provided a social scene for empire's operatives from Malta to Melbourne. Based on gentleman's clubs in Britain,[1] they were oases of European civility and "native" exclusion. A microcosm of racialized class sifting, exclusion, and spatial separation, the club is a colonial icon. But how does it operate, and what is the point of it in postcolonial times? Clubs are a neat capsule of the things we are exploring in Hong Kong. Remnants of the recent colonial past and the postcolonial present fetch up in the fabric of the club and the lives of its members. In rapid transition from bastions of European privilege and Chinese exclusion, clubs have new members, new purposes, and new activities. Like the rest of Hong Kong, they are in transition. They are becoming more distinctively Chinese in their membership, and this has implications in the use of club space and activities. Relinquishing their function in the separation of European and Chinese bodies, clubs now provide their European members with new proximities to Chineseness. These new proximities are negotiated in mundane decisions about club rules, activities, and the disposition of space. At the club we can glimpse the salience of racial/ethnic and cultural differences in the little places where they cause small frictions. Clubs are postcolonial Hong Kong writ small.

There are forty-two[2] private social clubs in Hong Kong offering special interests, dining, and recreational facilities. They offer (selectively) communal indoor and outdoor space in a place where these are limited and expensive. Special interests include sports such as golf, sailing, football, rugby, cricket, field hockey, and horse racing. They include cultural/intellectual activities such as the Helena May, which we visited above. They provide an occupational focus like the Foreign Correspondents Club. They vary in fees, accessibility, and niche within the bigger system of social differentiation that is Hong Kong.

At the upper end of the hierarchy the (Royal) Hong Kong Jockey Club[3] only accepts new members with an endorsement from two of its two hundred voting members. Through this small window of personal recommendation it operates as a most exclusive social club; filtering and facilitating social connections at the highest levels in Hong Kong society. It is now firmly in elite Chinese hands. Social stratification is built from the ground up: through the intimacies of personal association.

Social strata are made in people's patterns of choices. Even close relationships negotiate hierarchy and its tiny differentiations.[4] Jockey Club land occupies a central location on the northeast side of Hong Kong Island, at Happy Valley, below the lookout at Jardines. The Hong Kong Golf Club, situated in the outer edges of the New Territories, between Shatin and Fanling, is another exclusive club, which is expensive in membership fees and has a thirty-year waiting list. Only the well-connected succeed in joining, although being a talented golfer enters the decision making as a supplement to social connection. Its general manager, impeccably dressed and well-mannered in an English public school way, staunchly defends the privacy of golf club members. These now include those in elite positions in "old Hong Kong society": the golf club is now 90 percent Chinese. In the hierarchies of clubs this is one to join for those who seek influence and connections as a route to (further) social success. Women have a niche, but they are not on important committees and their game is clearly separated from men's.

At this level clubs sift degrees of elite status. These are delicate and subtle matters of social position in public and working life. Elite status is about social influence, wealth, and historic standing in the colony, as well as interest and aptitude in the sport or activity the club offers. Corporations offer debentures that parachute new migrants into membership of elite clubs as part of a package of relocation benefits. This is ideal for those on short postings as this would otherwise exclude them from membership of the most exclusive clubs and the social connections they enable.

The Aberdeen Yacht club, where we observed our ladies at lunch, has sumptuous decor and facilities but is not part of this top tier. The Kowloon Cricket Club has a certain caché that extends beyond its cricket fans. But it is modestly priced and accessible in comparison to the Hong Kong Golf Club and the Jockey Club. The clubs with more modestly priced membership fees and facilities are more accessible to people at the lower end of the social strata. Mary and Peter Trent, you may remember, are members of the United Services Recreation Club. They like this club because they dislike pretension. It is also cheaper in membership fees and the Trents earn modest wages and pay their own fees. Clubs also attend to other dimensions of social sorting. Journalists, photographers and other media types use the Foreign Correspondents Club. This is located in one of few remaining colonial buildings in Central; and its talks and activities reflect its membership's inclination towards intellectual and cultural issues. It recently hosted a talk on "Chinese flair and fashion." A roll call of photographers and journalists killed in their line of duty as war correspondents is prominently positioned inside the entrance way as a tribute. In and around their key activities clubs are places to socialize, eat, and drink with like-minded people. They provide homes away from home for locals and migrants alike.

United Services Recreation Club

We will tour the United Services Recreation Club to get a closer look at how things work. USRC, as it is popularly called, occupies a tranquil green space of trees, shrubs, and lawns in Kowloon's tangle of elevated motorway intersections connecting Nathan and Gascoigne Roads. It sits at a confluence producing a relentless roar of traffic not far from the Trents' apartment. We will walk around it, starting in the grounds where multiple games of tennis are played by expats and locals into the night on floodlit courts. This is the only activity where demand exceeds supply. The lawn bowling green at the front of the old low white building, on the other hand, is underused. The bowling teams present are all Chinese and have given up after an energetic Sunday afternoon and departed for prearranged family dinners. The pool glistens in the floodlights and one or two British or Australian expats still sit around the edge, reading newspapers. A scattering of small children take their last swim of the day and two women practice the "pool section" of their deep-sea diving training. You wouldn't know to look at it now that it was once difficult to get a seat around the pool on a Sunday afternoon for the crush of families wanting to cool off. This is how the Trents' remember it from

when they first arrived, and the club provided the only outside recreational space available for their children.

The pool has had more sinister uses, too, in the past, before it was crowded with expatriate families. It was used for executions during the Japanese occupation of Hong Kong (1941–45). Unless you knew this you would swim past these ghosts without noticing them. But once you know this piece of local history the pool takes on a new, more sinister countenance. It is a place fabricated by layers of time and bodies: simultaneously a place of death and leisure. Places constituted in the sedimentation of temporal layers and discrepant uses are not always what they seem.

Walking inside, through the main door and the newly refurbished reception area, the notice board announces pilates and yoga classes. There is a tiny gym with a couple of treadmills in an outbuilding with a code-protected door. On the ground floor of the main building is a restaurant partitioned to accommodate three different styles of dining. There are tables for four in one section. There is a back part with three large round tables seating larger groups of up to twenty people each. Then there is a shabby coffee lounge area with newspapers and tired-looking colonial-styled wicker furniture. The menu sports a range of food, from fish pie and baked beans to Indian curries and standard Chinese fare. At one of the big circular tables in the back part of the restaurant on this Sunday of our tour is a Chinese party of twenty eating dinner and singing happy birthday to one of their party in English. At the small tables a family and two couples, all expatriates, dine in a quiet and altogether more private style. Next to the restaurant is Gunners' Bar. As its name suggests, the aesthetic of the bar is military. Regimental plaques hang on the wall, personal tankers are kept in a cupboard over the bar, and a large flat-screen television broadcasts a British football match. The Gunners' Bar would not look out of place in a British main thoroughfare.

Only one barstool in a row of eight is occupied. At ten o'clock, thirteen Chinese tennis players arrive with one *gweilo* man in tow. They come to the Gunners' whether they have played tennis or not; tennis is the most readily deleted part of the evening. It provides a reason to enter a space occupied by (white) expatriate men from Britain, Australia, and the US watching sports on TV. The *gweilo* is either a mascot or an entry ticket. Upstairs is a smarter restaurant with small tables covered in crisp tablecloths for candlelit dinning. At the other end of this upper room is a bar and soft chairs overlooking the swimming pool. All are seductively lit and served by the attentive eyes of several Indian and Nepalese waiters. Only one table is occupied. This restaurant, too, is not much used.

Emptiness is the pervasive feeling in the club. It has a slightly crumbling, abandoned shabbiness. While the central parts of the city gleams with newness and modernity, the club crumbles into the artifacts of the military side of colonial occupation. It needs a makeover, though opinion is divided on this. Chinese members representing the spirit of modernization favor marble. Marble is the surface of the future. British expatriates favor the preservation of crumbling tradition. They favor the colonial shabby-chic of wicker and keeping the plaques on the wall of the Gunners'. Wicker is the fabric of the past.

Who has abandoned it? A middle ranking layer of military personnel, police, civil servants, and government workers of varying trades, including building and surveying would once have filled it to bursting point on a Sunday. In the past applicants for membership were interviewed by army officers who assessed their capacity to "fit in." Chinese were excluded, still in the fifties and sixties and were later, in the eighties, understandably reluctant to join. This was never a prestigious or expensive club, and Hong Kong's particular style of decolonization served it badly. On the day Hong Kong was handed back to China, the club lost 350 members, as a cluster of people entangled in the colonial apparatus decamped, returning to Britain or moving on to posts in other places. Today's expatriate club mem-

bers are a dwindling group of people who have decided to stay on. Sometimes they are boosted by recent arrivals, but the trend is one of outward migration. The club was not just decimated by the end of empire and the retreat of the lower echelons of its governing class. In 2002 sixty people who had lost their jobs in the economic downturn departed to take new jobs in other locations. We will move in closer and speak to two of those who remain.

Poolside with the Vicar's Wife

The vicar's wife is furious. Not obviously so: she seethes quietly with a sense she has no right to be angry. Yet she is. She sits on a sun lounger by the pool fuming. Slim, blonde, and barely forty, she doesn't look angry. She looks sad and wistful. It's Monday and she likes to take the day off with the vicar. Sundays are busy. Needing a break on Mondays is her justification for club membership; she would otherwise consider it a frivolous luxury. She is in Hong Kong living the vicar's dream job. She has "always known he'd wanted this job and when it came up it was obvious that he would take it." It was so obvious that "I don't remember really being asked." Driven people are like that. They drive others all over the place without even asking. It's two-and-a-half years now but it still brings a lump to her throat when she thinks about it.

Coming to Hong Kong meant giving her life away. Living at the vicarage in Gloucestershire meant they lost the house when the vicar gave up the job.

> So having spent twenty years saving and whatever to try and buy the odd bit of furniture I was then giving everything away and getting rid of some nice things. So that was quite hard, I think it took me quite a long while [*pause*] of grieving just to give away so much of what had been home.

Things accumulated through effort and struggle; objects and bits of furniture that enclosed the family biography, her four boys' childhoods, are disposed of in the move. She grieves.

The church is thriving and the vicar is happy. Twelve hundred come through the door on a Sunday for all three services. The vicarage is in a very busy part of a main road, a stark contrast with their quiet rural parish in Britain. She finds it difficult to get used to the bustle of the area. She feels a "failure" because of this. She thinks that it is "just her." The vicar loves it and she should somehow love it too. Only she doesn't. She articulates the difficulties of living the life she wants to live in Hong Kong.

> The biggest things are shopping. What you buy, where you buy it. I still, I can get quite upset that I can't just walk out of my home into the nearest shopping area and there is a wet market and some local food shops near me. But buying food here is quite difficult. It's fine with fruit and veg. But things like meat I can't just think, oh, we've got a dozen people coming for Easter, I think we'll have lamb curry, I'll go and get three pounds of stewing lamb. It doesn't work like that. So that's one of the biggest problems. . . . And I think years ago it would have been easier because there were butchers that were set up for expats, and you phoned them up and told them what you wanted and they delivered it. . . . You have to be a bit flexible, I suppose. I think it's important that we have roasts and sausages, and cheese and milk. Not roast every week, but certainly occasionally. . . . I can buy beef more easily than lamb . . . you can get lamb but it tends to be tiny lamb cutlets and if you've got a family of four hungry boys and visitors you want three pounds of stewing lamb! . . . Sometimes I can get a big chicken . . .
>
> My supermarket on Kowloon side takes about an hour to get there and back . . . You pay a lot for dairy products, and for me that was a major, major change because as a

vicar's wife bringing up a big family, economy was . . . you know [obligatory] I can feed a large family on a shoestring. I've learned how to do that; and moving here you spend your money differently. And there's more money because you get paid more . . . little things I still can't get used to . . . So I walk to the star ferry . . . and I think that marks me out. Most expats don't use the MTR for a start. Most expats wouldn't think twice about just paying for the tunnel; and paying for parking. I'm told, "You'll get used to it." And I still haven't after two-and-a-half years. . . . I struggle with that.

I think I got very down just before Christmas just because of the materialism and the way people spend money. Sometimes I think I just don't belong to this spendthrift society.

Small things ground bigger thing. Food is a way of missing home and acknowledging the difficulties of adapting that is expected. Isolation and marginalization anyway come with being the vicar's wife. The vicar is the nearest thing in the parish to God and the vicar's wife is the nearest thing to the vicar. She moves among parishioners, her key contacts, but is set apart from them. This was true when she lived in Britain, too. In migration her isolation and marginality takes new forms. She is separated from other expats by where she lives and the amount of disposable income she has, and the rules she makes for herself about how it may be spent. She'll either have to make further efforts to fit in or hold out to go home. Meanwhile her boys drift back to Britain one by one as they go to university and don't return. Soon it will be just her and the vicar. What next?

Poolside with the Diver

The diver is impossible to avoid at the club. He teaches the practice part of his diving lessons in the pool. He teaches the theory part in the upstairs bar overlooking the pool. When he is finished teaching diving, he props up the Gunners' Bar late into the night. If we are unable to avoid him we may as well get to grips with him. The best way to understand the diver is to become his diving student: total immersion. There is no other way. One of us has to become his diving student for the evening. I (Caroline) volunteer. I am no diver. I don't even like being in water. I hope that he will have other students, that I can flounder wetly at the back of the class and beat a hasty retreat. No such luck. He is waiting when I arrive at the pool and I am the only student. He is happier in the silent graceful world of underwater than he is on dry land. I, on the other hand, am acutely uncomfortable on so many levels I don't know where to begin describing them. There is equipment and it's very uncomfortable. A belt with weights takes you to the bottom. The bottom! I'm weak with fear. Then there are the rubber boots you wear under your flippers, which are done up very tightly and hurt. There's an inflatable jacket that buckles up tightly across the chest with a tank of air I'll have to use to breath underwater. There is lots of body contact involved in getting the equipment on. I try to think about why I am so out of place in his world. I tell myself, "Don't panic." Panic! I'm hyperventilating with an anxiety that appears to center on putting the mask over my face. I tell him feebly that I don't really do underwater. I have, in fact, been to the world's top dive spots, I explain, expanding on my argument—the Great Barrier Reef, the Cayman Islands, Mexico, and the Red Sea—and not once in any of these places have I felt the need to put my face in the water.

The diver is unimpressed by my humiliating explanation of how I feel about being underwater. I tell him I am claustrophobic. He says we'll take it slowly. I can stop at any point. Good. The mask is the bit that most disturbs my claustrophobia, but he helps me with it. I struggle to continue breathing through my nose. I run out of air inside the mask in seconds and start to hyperventilate. He helps me take it off. He points out that it would be best to breathe through my mouth, which is connected to the rubber tube and the oxygen. I concede the point. I put the mask back on and practice breathing through my mouth, gripping the rubber tube between my teeth like my life depends on it, and actually it does. Slowly he gets me to kneel down in the water. He holds my hand so I don't panic. In the circumstances I overlook the fact that he is touching me! He gets me to lie face down on the bottom of the pool, shows me that I can come up anytime by reinflating my jacket to bring me to the surface. We go under water and I swim around. I can breathe and it feels pretty good. There are no ghosts from the Japanese executions, and I see an angle on things I hadn't seen before. I swim around some more. On my own!

The underwater version of him is porpoiselike, big and soft and slightly fuzzy round the edges, I don't see him at all clearly, only as a looming indeterminate presence. This after all is his world: the world under the sea with its silence and sudden seabed curiosities. What he likes about being under water is that things look totally different. On the surface you can take things for granted: but under water you take a closer look. Best of all, it is totally silent under water. You can walk around slowly and let your mind float because it is difficult to think. Your thoughts drift into suspension and time slows down. Depth provides a slight narcotic effect. He says its "like going to war"; you have to "to worry about it a bit or you are going to get shot."

On the surface the diver is a recycled soldier. He joined the army cadets at the

age of thirteen. He fought in Britain's later colonial wars. He did three tours in Ireland and the Falklands.

> I'm a service guy, that's the way I am . . . You can pick an ex-military guy out in the street: the way they walk, the way they hold themselves, the haircut, the bearing. . . . If I am dressed up I look like I've just stepped out of a mess. That's the only thing I miss is mess life. That's why I like to get down here.

He first came to Hong Kong because the army posted him there. His wife refused to join him. He meets and marries a Chinese woman. After a stint back in Britain they return to Hong Kong when he retires from the army. Supported by his army pension he turns his passion and hobby into a job. Hong Kong is close to some really good dive spots in the Philippines and other places too where he runs courses: "I've done 220 dives this year. I'm happy with that."

The diver's wife is an investment analyst working for one of the big banks. With local family, friends, and business obligations, she is busy with her own life. This is why he sits in the bar until midnight: he is waiting for her to come home before he leaves. Pondering the benefits of mixed relationships and stereotypes of "Oriental women," he says:

> She's top-notch, and she doesn't serve me. That's why we have a very good relationship. Last night she [pauses]; and this other couple are exactly the same. The wife does her own thing. The husband does his own thing and we are happy with that. So there's no controversy . . . She's got her own social life, I've got my own social life. So that makes the relationship work. It was neat today. I haven't seen an octopus in a while. . . . There's so much to see underwater . . . Hi ,Pierre, I saw an octopus today.

"It's time to pack up and go home"

Pierre, the club's round French manager, huffs into the bar from a meeting of "the committee" that makes major decisions about the club. The meeting had been mercifully short by the standard of these things. The chairman is experienced in driving the business through and leaving Pierre to get on with things. But Pierre is agitated. "It's time to pack up and go home," he announces quietly. Another club has closed. Two more are rumored to be closing. The writing's on the wall. The "clubbable" population is declining. The committee is (unrepresentatively) overwhelmingly composed of expatriates. Yet the club membership is now more than 70 percent Chinese. Pierre, his own baggage collected from another (French) version of empire in the East, deals with this shifting demographic indirectly. The problem, he huffs, is "mentality." The spirit is not there. The new members are not "clubbable." He's tried endless combinations of activities. He's tried BBQs, cravat knotting, plays, flower arranging in attempts to create the right level and type of sociality among members. No takers. This includes Peter and Mary who see the club as a place to have private family dinner when they don't feel like cooking or for a quiet drink or to use the gym. They would rather it wasn't a place in which they felt obliged to join in collective activities.

"OK, it is shabby," concedes the agitated Pierre. But it's a club, not a hotel. It's there for its members to get together and do things together. He contrasts what the club should and could be, and perhaps once was, unfavorably with the pressure towards it becoming more of a "business" in marble and gold and "Have a nice day." Marble, gold, and service are, he implies, the pressures brought by new Chinese members who regard colonial shabby-chic as unacceptable. So decoration is also a way of speaking indirectly about ethnicity, about the social relations of empire, about change, about the way things were and the new, more difficult proximities with Chineseness.

He stops circling and goes for it head-on. They "have let too many local people in," and they have a "different mentality" of self and immediate gratification. Gold and marble are a decorative manifestation of the "wrong mentality," the "wrong set of activities": the wrong ethnic group. Pierre is smart. He knows this is part of a bigger picture. Hong Kong was once a booming city with movement and opportunity. Now it's a "gloomy city," being bypassed by Shanghai and Beijing, places business and people are moving on to. In contrast, government in postcolonial Hong Kong is atrophied and dysfunctional. He tells his story about the difficulty of getting recycling going among the clubs to anyone within earshot and willing to listen. He concludes that the business of governance is being mishandled. The return to China has left postcolonial Hong Kong weak and vulnerable. The Chinese cannot be trusted to maintain the status of Hong Kong as an important node in the global economy. The club and the city are part of the same malaise, and Pierre is looking for a new job, somewhere else. The diver stares morosely into his Coke, considering whether or not to order another before heading home. Conversations like these have a ritual quality he enjoys. His wife will be back from work soon and there will be someone to talk to at home.

The dramas of the club are managed by the work that takes place backstage.

Backstage sustains a version of service that is subtly different from the one that operates in private homes. Backstage the serving class is more Chinese and Indian than Philippine. The Gunners' barman is originally from Nepal. He was deposited in Hong Kong by the British military apparatus and now hovers attentively on a very small salary. He has other relatives working in the kitchens. His wife and child are in a small apartment nearby. He's memorized everyone's order. He knows who has a beer tanker stored behind the bar with their name engraved on it. He knows what to put in it and how often to fill it. Raminder and other (Nepalese) women work as waitresses in the coffee shop and pool bar in the daytime. Old Chinese men with wizened faces and blue overalls groom the grounds and keep it free of leaves. Indian cooks and kitchen hands work in the kitchen. The food has a popular Indian orientation. Laundry is washed, the guest rooms are cleaned, and cleaners keep the club pristine in unobtrusive ways. Young Chinese women who speak excellent English run the front desk and deal with members.

Kowloon Cricket Club

We are back on our tour. It's a short walk from the United Services Recreation Club to the Kowloon Cricket Club. The problem with the Kowloon Cricket Club is cricket. The field, or pitch, is bright green, lovingly manicured and watered, maintained at great cost and once a matter of no controversy. Most members played cricket, or watched it, this was why they joined. No one minded that the pitch occupied 90 percent of the land area available for sports activities: until recently. Rumblings about space for other activities are beginning to make themselves heard. Only 3 percent of the club members actually play cricket. They need more tennis courts and field hockey pitches because more people play these games than cricket. Reallocating the available space has become a hot issue in the club. What could be more British, more colonial than cricket? Kowloon Cricket Club— KCC—is over a hundred years old and was once a predominantly white domain. It opened up its membership in postcolonial circumstances when they needed extra income for its development. Now its membership is approximately 70 percent Chinese who have less interest in cricket and lean towards tennis. It is roughly 15 percent Australian and British combined and 15 percent Indian subcontinent. The cricketing nations are seriously outnumbered. Neither expensive nor pretentious,[5] it has a caché that generates a ten-year waiting list with accelerated entry for cricketers of the appropriate playing level.

Overlooking the manicured cricket green, Alice sits on a balcony in the sun eating her lunch, reflecting on the theme of change at the club.

But it has changed a lot, this is all new and so, because it used to be just the old building and it was a bit run-down. I think funds were a bit limited so they've attracted a lot of new members, which they had to, to get the new extension, got a gym and a teenagers' room. But unfortunately there's not, the percentage of members who are actually interested in cricket is very small . . . In fact, cricket is a sort of dying thing in Hong Kong anyway. When we first came there were a lot of cricket teams because there was the army and the police and all those people who played a lot of cricket, and a lot of the clubs ended up selling their grounds. It's just the space, really. There isn't the space.

The club is part of the furniture of Alice's life. She grew up in Nigeria while her father, who grew up in colonial India, worked as an engineer on the construction of the Jos-to-Maiduguri railroad. This was one of colonialism's transport and engineering accomplishments. She recalls childhood memories of the prefabricated houses they lived in, enamel bowls, smells and sounds, their houseboy, the crafts, ordinary things.

My father was born in India, he lived there all his childhood. My father's father was in the army [in India] but then stayed on. He was a musician in the army but then went into business and was a coal merchant . . . my father was born in '27 in Darjeeling. They lived in Calcutta but lot of people in Calcutta used to go up to Darjeeling. He was born there and went to school in Darjeeling. But his parents lived in Calcutta. My grandmother stayed there, my grandfather died there, and my grandmother, well, they both did. They stayed till they died, they never came back. They'd been there such a long time they just wouldn't have fitted in [in Britain]. There are people here actually. . . . a lot of people aren't retired because they can't afford it and worry about the medical and so on and just think they don't want to be anywhere else and you *can* actually afford to live here quite cheaply. If you know where to go and live up in the New Territories you can get a property very cheaply if you are prepared to convert an old pigsty or something and there are people who do that: real hangers-on, stayers-on.

Empire isn't in the genes. It's in the bodies and social practices embedded in the genealogies of family life. Yesterday's colonials are today's expatriates available for overseas postings; and the club is now part of the furniture of expatriate postcolonial life.

> When we came here [in the eighties] everything was provided, a house, a car, the schooling, the airfares, accommodation, just everything was provided, sort of expat life and joined the club . . . Now you look around and actually it's very Chinese now. Which isn't a problem, but it's not what it was. Whether that's a good thing or not, I don't know. Now my husband works for a Chinese company, we don't get housing, accommodation, medical, anything like that. So you sort of think, is it really worth being here? Except I love it and I don't want to go. I love the weather, the social life, my job, I love everything about it.

It's worth staying despite the withdrawal of colonial privilege transformed into expat employment conditions. But there are foundation scandals. Some of the high-rises are not sunk deeply enough into the ground. Corners were cut on the subcontracted work. Alice's husband's firm is implicated and can no longer secure work, and employees are laid off. He's had to find new work in worse conditions, which don't match his qualifications. So staying on is demeaning. The erosion of entitlement is a difficult burden to bear, bemoaned and traded against other privileges, including a lifestyle that makes it "worthwhile."

Alice, like the others, remembers the day things changed forever.

> It was exciting [living through the handover], it was interesting and it was all kind of a big pageant. Some people were, you know, scared, people back home like my mother thought they were going to line all the Brits up and shoot them: and when the tanks came rolling in, because they came in at 4 o'clock in the morning. We thought we'd get up and go and see them, because the barracks is just here. This building here. . . , because it was a two-day thing . . . a big build-up it was the last day of British rule so they had a big ceremony, and it rained. It rained during the handover . . . and Prince Charles was there . . . and it just poured and everybody got soaked, and there was Chris Patten and he was crying and his daughters were crying and Prince Charles was there with the umbrellas and everybody had big parties and you went and watched in on the TV so it was very emotional. . . .
>
> Everybody had their flags and . . . you thought, well, let's all pretend we are British overseas colonials in the days of the [empire], when you thought about it you thought it was sad in a way . . . and you thought, well, what is going to happen in the future? . . . And, but then things haven't changed dramatically, but then things are gradually changing.

Hong Kong changed and the club changed with it. No longer an oasis of European civility, Alice shares it with people who spit in the pool and stand on the toilet seat, who bring their servants with them and use their mobile phones, which, she says, is supposed to be against the rules. It's the minutiae of daily life that grates; small changes that log bigger ones. Although she doesn't "mean to be racist" and knows that "we are in someone else's country," we see in these unguarded moments some of the little places where race and empire still matter and make matter.

ON PATROL

This is the last part of our tour. We are in the open areas of the New Territories in the low, hilly green spaces that join the border with mainland China. We will shift to a different pace and style of walking from the stroll composing boys' night out—that is, to patrol. Patrol involves a particular kinetic, a use of the body in surveillance and intervention. It involves stealth and high visibility, patient watching without being seen, and overpowering at the right moment. It involves high mobility and immobility. In addition to its bodily rhythms, patrol involves particular intersections between body and space. It also involves space becoming territory. From one perspective, territory is a special configuration of space. Territory is space in open contention. It is land that must be reclaimed or protected from the threat of alternate use.[1] Patrol is part of the constitution of space as territory. These are routine strategies in military occupation and routine policing. Patrol is a tactic serving all regimes and the forces that seek to undermine them.

Bill patrolled the New Territories around the border with China as a British officer in the colonial Hong Kong police force. He joined the Hong Kong police force from Britain as a trainee inspector[2] in 1977. This was a defiant gesture at the time. His parents were horrified that he was moving to the other side of the world from Cleethorpes and forbade him to go. But he left, and by the late seventies he was in the Police Tactical Unit (PTU) trained in riots and emergency situations to support local police as a mobile patrol unit in the New Territories. This included what police call "swamp" duties. The PTU was more like another colonial policing outfit, the Northern Ireland police force, in its equipment, style, and training, than any police force in mainland Britain. Its focus at that time was dealing with illegal Chinese and Vietnamese migrants crossing the border from China. Bill refers to these people as "IIs." They are not refugees but "illegal immigrants." The term both clarifies their status and justifies their treatment. Denied mainstream legitimate means of subsistence by their status, the IIs arriving in the New Territories are associated with high rates of crime and prostitution. But Bill's job also has larger geopolitical significance. Hong Kong is also about the space behind Hong Kong in the New Territories and in China. He was not just enforcing the boundaries between illegal immigrants and those who had a right of entry and abode; Bill was enforcing the boundaries between China and Hong Kong, between Communism and the British Empire. Hong Kong was a listening post for China and it was the height of the Cold War. Bill's patrol would go to high places and look down over great distances. Hilltop fortification allowed easy observation of the conduct of people within the territory, and enforcement of the boundaries between states by controlling the flow of people from one to the other.

The best way to understand Bill's activities is to go with him "on patrol." His

patrolling activities are on a landscape defined through memory, as Bill's patrols were part of his job as a colonial police officer in the seventies.[3] The pace and movements of his body contain the memories of patrol, which he struggles to compress into walking. Bill see things in macroterms, pointing to great tracts of land and discussing population movements, across borders, and internally, as the population grows through migration and the government struggles to house it. Now on the same border that Bill once patrolled, he and Lisa stand and look at the barbed-wire fence. This border separating the Special Administrative Region of Hong Kong from China at Shenzhen is now guarded by motion detectors and cameras. It is guarded by the authorities in Beijing as a way of separating the territories over which they exercise jurisdiction. Immigration is permitted but strictly controlled. A steady flow of trucks in both directions move the produce of Hong Kong's off-shoring arrangements with China.

Standing in this place Bill remembers that the "IIs"—the objects of his patrol—came in two varieties. Most were Chinese, but there were also Vietnamese refugees in the period following the end of the Vietnam War.

> We had Vietnamese illegal immigrants . . . and the authorities wanted them back . . .
> we did one or two operations whereby we had a sealed train provided by the main-

> land authorities . . . filled them up with Vietnamese and we guarded the train. . . . we put them on the sealed train and cordoned the area. . . . and it used to be. . . . a single line railway line covered over, and there was this gap that marked the border. . . . My idea . . . for transporting the Vietnamese back on the sealed train, was to use cattle trucks. . . but no way can you do this.

Sealed trains were used by the Nazi for transporting Jews and Bill acknowledges this problematic connection.

Being returned to China as an escaped Vietnamese refugee was a dangerous position to be in with the Chinese authorities. Chinese returnees were equally vulnerable, and it was Bill's job to send them back too. He points in the distance and remembers.

> We would have to go through here when we were picking them up off the marine launches lacerating their feet. . . . and loading them into lorries and bringing them back along here . . . following the road that runs parallel to here,. . . . the holding center for illegal immigrants. They'd gather so many, then they'd have a day they'd move them across the border. So we'd pick 'em up in lorries . . . We just watched the lorries. . . Walking up and down the lorries and "Excuse me, sir, excuse me, sir," from the back of one of the lorries. A Chinese lad, speaking better English than I did, educated in Beijing and wanted to get out. Amazing.

His memory of sending an attractive young Chinese woman back even though she pleaded with him not to is particularly vivid. He knew that she would be raped by the guards on the train once she was in China. Did he feel bad about this?

> No, to be honest with you. I know it might sound callous but it's a job. All right, yeah. You remember it. Yes, that may be. But you were upholding the law of Hong Kong. When we arrived we swore allegiance to the Queen and her successors to uphold the laws of Hong Kong.

Bill has remembered this for almost thirty years because it contradicts his sense of himself as a gentleman. Bill is a family man with a respectful relationship with his wife. He is close to their three sons. On patrol he is regularly caught between duty and his sense of self. Police have to do things "the public" doesn't like to think about.

Bill's relationship with Chineseness is shaped by empire. Once part of its ap-

paratus of enforcement his skill is still valued in postcolonial Hong Kong. Swimming against the tide of decampment by British officers in 1997,[4] Bill stays on. His prospects are held in a careful structure of expectation. Only the top three posts are closed to non-Chinese officers. He can be promoted all the way up to senior assistant commissioner. With his recent promotion he has done well for himself and learned some Cantonese. He says, "These jobs no longer exist. HK was the last jewel in the crown of the colonies." He regrets that the opportunities from which he benefited will not be extended to his three sons. Patrolling is one of those plastic activities not tied to styles of regime. Policing provided Hong Kong with "stability," and in an "international city" stability maintains the confidence of investors. Local Chinese police don't mind working with expats. Bill thinks this is because outsiders like him are not in on the politicking that goes on among those more in the know.

Now too-senior Bill has not been on patrol since 1984. Instead, he manages patrols in more central locations than the border area. He deals with the densely populated apartment buildings. These vertical communities of 50,000 are problematic from the vantage point of patrol. High-rise patrol requires special kinds of maneuvers. His position in law enforcement exposes him to versions

of Chineseness in a side of life most people—local and expat—never come into contact with. He and his officers deal with savage disputes between neighbors and family members, territorial disputes between rival gangs, drug dealing and robbery. They do this all in the context of densely packed vertical communities.

> We suffer the same problems as any place or any Western country. . . . High-rise may be different, of course, in the UK you've got low-rise patrol. . . . the majority of the population is in high-rise flats . . . it takes it to another level. You do have high-rise patrols where you swamp an area picking up from your intelligence that you've got a particular problem with a particular housing estate or a particular block in a housing estate and then you'd cover the housing estate with high-rise patrols. Basically sweeping across one floor on the way down, so geography wise, urbanization-wise, high-rise flats and illegal-immigration [are Bill's business].

Bill and his family live in the same apartment building as the Trents: the only other expat family in the high-rise development. His relationship with racialized and ethnicized difference is more intimate than theirs. One foreign adventure leads to another. Bill's wife Lisa was a Filipino maid working for a wealthy family on the Peak. He met her through the Filipino date of another police officer soon after he arrived in Hong Kong.

His relationship with Lisa added new complexities to his parents' disapproval of his posting in Hong Kong. Bill's parents' early relationship with their new daughter-in-law during infrequent visits to Cleethorpes was fraught with difficulties. It settled around routine domestic tasks and called Lisa's level of civilization into question.

> I did take Lisa home . . . This was the first time I'd been back since I got married. It was the epitome. The mother-in-law–daughter-in-law clash— terrible, absolutely terrible . . . This was just a clash. . . . Things that Lisa was used to doing you couldn't do in the UK, washing clothes in the bath, that was a no-no in my mother's house. . . . She was whisked off by immigration [as they arrived in Britain].

Bill takes up this theme in a more humorous and forgiving way; perhaps allowing his parent's anxieties to stand in for his.

> I think it broke her heart basically. . . . Came out here, of course. The next thing was December 1979, met my wife. March '80 we were married. I phoned up and said by the way I'm getting married. Next thing I got this telegram. Oh no, I'd told

them in a letter I was getting married. Next thing I got was this telegram—"Phone home immediately." Not "Congratulations" . . . Phoned up. "What on earth . . ." They didn't make it [to the wedding]. Lisa's parents didn't make it. Different situation: difficulty of traveling from the Philippines. Got married. Then my leave came. In those days I was on whole terms and we got 120 days leave after a two-and-a-half-year tour. First six weeks I spent down in the Philippines. . . . . She comes from a little village [on an island] . . . Get taken down to Negros. . . . Drive fifty kilometers down to a small town where my wife deserts me. Having seen her mother we then go off to the market . . . in the middle of nowhere. . . . That was culture shock, no electricity, no running water, when you want to get a wash you walked a mile to the river . . . Got married again there in a Catholic church. Got married here [Hong Kong] in a registry office. Not recognized of course. . . . And then got married in a Catholic wedding [in the Philippines]. I was brought up a Methodist . . . Went to my wedding. Didn't understand a word, apart from Henry VIII. . . . That was my wedding. But before that there was a ritual you had to go through—I'm talking about culture shock—they had to find a black pig . . . it's a story which I like; and the job of the groom was to kill it. My father-in-law's cousin, I will be forever grateful to, he took the job of killing it. No way. You put it between your thighs and placed a dagger in its jugular vein and let it bleed to death. . . . About thirty minutes, squealing . . . then cook it and the next thing I saw of it, it was lying on this table. They had this long table with a pig on it, ribs, cage, innards . . . and all this is laid out. . . . Sorry, I love telling this story. In the corner is a witch doctor mumbling nonsensically like the red Indian you see on the telly and suddenly he stops. And I looked at Lisa and she said: "Right, you have to eat something of everything that's on this table, starting with the pig's rear end." . . . You go round and round the table . . . local libation: it was awful . . . I'm the apple of my mother-in-law's eye because none of the other sons-in-law did it, two of which are expats, one from the UK, one from Canada.

Intimacies negotiating tightly held cultural, racial and ethnic differences reveal bigger difficulties and anxieties. Bill takes for granted that he is a positive addition to his in-law's family just as he knows that Lisa is problematic in his, with its rooted approach to life. And yet their life together and their children have bridged these difficulties in a practical way made possible in Hong Kong. We don't know how. Bill and his boys visit Lisa's family in the Philippines annually. But they do as bored tourists and complain there isn't much to do. The proximities that bore her family are important to Lisa. What accommodations and trade-offs did she make in this route out of her life in domestic service? Intimacies open onto bigger landscapes and hers is about the global organization of labor and migration as ways of managing.

This is the end of our Hong Kong tour. It is time to return to the theme of migration and gather up what we have learned.

MIGRATION REVISITED

We suggested at the outset that migration constitutes the global world. Through migrants' activities (settlement practices) we tracked global circuits that pass through Hong Kong. Alongside mainstream financial circuits we found smaller ones working in parallel. We found large volumes of trade between China and developing countries, all in small-scale activity. We found Indian food, Islam, domestic services, exotic dancers, and prostitutes. All part of the same system, these circuits differ in scale, in their rewards and in the lives they organize. These circuits parallel and interconnect with those that are generated by locals. The city and its social architecture are composed through these circuits.

But migration's social significance exceeds its composition of globalization. In a world on the move it is not enough to know that people move from place to place generating new activities and connections. We also need to know how people live these routines of long and short-term mobility, and our tours have shed light on these issues. The migrants we met showed us their worlds and the skill it takes to live in them. Our tour provided close-up portraits of migrant lives, concerns, calculations, movements, and opportunities while they were looking after pets, buying food, cleaning the kitchen, dancing, or trading US dollars, tape recorders, and manicures.

We began with some clunky categories cut from the patterns that migration scholars use to understand the world on the move. Lifestyle and serving-class migrants provide two categories that fade into each other. They allowed us to frame migration through the lives and settlement practices they sustain in Hong Kong. They revealed the social inequalities that migration produces and circulates while constituting the world on a global scale. These inequalities are elaborated from two key macrofactors.

The first are social conditions in migrants' countries of origin or citizenship. Thailand and the Philippines have developing low-wage economies with limited social opportunities even for its middle-class college graduates. This is less true of India, where accelerated industrialization has provided more opportunities. These circumstances are tangled in old alignments of the global world drawn around European empires and the new matrices of US global dominance. In both systems these countries occupy subordinate positions. Britain and the United States, on the other hand, sustain high levels of development and (unevenly distributed) social opportunities. These contrasting circumstances tag migrants in global circulations through conditions of exit establishing degrees of desperation and need. This only maps roughly onto race and ethnicity. While generally privileging whiteness, this system allows British and American ethnic minorities to trade on their British or US citizenship. Likewise white ethnicities carry differential value accumulated through citizenship. Moldavians and Bosnians are tagged by the circumstances of low development and opportunity that propel them outward. There is much to untangle in the circumstances of migration that scholars call push factors and that configure social hierarchies on a global scale.

The second set of macrofactors configuring global social inequalities are also tangled with the first. These are entry conditions in receiving counties. The skills and qualifications migrants carry from Thailand and the Philippines are not permitted to transfer. They are only allowed to enter as live-in domestic labor. Moreover, they are contract laborers with no accumulated rights of residence. Worse still dancers and prostitutes live beyond their (tourist) conditions of stay and this makes them vulnerable to a range of abuses. These circumstances result from decisions made by the Hong Kong immigration department, and we saw their consequences. They could make other decisions that avoid these inequalities. British migrants, on the other hand, were able to make use of the air routes and occupations opened by empire and translate them into something else after 1997. Their rights of residence are not tied to specific jobs and they can move freely in and out of Hong Kong and on to other places. They have rights of residence and employment in member states of the European Union. These migrants have many attractive options for relocation.

Macrocircumstances reverberate through lives, as our tour showed. It drew fine distinctions within our clunky categories exposing variation through biography and circumstance. We saw that serving-class migrants are highly differentiated. Service has a different meaning for Indian waiters than for maids and waiters have clear avenues of upward mobility. Maids exemplify service in their forced entanglement in others' lives, but they manage this in different ways. Exotic dancers and prostitutes have other intimate entanglements. Routes out of these positions are difficult and dangerous. Personal routes around the city are circumscribed by work commitments and lack of money. New lives are made in new terms at a distance from long-standing commitments in the Philippines. Service migration, as we saw, involves many ways of living with the constraints operating at macrolevels. The migrants we met supply a moving and complex portrait of their lives that defies easy description as well as the application of categories like gender, race, and ethnicity.

The macrocircumstances shaping lifestyle migrants' lives reverberate in fine distinctions. We saw this in how the "good life" that lies at the center of lifestyle migration is produced in trade-offs between work and overall quality of life. We saw many variations in this. At one end of this spectrum life is a tropical beach, and work is what pays to sit on it. John and Lyn provide examples of migrants

who will do what it takes, workwise, to stay in Hong Kong. If this option is re-moved they will find a beach somewhere else. Vacation, for some, provides a tem-plate for the good life. For others, like Zoë and Daniel, immediate gratification in the good life must be delayed while Hong Kong provides the resources to live somewhere better, later. For others, like Jake, the good life is all about work and making money. Others qualify the good life with the requirements of ordinari-ness. We saw some of the ways in which gender and class matter in these life productions. We saw that men, women, and children in the same household live different versions of migration. Hong Kong has freed many women from the ne-cessity of work and some like this more than others. Lifestyle migrants come in as many varieties as serving-class migrants. We offer these as different versions of white Britishness operating form postcolonial Hong Kong.

As we conclude, we will further explore some of the subtleties of lifestyle mi-gration. We will use the idea of *migrant skill* to develop our thinking. This inverts the term "skilled migration" discussed at the beginning of our tour as one of the terms used by migration scholars to think about (white) expat migration from developed countries. As we noted then, the problem with "skilled migration" is that it is not applied to differentiate levels of skill among migrants. It is instead applied only to those who are permitted to transfer their skills to new locations. It denies, for example, the high levels of skill we noted in maids living inside others' lives. It promotes a narrow, work-focused notion of skill. It has indirect racial and ethnic resonance, as we also noted in suggesting the invisibility of white mi-grants and the positive benefits they bring to their landscapes of new settlement. We would like to propose instead a broader notion of skill, so we will end with an evaluation of the skills white lifestyle migrants in our study display.

What do we mean by "skill"? Skill is compressed knowledge about the world and how to operate within it.[1] It is not confined to employment. Skill is generally demonstrated in the practical operation of routine activities in everyday life. Our question then becomes: what skills do lifestyle migrants display in living in their world?

All migrants live in translation. We think of translation as provisional ways of coming to terms with foreignness.[2] This is a central skill in migration and all other forms of travel. In a world on the move this is an important issue. From Britain alone six million people have moved to live in other countries. How do they live? How do lifestyle migrants operate in coming to terms with foreignness? The foreignness in Hong Kong is Chineseness. So how do British lifestyle mi-grants live with Chineseness?

Chineseness, as we noted at the beginning of our tour, compresses many elements of life in Hong Kong. We know that serving-class migrants live on intimate terms with Chinese people. Maids manage their entanglement in the domestic regimes and emotional landscapes of employing families. They bring up Chinese children, deal with grandmothers, and know the intimate recesses of Chinese homes. Such proximities demand high levels of skill in cultural translation in the minutia of Chinese lives. Exotic dancers and prostitutes manage still greater bodily intimacies than these. Failure in these skills has dramatic consequences in summary repatriation. Maids speak Cantonese. So do the traders we met from the Indian subcontinent. They manage intricate negotiations between Chinese suppliers and customers involving complex patterns of risk and trust. Lifestyle migrants compare poorly with serving-class migrants in terms of the skills they demonstrate in living with Chineseness.

We saw on our tour an uneven picture with many positives. Women lifestyle migrants manage the interface with Chineseness in ways that transcend language in fabricating daily life on behalf of their families. We saw them supporting children's social and sports endeavors, going shopping, and participating in hobbies and activities that draw upon Chineseness in fragmented and fleeting ways. We saw the vicar's wife struggling with Chinese food, looking for lamb and sausages. Affectionate connection with the energy and exotic aesthetic of streets, shops, and Chinese festivals reveal admiration for (versions of) Chineseness and skill in interacting with them. Men and women manage in Chinese workplaces, albeit in limited and partial ways. Policing the city requires certain skill in interfacing with Chineseness even though much of this is confined to its seedier and dysfunctional underside. The idea, advanced by migration scholars, that some migrants live without connection to landscapes on new belonging is an exaggeration of what happens in practice.

Those with Chinese partners—Julia, Jack, Hamish, and the Diver—have privileged access to Chinese languages, cultures, and families. Let's think about linguistic levels of Chineseness as a platform for others. Of those with Chinese partners, only Jack is fully operational in Cantonese. Hamish and the Diver irritate their Chinese partners by refusing to take Chinese-language instruction seriously, knowing they can get by in English. Others we met on our tour were prepared to try Cantonese and had varying degrees of operational effectiveness. Recycled employees of empire like Peter and Bill have intermediate-level Cantonese-language skills. Lyn, John, Stephanie, and many of the others were at least on greeting terms. Language is a key route into a place and its culture: a key route into Chineseness. Those without it are cut off from Hong Kong public culture, workplace culture, news media, and gossip. They can't eavesdrop on the bus. The privilege of being able to operate in English, as we saw, brought further lines of separation that make it unnecessary to learn Cantonese to operate on an everyday basis. This privilege is a disability in migrant skills. Speaking the colonial-rebranded-international language promotes this disability and disables key connections with Chineseness.

Many British migrants, as we saw, operate in workplaces where their exposure to Chinese people and languages is limited to security guards and cleaners. In many cases they live and work among significant concentrations of expats, and this limits their exposure to Chinese coworkers and neighbors. Peter works in a Chinese context but his path is smoothed by Chinese interlocutors and translators. Social networks are commonly composed solely of expats. Even those with privileged access to Chinese families through their partners appear not to take much advantage of this in making local networks. The Diver lives in happy social separation from his wife. This shows both respect for her position and independence and reluctance to engage with her Chinese family and social networks. This frees him to socialize with other expats. This is a lost opportunity in fitting in and establishing better connections through the resources available.

The image we were offered of the expat bubble exaggerates separation. The view that British lifestyle migrants' work and social networks are internally focused on each other lies closer to the situation we discovered on our tour. No migrant can live completely in a bubble. They all have connections with Chineseness that work across different planes of activity at different depths and require varied levels of skill. We saw infinite degrees of respectful segmentation. We saw not only a lack of Cantonese but also a shortage of curiosity and eagerness to engage with new people and situations. We saw that British migrants are self-absorbed in the minutiae of their private lives and socially focused on each other. Their exposure to the everyday concerns of local Chinese people thus depends upon their hosts' readiness to translate these things for them into English. In being rendered in translation, their world is presented to them by translators and interlocutors. In living through these forms of translation they operate at a level removed from the local population. We think this is what they mean when they speak about the expat bubble. They mean there is a lack of immediacy about their world, however good the translation and however interested they are in puzzling over it. Their lives are lived in English and lost in (multiple levels of) translation. In these same processes their lives are also made small. They live among each other and rely on each other for entertainment and social contacts. Old China hands develop expertise drawn from colonial ideas about local cultures circulated as advice. This further reduces the need for newcomers to grapple with local people and circumstances or to try to interpret their new world for themselves. Worse, proximity with Chinese people at the club quickly reveals some British migrants limitations. We saw some startling examples of cultural grating and conflict over personal habits and conduct. We saw competition over the use of space and activities in the clubs that exposed some of the limits of tolerance. These are not the skills of multiethnic or multicultural coexistence we might like to think global migration requires and develops in migrants.

Moving to another layer of Chineseness, what of migrants' skill in connecting with the city itself? We saw that migrants had quite different versions of what Hong Kong is and what it means in their life. In the configurations of work and life we witnessed, Hong Kong has varying significance as a place to live. Sometimes we saw that it was interchangeable with other places, supplying the same or similar things in life. Those for whom life is a beach can always find other beaches to sit on. Those who see Hong Kong as a high-status job locale do equally well elsewhere. They do not necessarily have a special connection with Hong Kong. Specific places don't matter so much in migrant calculations and connections. The mobile can always, well, move. Sometimes we saw that Hong Kong was a default option when families could not resolve conflicting views on future locations. In these cases it was easier to go on as before than to negotiate change. Sometimes we saw that migrants were instrumental in their relationship with Hong Kong. It is a means to an end, to a future that lay elsewhere. It was sometimes admired and sometimes not. It was better than some places and worse than others. Hong Kong is an object in migrants' calculations. It is not a place of deep connection although it is sometimes held in considerable affection. This is how lifestyle migrants live: without deep connection. This is part of the temporariness we saw in the casting of migrants' lives on our tour.

Inevitably temporariness works against deep connections. Skills that might be channeled into connections are instead channeled into managing temporariness, managing connections outside of Hong Kong and lining up other options. Lifestyle migrants' lives, as we saw, are permanently temporary. They are easily packed up and relocated. This option may not be exercised, but it forms one of the verities of migrant lives and the calculations on which they are founded. While living temporary lives takes considerable skill, as we saw, temporariness supports limited local material, emotional, and social network investment. It limits these investments to things that can be easily packed up and moved to the next place.

British lifestyle migrants diminish the significance of Hong Kong as a place

while choosing to live there and, in many cases, enjoying living there. While strong clues about their future are doubtless supplied in their (official and street-level) treatment as foreign residents, connections with Chineseness only recently stopped being synonymous with colonial connections. The way that colonial connections are premised on racial and ethnic superiority and subordination is a source of comfort-in-familiarity for some and discomfort for others. Our tour displayed migrants' reactions to empire in its many manifestations in their lives. For some this was a past that cannot be buried fast enough. Many migrants actively wanted to reconfigure their connections with Chineseness on more equal terms. What is striking is how little idea they had about how to go about this. But we also saw examples of migrants fabricating now with materials recycled from the past. We glimpsed nostalgia for the old China aesthetic of fishing junks, typhoon shelters, and Hakka fishing huts. We saw empire employment and conditions of service extended as expat advantage: even by those who wished to strike a distance from it. We saw colonial genealogies taking newly animated forms in Hong Kong. We saw the little places where empire and race still maters, and make the matter, that forms the substance of now. New, tentatively formulated, and ambivalent (racial and ethnic) superiorities inevitably reduce the importance of fitting in and the skills and effort that might expend in doing so. In a competitive global system it is important to maintain and further advantage over other migrants. The transformation of old hierarchies into new ones are actually rather convenient.

Maintaining a competitive edge provides a curious series of discordant dis/connections with Britain. It also provides an outlet for energy and skill that might be channeled into fitting in and forming deeper connections with Chineseness. Britain provides its migrants with credentials that play well in global scenes. Our tour shows how being British works well compared to being South Asian or Southeast Asian. Migrants' ambivalent connections with Britain provide resources in the production of what are actually rather valuable versions of whiteness. Of course the value of these connections and their place in the production of whiteness remain unacknowledged. As we saw on our tour, Britain provides migrants with resources in self and "proper" child production. It provides schooling and university places. It provides language skills that are highly valued and rebranded as "international." It provides connection with kin, time out from being a migrant, and cultural resources and artifacts that embellish life in Hong Kong. Most importantly, it provides measures of migrant advancement in the contrast between their lives in Hong Kong and the lives of more sedentary relatives who remain in Britain. It provides evidence that migrants' lives have changed: for the

better. Britain provides a measurement of upward social mobility. This is one the key goals of migration measured in quality of life and disposable income. The migrants we toured were clear about this.

For a minority (remember Hamish and John) Britain provides a reminder that the unacknowledged privileges of white Britishness have been eroded by multiracialism. Multiracialism, as you will remember, was seen as responsible for creating violence and a breach of civility in British inner cities. It skewed proper hierarchies in favoring "black lesbians." In this scenario the privileges legitimately due to whiteness are only properly restored in migration. They are restored in opting to live as an ethnic minority in a postcolonial Chinese city. A minority of British migrants live in Hong Kong with this knowledge and skill.

It is not that British lifestyle migrants lack skill. It is a matter of the social priorities embedded in where their skills are focused. Focus betrays the framework from which they operate. Their skills are focused on building connections that sustain relative advantage in global systems composed in migration. Their skills are not directed at fitting in to a Chinese city. Social integration in places of new settlement, the skill that must be demonstrated by those who come to live in Britain as migrants, is not part of their framework.

Lifestyle migrants are rich migrants in terms of comparative advantage, wealth, and resources. But the global mechanisms that work to make them rich also make them poor. They make poor migrants in terms of the skill it takes to live in a connected way in multicultural, multiracial contexts with (social, cultural, ethnic, and racial) difference. In these respects they are indeed poor migrants. Poor South Asian and Southeast Asian migrants, on the other hand, are rich in migration skills. They have no option. Their survival depends upon it. We can learn from the way they live as migrants. And we can be less critical of the way they live among us. In a world on the move fitting in and forming connection across multiple planes of difference are indispensable skills. The alternative is to live on the surface. In this case migration and other forms of travel do not enrich and broaden through exposure to other people and places. They simply work to provide new venues for the development of social advantage.

ENDINGS AND BEGINNINGS

Bringing It All Back Home: The Village

What happens when versions of (white) Britishness formed in migration are re-patriated? How do they play locally? What difference do they make? We know by now there is no single or simple answer to these questions. The end of these stories is also the beginning; the place from which we picked up the road to Hong Kong. It is paved with the memories of an old lady who lives in a Devonshire village in the southwest of Britain. She spent "the best" twenty years of her life in Hong Kong. While we were on our tour, the old lady lives on in Britain.

Place. There is more to the English village than you think. On the surface, the built and "natural" (highly contrived) environment and its social relationships seem straightforward enough. There is the old church set in its ancient grave-yard, no longer receiving the dead but a social archive of life in the area. It has gloomy stained glass, an elderly dwindling congregation, a vicar on rotation from the nearest town. The church was a social hub even in the years after the Second World War when it had long ceased to be the basis of the social order. It is now neglected by the commuters, the newcomers, and the locals with better things to do on a Sunday. The public housing was a monument to British postwar housing policy. Once a source of unease and quiet protest, it is now owner-occupied and an accepted part of the landscape on the edge of the village. New, expensive de-tached houses with built-in garages are springing up in fields beyond the estate. This adds to the housing stock of older single-family homes and bungalows with ample grounds. A smattering of thatched cottages once occupied by farm labor-ers pepper the landscape. Sometimes a whole row of them is made into a single low-ceilinged gloomy dwelling. A smart car parked outside. The new social order, like the one it replaced, is inscribed in buildings. Farms, once much busier and a source of local employment, are unnaturally quiet now. The farmer has a part-time job in town. One main road runs through the center of the village, and four buses a day carry those without cars—the young, the old, and those of insuffi-cient means—to the nearest town. School kids are bussed out and back in. The village school was closed in the forties. There's not much to do in the village in the contemporary way in which these things are counted. The Women's Institute, the Mothers' Union, and the Youth Club have seen better days. There is no great demand for collective activity anyway. The old distinction between local and new-comer takes on new substance as young people in search of jobs and affordable housing move into town and new people with higher incomes arrive to enjoy the "village atmosphere."

Closer examination of village bodies and their social alchemy reveals people you may not have noticed. There are a couple of relatives of the Earl of Devonshire, women of course, living in elegant unmarried simplicity. There is a smattering of ex-military personnel who still insist on being addressed as "Colonel" and "Major" though now retired and long back from India and postings in the East. There is an old lady, now widowed, who spent most of her life in Hong Kong. There are others whose lives were spent in east Africa and a family back from Sarawak on Borneo. These were the functionaries and beneficiaries of empire: now back in the village.

Ethnicity is silently present here. Unannounced forms of whiteness were forged in intimate proximity with the subjects and practices of colonial governance. The husband of the woman who runs the post office is Irish and is made to feel it although he fought in British uniform in the Second World War and almost never goes to Ireland. The ethnic cartographies beneath the surface involve a range of colonial encounters, far away and near at hand, only partially resolved with the partition of Ireland, which is when the woman's husband left, or to take another example, Indian independence. Things are never quite what they seem.

The English village, on the surface the most parochial of places, with its yeoman resonance and feudal theocratic accents, is actually created in intimate association with distant places. The village is not just on the road from Exeter, it's on the road from Delhi, Mombassa, Nairobi, Kampala, Auckland, Sydney, Fiji, Toronto, Hong Kong, and other places too numerous to name. The village is connected with these places through people's journeys and what they bring back with them. The routes that pass through the village are not the disused routes of the past. The road to and from Hong Kong, Toronto, and Mombassa, are also the new highways of globalization just as surely as they were once the highways of empire.

Joyce

It is a bright autumn day in 1997, and Joyce sits on her floral sofa looking out of the picture window of her sixties house. She is focused on her back lawn and the shifting boundary between the birdfeeder and her cat. The lawn and house form part of a quiet cul-de-sac tucked away behind the old church, in the center of the village. Her cluttered living room is full of Chinese furniture, ornaments, and wall hangings: mementos of a life spent in the East. She shifts her gaze from the lawn to her photograph albums scattered over the coffee table. Around these visual fragments episodic memories of her life in Hong Kong and other places too, are marshaled into stories that can be spoken into the tape recorder.

Joyce's life in Hong Kong ended abruptly when Arthur—long since deceased—retired from his post with the colonial government. They "returned" to this unfamiliar corner of Devonshire, where they had never lived. But Joyce has another ending, another "return" on her mind on this particular afternoon—the return of Hong Kong to China. She and her middle-aged daughter Jane—who spent her childhood in Hong Kong—had the same reaction.

We couldn't bear to watch it on the telly or listen to it or anything. It was just so upsetting. And people couldn't do anything about it. Course—oh dear, he always does this.

Joyce's slight tone of exasperation is prompted by the package that had just landed on the doormat and which she is tearing open with faltering fingers. "It is from Peter," she announces, "one of Arthur's Chinese employees." They've kept in touch over the years, even since Arthur died. Letters, a circulation of stamps they both collect, and even (infrequent) visits between Hong Kong and Devon form their current connection. It was quite different when Arthur was alive; when he ran the Public Health Department in Hong Kong and Peter worked for him.

Trouble is, there's stamps inside. He's mad, 'cause, you know, they changed all the money. Obviously it's going to change over to Commies, and he gave me about fifty pounds' worth of notes that'll be worth a fortune one day . . . Oh thank God, he's typed it, I'll be able to read it.

"Dear Mrs. Jones, I am sorry to have taken so long to write, and thank you for all the beautiful stamps. . . . Apart from being loaded by all the work—much of which is brought about by politicians, and not all of which is called for, I'm afraid—I had recently moved house and that had further involved us both day and night after, as well as before the actual move."

She explains:

His daughter's at university in America and his youngest son's in Hong Kong, and you see, trouble is, he can't get permission to come and live in England, but he might be able to get to the States because of his daughter. Very Chinese! [*She returns to her letter*] "The previous unit that we occupied since 1972 was too small and very inconvenient, actual total size under 500 square feet." This is minute, isn't it? "to accommodate the entire family. The new one is slightly larger." [*She considers this*] '650's still small. It's some of the most expensive housing in the world, Hong Kong. It's, I mean, our flats . . . You know, if we'd had to pay for it.

They didn't; they were on the colonial government payroll. She continues:

"It's a twenty-five-year old building, three years older than the previous one, and noisier due to its proximity to heavily used fly-over. But the spaciousness is the main concern." 'Cause you know, he came to stay in Jane's house, absolutely, he and his wife were shaken rudely. By the size. And the environment is upper middle-class. . . .[*She continues to read*] "We had major renovations carried out to render the not-large unit suitably . . . to fit our family. The floor tiles needed replacing, the walls repainted." [*She looks up*] Hasn't said anything about the handover, has it?

[*And returns to the letter*] "Electrical fitments changed, the mason did promise us three weeks in which to complete all the work, but in the end it took two months."

Sounds like England there. "During that time we had to be constantly involved with the planning, discussion, materials selection, work supervision." [*She looks up again*] That's very true, now see we had that table, the chairs made, and it nearly drove me mad. . . . How did we want it carved? How deep did we want it? How did we want the legs . . ."

Finally Peter gets to the topic of the handover. Joyce reads his description:

So, the historical Hong Kong handover is done. To those of us who had grown up in, and further spent our life serving under, the old system, it had some very special sentiments when the last moments arrived, as the Union Jack lowered, folded, and presented to the last governor who somberly accepted with drooped head. Then him farewelled for the last time by the representatives of the military and disciplined services who wore the crown insignia for the last time. Then "God Save the Queen," the last bugle sound, then "Olde Lang Syne," the crown car circulating three times. All these taking place in the drizzle that God had seemingly taken care to arrange. These had caused much more eye wetting than the ensuing formal ceremonies of marching bands, speeches, lowering and hoisting of flags and the rain." [*She looks up from the letter*] 'Course he won't be.

She stops to consider Peter's relationship with colonial governance, as though she hadn't thought of it before:

Don't know what he was. Never asked! "It's now eighty days since the above, they had really seen to it that things continue as much as possible unchanged, e.g.. PLA confined to camps. . . , street names unchanged, viz. Queens Road, King's Road, Princess Margaret Road, etc. But you can see the Royal Hong Kong Yacht Club and the Royal Hong Kong racecourse. Oh, horseracing regularly held, the existing common law system continues, and the foreign judges, though diminished in number, remain on the bench. British police officers, those who opted to stay on, remain, though fewer, especially on top levels, even the counter-productive political government system goes on. Of course some changes have taken place, for example. The official imperialistic connotations have been dropped, the crown, the logo, some holidays, Queen's birthday. The Chinese name of many government departments and some post titles renamed or converged with their mainland counterparts. The increased use of Chinese in official documents and files. The SAR flag is flown over Government House."

She tosses the letter aside and continues looking at her photograph album. How to excavate her world? What questions would reveal it? What circumstances had led her and Arthur to Hong Kong and to Peter's world? What was her life in his world like? How had she spent her time? How were the worlds of colonial governors and the governed in Hong Kong entwined? What fragments of empire remain in her way of being? What did she bring back with her, apart from furniture? What ideas about the East? What ways of living? And what might be the influence of these thoughts and practices on the village and the countryside beyond? She circled and she jumped. She dipped in and out of the photographs and marched off at odd tangents. This is the story that unfolded.

Joyce is in her eighties. She has uncles who were killed in the First World War, and her father, too, was quite badly injured when Joyce was a child. In the aftermath of war Joyce and her parents move to Manipur in India. Her father teaches in a local Indian school and deals with his war ghosts. It's the 1920s. Joyce and her mother are photographed with the maharaja of Manipur. The family has nannies and servants who take care of Joyce. Exhausting the possibilities of teaching and life in India, the family moves to South Africa, where Joyce says there was "no school or neighbors or anything" because her father is trying his hand at farming. It is the time of the great agricultural expansion in the settler colonies. When Joyce's paternal grandfather dies the family returns to Britain to shoulder broader family responsibilities and see Joyce through her secondary schooling. Her father returns to teaching and they live in Kent. Joyce's brother is born and cared for by a very "unpleasant nanny" in a stiff white uniform. On the eve of the Second World War and after her father is turned down by his old regiment on account of his First World War disability, the family return to South Africa. They leave without Joyce, who is twenty-one by now and has met Arthur, but they take her younger brother. Joyce's parents sit out the war in South Africa. In fact they both remain there for the rest of their lives. Her father dies in the 1950s. Her mother lives on into her nineties: alone in her personal version of apartheid-turned–black majority rule.

Optimistically the young couple marries as war breaks out. Arthur is instantly posted to the Middle East and then to the Far East. Never faint of heart, Joyce joins the First Aid hospital ships coming from Chengi Prison and other Japanese prisoner-of-war camps. Her long-distance connection with Arthur at this time is gruesome. Arthur—by now a captain—is loading the ships in Singapore with the emaciated bodies of released Japanese prisoners-of-war. Maybe Jack was there too. Joyce meets them off the ship in Madras and drives them to hospital treatment. They dash about in uniform doing things that must be done by young people at that time in those places.

The shifting rhythms of the young couple's lives in many ways extend those of Joyce's parents. The immediate postwar period finds them in Manchester living

249

near Arthur's family. They are less mobile, less connected with the practical arrangements and opportunities of empire, than Joyce's family. They last only a few years in Manchester before getting restless and move to Fiji. Here Arthur secures a job as a public health inspector with the colonial government. They slot easily into colonial life. There isn't much to do, at least from Joyce's vantage point. They sail and play golf for two "tours." As in other regions of the Colonial Civil Service, the Joneses did two-and-a-half year tours, at the end of which they would be expected to leave the colony for six months. A guard against going native and an opportunity to absorb the benefits of home leave; they would be allocated new accommodation on their return.

She leafs through the album. The Queen visits and they all wear their medals. There are local chiefs (she thinks they may once have been cannibals) and a governor. There are functions and ceremonial occasions; photographs and well-preserved embossed invitations. And so they spend the 1950s and the arrival of their daughter, Jane. There are nannies and servants. Joyce supervises; she has hobbies and social obligations rather than housework and childcare.

An abrupt change of pace and place in 1959 sees them moving to Hong Kong where Arthur is promoted he becomes senior superintendent for urban services.

He is eventually to be in charge of the colony's health and hygiene: its swimming pools, sports facilities, abattoirs, and graveyards. The album is bulging with official photos. European couples in evening dress pose for the camera at the many functions composing their daily life. Joyce learns to water ski, do Chinese painting, and play mahjong. Their daughter attends one of the many international schools for children from British and European families. Arthur takes his place in a very hierarchical, status-conscious, Colonial Civil Service where life is all about comparison. It matters who has the biggest flat, whom is seated next to whom at official functions. It matters who is served first at the club or at the dinner party. There are protocols governing when you are allowed to leave a function of this kind and you don't leave before your superior. We keep flicking through the album. There's News Year's Eve at the Magistracy. There are consular functions, swimming pool openings, parties at Government House. There is a menu from a dinner held at Princess Gardens. She reads it out. "Two hot dishes, crisp fine scallop and broccoli, brazed fish and asparagus, shark's fin and minced chicken soup, BBQ-ed Peking Duck."

Against this backdrop of colonial life there are riots throughout 1966 and 1967. The 1966 riots began as a popular protest against fare rises on the Star Ferry, which (still) connects the Kowloon Peninsula with Hong Kong Island. The 1967 riots began as young followers of Mao Zedong besieged Government

House, the epicenter of colonial administration. There are anti-British slogans on Chinese-owned buildings, bombs are planted, and there are demonstrations. British forces retaliate, and order is restored.[1] Refugees from China and Vietnam pour over the border as the colonial police struggle to contain and remove them. A massive program of slum clearance is underway and new apartments are built to house the population swelled by these more desperate forms of migration. Joyce is aware of this political backdrop to her life in the colony although her life continues in much the same pattern through the sixties and seventies. There are dinners, celebrations, civil disturbance, migration, building, building, and building. The Joneses move up, topographically and socially. They live on the Peak in a better apartment with more space and ever more spectacular views over Hong Kong Harbor.

But then it's 1978, and Arthur must retire. The rules are clear. They return reluctantly to Britain. Staying on is impossible. Their lifestyle was tied to the job, and the job will now be done by someone else, someone younger. Apartments are expensive and small—as Peter's letter points out—and, as the official functions end, socializing too, is both expensive and more limited. Staying on is not an option.

Instead they are "back" in the village, somewhere they have never lived: so return involves new beginning. "And we brought everything you see, we brought this table and that table, that table, these two end tables, dining table, chairs, my desk, sideboard, that cabinet." She traces with her fingers the intricate embroidery on the traditional Chinese silk robes of local members of the Hong Kong Civil service: visual emblems of social position. She eyes her impressive, and no doubt valuable, wood carvings: artifacts such as these were easily available in Hong Kong after the Chinese Cultural Revolution. They arrived in the pockets and bundles of those who fled over the border escaping Mao's program for the eradication of revisionism. Marauding youth, party officials, and intellectuals were sent to the countryside to learn from the peasantry.[2]

Joyce and Arthur are not alone. The Devonshire countryside is bristling with returnees from different parts of the (British) empire: blown home on the winds of postcolonial transformation and retirement. Joyce and Arthur soon develop a network. In fact, they had one already. They were, like others, assiduous at keeping in touch and letter writing, at connecting the different postings and chapters of their lives. There are the Parsons from Fiji, just down the road in the next town; and the Nortons—"they were Hong Kong"—only a short drive away. Joyce and Arthur have more in common with the Parsons and the Nortons than with their more sedentary neighbors in the village.

Arthur's retirement is tragically short. When he dies, Joyce soldiers on in all sorts of positive ways that form part of village life. There's the mahjong circle, although they played by different rules in different outposts of empire and this can lead to tensions. There's the Corona Club, which gives advice to those going abroad to work and provides a social context when they get back. There's the W.I. (Women's Institute), who are, no doubt, pleased with Joyce's craft contributions to the summer fair and the bring-and-buy stall including the spectacular quilts she made and Jane designed in Chinese styles. There's her stamp collection, which contains stamps from all over the world: the product of a large transnational network with a penchant for letter writing. There's West Country Embroiderers, the Friends of the Village Surgery, and some military functions too. There are old regiments to keep up with.

She scans the Corona Club meetings—"beekeeping," "life in a Victorian kitchen,"

253

"the Brontë sisters," "Women in Russia Today," the "Headquarters Service Lunch on the Royal Yacht *Britannia*," "miniature doll making," a "talk by an auctioneer," "Exeter parks and gardens"—"dull as ditchwater," she snorts. Most of the Corona Club members are "Africa," anyway. This makes a subtle but important distinction. Their meetings are also difficult to get to since she surrendered her driving license after the third time she hit something with her car. She gets round the village in the "buggy." This is a battery-operated carriage in racing red. It has a button in the middle and if you push this it goes at "top speed" from her house to the village shops. It's hard for her to walk now. The photos have stopped. What does she miss most about her old life? "The servants!" she hollers at her home help, who timidly straightens up her lounge.

Beginnings and Endings

1. Calvino (1997:61).
2. See http://MapZones.com.
3. Abbas (1997:289).
4. Abbas (1998:194).
5. Lam (1997:265).
6. Skeldon (1997).
7. Cuthbert and McKinnell (1997).
8. Amin and Thrift (2002:105).
9. Bell (1998).
10. *Standard*. *Greater China Business Paper*, 17 February 2005.
11. Calvino (1997:11).
12. Some colonial historians claim that the impact of British imperialism on Hong Kong was only marginally significant in the forging of daily life in the colony. Others claim it had a big impact.
13. European empires were also (eighteenth- and nineteenth-century) global systems.
14. Giddens (1990), Held et al. (1999), Massey (1993, 1999), Hirst and Thompson (1995), Sassen (1990), Eade (1997).
15. Sassen (2000).
16. Martin and Martin (2006:6), Zlotnik (1999:24–7).
17. Sriskandarajah and Drew (2006).
18. Sriskandarajah and Drew (2006).
19. Grant (2006:16) provides an excellent account of resulting social justice issues.
20. McGee (2005).
21. Beaverstock (2005), Findlay (1995).
22. Castells (2000), Sassen (2002), Hannerz (1996)
23. Smith (2005:235).
24. Scott (2006), Conradson and Latham (2005), Clark (2005), Walsh (2006), O'Reilly (2000), Smith (2005), Amit (2007).

25. See Karen O'Reilly's (2000) work on the British on the Costa del Sol for example.

26. Castells (2000:446–7)

27. Findlay (1995)

28. Beaverstock (2005).

29. See, for example, Basch, Glick, Schiller, and Szanton Blanc's (1994) classic early account of social fields of transnational migration. This initiated a great deal of valuable small-scale research tracing other routes and connection.

30. Blunt and Dowling (2006), Scott, (2006), Conradson and Latham (2005).

31. Ingold (2004:329).

32. The concept of fabric is developed more fully in Ingold (2000).

33. Cohen (1995) suggests these categories.

34. Conradson and Latham (2005).

35. Clifford (1997:2). There is a large literature on economic migration including Kay and Miles (1992), Richmond (1992), Ongley (1995).

36. King (2002:100).

37. 2001 Hong Kong Census.

38. Colley (2002:4).

39. Clifford (1997:30).

40. Yeoh and Willis (2005:270–2).

41. Findlay (1995:515).

42. Beaverstock (2005:248).

43. Dyer (1997), Hall (1991). For detailed accounts on whiteness, see Bonnett (1996, 1998 and 2000), Cohen (1997), Gallagher (2004), Frankenberg (1993), and Ware and Back (2002).

44. See Gallagher (2004).

45. The work of Howard Winant (1994), Les Back and John Solomos (2000), Ware and Back (2002), and Claire Alexander (1996, 2000) have provided crucial direction and framing in developing our understanding of race.

46. Omi and Winant (1994).

47. Roedigar (1992).

48. Schueller (1999).

49. Gallagher (2004).

50. Alexander and Knowles (2005).

51. Winant (1994) elaborated in Knowles (2003).

52. Verdery (1994), Amit (1996) provide useful insights on the production of ethnicity.

53. Stoler (2002), Colley (2002).

54. See Wu (1999), Flowerdew (1998).

55. Analyses of postcolonialism developed from Fanon's (1986) analysis of colonized subjectivity and Said's (2003) *Orientalism* eloquently objected to the representation of the colonized other in Western scholarship. The scholarship this produced centered on issues of representation rather than the production of social forms and subjectivities. It has been criticized for its overemphasis of representation at the expense of practice and politics (Scott 1999), for ignoring internal colonialisms buttressing ethnic and gender exploitation (McClintock 1994), for a crudeness in drawing its categories of colonizer and colonized (Cannadine 2001), for simplistic racialization of these categories, which fail to acknowledge subtleties in the way they map onto the living arrangements that follow conquest and occupation (Stoler 2002, Colley 2002), and for presenting colonization as over (Spivak 1999 or Carby 2005).

56. Massey (1999), Hesse (1999).

57. Clifford's (1997:54) reference to Certeau's (1989) *Practice of Everyday Life*.

58. See Mills (1970) for a detailed discussion of private troubles and public issues.

59. Jack Edwards asks us to use his real name when writing about him.

60. Jack Edwards, *Banzai, You Bastards!* (Hong Kong: Souvenir Press).

Making New Lives

1. Amin and Thrift (2002:10).

2. Hong Kong Public Housing Authority, "From Shelter to Home: 45 Years of Public Housing Development in Hong Kong."

3. BBC News Asia Pacific, http://www.news.bbc.co.uk/2/hi/Asia-Pacific. This protest took place on July 1, 2003.

The English Business

1. Speaking English is "no longer a colonial issue," see comments posted by parents in 2006 at http://www.esf.edu.hk.

2. The sum HK$950,000/year is the figure sited on the parents' comment board on the ESF Web site (http://www.esf.edu.hk) as the average ESF teachers' salary, although there are great variations in teachers pay depending on length of time in the system, and it is not clear whether this includes the gratuity (25 percent) paid at the end of each two-year contract of the housing allowance. Income tax is 15 percent, leaving a high disposable income.

3. See Amit and Rapport (2002) for a critique of emphases on weaving connection at the expense of disconnection across national boundaries through migration in much of the literature on transnational migration.

4. Primary school fees are HK$83,300 for Kelletts School.

5. The ESF runs ten primary, five secondary, and one special needs school.

6. See http://www.esf.edu.hk.

7. See http://www.esf.edu.hk.

8. The amounts: HK$78,600 for secondary school, HK$47,300 for primary school. Audit Commission, "Value for Money Study," November 2004, http://www.esf.edu.hk.

9. Figures relate to 2001–2002 Audit Commission, "Value for Money Study," 2004, http://www.esf.edu.hk.

10. Http://www.esf.edu.hk (February 2005).

11. The amount, HK$13,780. *CNN Asia Now*, http://www.asiaweek.com (February 2005). Half a million Hong Kong workers earn less than HK$62,400/year (less than US$10,000 on exchange rates as of January 2006) with Hong Kong ranked fifth in the world for the widest gap between rich and poor. See *Standard. Greater China Business Paper*, 17 February 2005.

Old China Hands

1. Only 14 square kilometers big, this is the third-largest of Hong Kong's islands—Hong Kong Island and Lantau, containing the new airport, are bigger—and lies to the west of Hong Kong Island (http://www.travelchinaguide.com).

2. De Certeau (1989:97).

3. Deferential respect for superiors whether they are right or wrong about a decision.

4. HK$7,000 (less than US$1,500) a month and buys 700 square feet as a flat in a three-story building (buildings over three stories are banned).

257

5. This no longer happens because of the visa situation once Hong Kong was returned to China.

6. They were both British Conservative Party voters.

7. See Clifford (1994) for an elaboration of diaspora.

Working Global Systems

1. Dant (1999:24–32) cogently explores the social significance of objects and the ways in which they are entangled with our personal and social lives as markers of social status and much more besides.

2. Candy (2005).

3. This date isn't just significant for the return of Hong Kong to China but for the economic downturn in the Asia Pacific economies.

4. Between the US and China. Mission statement of the Hong Kong America Center, http://www.cuhk.hk/hkac/about/mission.

5. "International Report on Hong Kong," *Washington Times,* 6 April 2000, available at http://www.internationalreports.com/asiapacific/oo/hongkong.

6. Mission statement of the Hong Kong America Center, available at http://www.cuhk.hk/hkac/about/mission.

7. Michael Klosson, U.S. Consul General's speech to the Washington State China Relations Council 11 April 11 2002.

8. "International Report on Hong Kong."

9. Ibid.

10. The WTO, set up in 1995 to provide a forum for trade negotiations, is dominated by wealthy countries, and notably the United States, that can get away with flouting agreements over trade barriers protecting national economies. The United States is adept at ignoring international agreements that go against its business and trading interests such as those concerned with environmental damage. The IMF is a public institution based on the recognition that markets did not work well and needed collective action at the global level to secure economic stability. The G7 or G8 countries dominate the IMF with the United States having effective veto. In a dramatic shift to a belief in free markets in the 1980s the "Washington Consensus" between the IMF, the World Bank (which deals with structural issues around loans to developing countries), and the US Treasury heralded new thinking on economic stability and development. These institutions' financial and lending policies are typically dictated by Washington, with the collusion of other developed countries. See Stiglitz (2002:10, 12,16, 24) for further elaboration.

11. See Collins (2003) on the operation of the multifiber agreement and the quota system shaping the global apparel industry as an example.

12. GUPSHUP Archive (2004), available at http://www.gupistan.com/forums/showthread/t-54567.html.

13. Associated Press Bulletin (6 November 6 2000), available at http://www.guest.morris.com/stories/111600/gen-1116006911.html.

14. Hardt and Negri (2000) provide the substance for this argument. They suggest that America is an empire, although in pursuing this claim they have to redefine empire from its eighteenth- and nineteenth-century forms. They suggest that the American empire is an empire without boundaries; that it doesn't work through conquest; that it operates in all registers of the social world especially through biopower; and that it is dedicated to peace despite its military aggression.

15. Canthotrade (10 July 2003), available at http://www.canthotrade.com.markets/.
16. Ibid.
17. Sir James Hodge, interview (April 2001), available at http://www.feng.peopledaily.con.cn/english/200104/10print20010410.
18. Brigadier Christopher Hammerbeck, interview, *English People Daily*, online, June 2002, available at http://www.english.people.com.cn/200206/10/.
19. Theories of globalization now acknowledge some of this diversity, and research is capturing nonmainstream global networks. See MacGaffey and Bazenguissa-Ganga (2000), for example, for the operation of alternate trading circuits.
20. We do not intend to suggest they are not sometimes interconnected but intend to stress globalization's diversity of networks along the dimensions outlined.
21. These "businessmen" are predominantly from Nigeria and Ghana as well as from other parts of Central and West Africa. The African population of Hong Kong is uncounted: included in the "other" category in the 2001 census.
22. Hong Kong Trader (March 2002), available at http://www.hktrader.net/200203/200101/2001013.
23. Tata South East Asia Ltd an Indian multi-national has its regional offices in Hong Kong as the gateway to China. Hong Kong Trader (March 2002), available at http://www.hktrader.net/200203/200101/2001013.

Life at the Top

1. Isabella Bird (1879) cited in Hoe (1991).
2. Below the Peak is Midlevels, once the domain of middling colonial servants and others in comparable occupations.
3. Yiching Wu (1999).
4. Dant (1999:74): "atmosphere" is a term used by Bourdieu.
5. Jardines is one of the big trading interests in Hong Kong, dating back to the time of the East India Company and the Opium Wars.
6. We had extended discussion about what kinds of action on his part would provide a more locally integrated life. He is the most interested in what we will do with the research and wonders if we think they are racist, something we neither confirm nor deny.
7. Adapted from "MarchArt" at the *Helena May—A Celebration of Women and the Arts in Hong Kong* (2000) and the Helena May information booklet.
8. Ibid.
9. Ibid.
10. Ibid.
11. Ibid., based on documents from the Hong Kong Public Records Office.
12. Bottero (2005:8).

Service

1. A high proportion of Chinese women work and see work as an important commitment (Pearson and Leung 1995:11).
2. The total is 142,500 in the 2001 Hong Kong Census, or 2.1 percent of the population, by a long way the largest immigrant group out of the 240,000 foreign maids in Hong Kong, the others coming from Indonesia, Thailand, Nepal, and the Indian subcontinent http://www.imdiversity.com Global News Digest, February 3, 2005.

3. Nicole Constable's (1997) scholarly study of Filipino maids in Hong Kong details Philippine/ US military bases and other forms of contact forming a bridge on global routes for Filipino women migrants. Sassen's (1990:376–7) analysis of the geographies of migration into the United States stresses the significance of technical and economic "bridges" in military and off-shoring connections that form significant conduits for migration.

4. Elias (2000) establishes the construction of normativities around things such as spitting, eating, and nose blowing—bodily habits that have a bearing on the practicalities of cross-cultural proximities.

5. Constable (1997) provides a more thorough and systematic study of Filipino maids than anything that can be offered in this chapter. She points out that being treated as part of the family is something the maids appreciate and a model with which they operate.

6. More traditional, segregated, and hierarchical relationships between maids and Chinese employers reported by Constable (1997) may well be rooted in their historical relationship with colonialism and between wealthier local Chinese families and their Chinese serving class. Constable (1997:22) cites Andrea Sankar (1978:52) in arguing that in the 1870s, 77 percent of the Chinese people living in the colony were employed in some kind of domestic service and only a small proportion were women. This reveals that the local traditions of service have quite different conditions of production in class and gender terms.

7. Maids' lives don't map onto categories like race, ethnicity, gender, and class in any straightforward way. The significance of these intersecting forms of social distance is a complicated puzzle requiring empirical work.

8. Constable (1997:4).

9. Employers who impose restrictions cite anxieties about appropriate places maids might visit and behavior they might engage in. Prominent is the concern that they will "freelance" in various capacities in and around the red-light districts and that this might taint respectable homes.

10. See Constable (1997).

11. Parrenas (2000).

12. Since 2–3.5 million Philippine citizens live in 140 different countries. See Migration News, http://www.Migration.ucdavis.edu (1995).

13. We know little about how decisions to migrate or not are reached among this group of women, and these are likely as varied as their individual biographies.

14. This is approximately one-third of the average income (approximately US$500).

Boys' Night Out

1. Thanks to Veronica Person for her insights on this.

2. Friday is a boys' night out, too. Parts of Sunday are also reserved for a "boys focus," but centered on sports rather than sexual fantasies.

3. This offended a generation of Asian and Asian American women who grew up in its simplistic shadow, ostensibly, as passive objects of Western male gazes. See Asian American at http://www.www.goldsea.com.

4. Hoe (1991): a reference to 1860 and to the activities centered on Wanchai.

5. J. J. Francis, a barrister, suggested this figure, see Pearson and Leung (1995).

6. See Hoe (1991).

7. Pearson and Leung (1995:245) suggest that Hong Kong's sexual services industry is run by men and dominated by Triads, that is, Chinese gangs, and the middle management level of mamasans in a club or bar is as high up the hierarchy as women rise.

8. See Pearson and Leung's (1995) excellent essay on this.

9. This depends on where they work. Pearson and Leung's (1995) study points out that provision of sexual services is highly stratified and context-driven: Women may enter the sexual services industry as beautiful young women near the top, but there is only one direction in which mobility works. Older women, who work the streets in an area of Kowloon called Shamshuipo, which is the most independent of men and infrastructure, earn about HK$1,200 a month (Pearson and Leung 1995:256). Women working in upscale clubs and bars earned much more—HK$1,500–$2,500 a client at 1995 prices (Pearson and Leung 1995:272) but had less control over clients, money, and work conditions.

10. Maids freelancing as PR girls can earn HK$300–$500/night and HK$1000HK at weekends which compared to the wages they get from being a maid is an attractive option. See International Press Service, "'Hong Kong: For the Money, Foreign Workers Cross Over to the Sex Trade," http://www.aegis.com/news/lips/2002.

11. Pearson and Leung's (1995:269) study suggests that even women unambiguously working in sexual services kept the boundaries between affection and commerce deliberately fuzzy for reasons of self-esteem.

12. Western as well as Chinese men operate in this way in this area, but certain bars and clubs are overwhelmingly Western expatriate. The market for sexual services is also highly segmented but in a different way from the 1960s. Wanchai is at the center of the more up-scale red-light district. Mongkok has a less expensive red-light district from where poorer Chinese prostitutes—local and mainland—operate. Western men do not usually go to this area, which is associated with danger and disease. Upscale hotels like the Grand Hyatt are also places where equally upscale prostitutes operate among Western and Chinese men. This observation is based on fieldwork.

13. Constable's (2003) *Romance on a Global Stage* provides a delicate pathway through the connections between emotion and money.

14. There is etiquette to consider here: Hamish says you don't just walk straight into a strip bar, but work up to it.

15. Organizations devoted to monitoring trafficking of girls into sexual services claim that (uncalculated) but (presumed) large numbers of Thai, Chinese, and Filipino women are trafficked into Hong Kong's Wanchai district to work in exotic bars and the activities connected with them (http://www.humantrafficking.org). Bales (1999), detailing what he refers to as the new slavery in which people from developing countries work in bonded labor conditions, says that young Burmese and Cambodian women are trafficked into Thailand's sex industry and that young Thai women, especially from the hill tribes in the north where they are acquired through village elders and even close female relatives, work in countries like Japan and Germany (and Hong Kong) in girlie bars. As in China, prostitution accompanies rural-to-urban migration that often accompanies rapid industrialization. With attention turned to trafficking from northern Thailand and Thai government initiatives to stem this migration flow, Burmese and Chinese girls aged 12–18 are taking their place. See Fact Book on Global Sexual Exploitation: China and Hong Kong, http://www.uri.edu/artsci/wms/hughes. Not all women in these circumstances, of course, are trafficked.

16. See Constable (2003).

17. Pearson and Leung (1995:261) suggest that women from the Philippines and Thailand are the most vulnerable to exploitation, partly but not entirely on account of their immigration status, and disliked by local Chinese women because they are cheaper competition and associated with AIDS.

18. The details here are difficult to establish. Pearson and Leung (1995) record the difficulty of investigating this end of the sexual services sector in view of the fierce gate-keeping that protects the women, the agencies, their managers, and Triad involvement and cites this as shaping their decision to study streetwalkers in Kowloon.

19. Prostitution is legal in Hong Kong, but pimping is not. Girls like Amee and Kandy are usually processed under immigration laws and sent home if they are discovered.

20. Complaints by organizations monitoring trafficking point to the ways in which young Filipino girls are trafficked to Hong Kong's red-light district like Thai women and held against their will (http://www.humantrafficking.org). There are no specific laws against trafficking and so prosecutions tend to take place—if at all, girls are often just sent home—under legislation related to trafficking or are treated as immigration offences. Critics of this position point out that most women in the industry are volunteers and there is an easy line between Filipino maids, PR girls, and prostitution with maids freelancing in clubs as PR girls who may or may not also sell sexual services to bolster their income.

Clubbing

1. The Traveler's and the Athenaeum, for example, as well as those whose establishments were more directly linked to empire, like the East India United Services Club. Sinha (2001) provides a more thorough discussion of the links between British and colonial club-lands in the context of India.

2. Calculated from the Club Managers' Association to which those managing key clubs belong.

3. Established 1884 and now has dining and recreation facilities for 20,000 members, the Royal was dropped post 1997. Its 2002–3 turnover was HK$71 billion, US$9 billion. It operates as a not-for-profit operation and large-scale benefactor to charities as part of a government-granted monopoly providing over 11 percent of government revenue. It funds Stephanie's information bureau and many bigger projects too.

4. Bottero (2005:8).

5. Corporate membership is over US$80,000/year.

On Patrol

1. Feuchtwang (1992).

2. British recruits joined as officers, unlike local Chinese recruits.

3. Not a privileged point of access to the past, but the point of access available to us thirty years on from the vantage-point of postcolonial time.

4. From the 1980s the Hong Kong police force took local recruitment and promotion seriously, so there was no crisis in 1997.

Migration Revisited

1. Ingold (2000:289–291) provides a useful discussion of the social dimensions of skill.
2. This is taken from Benjamin (1999).

Endings and Beginnings

1. See http://britains-smallwars.com/RRGP/HongKong.
2. Zhensheng (2003).

BIBLIOGRAPHY

Abbas, Akbar. 1998. "Building, Dwelling, Drifting: Migrancy and the Limits of Architecture; Building Hong Kong from Migrancy to Disappearance." *Postcolonial Studies* 1, no. 2: 185–99.

———. 1997. "Hong Kong: Other Histories, Other Politics." *Public Culture* 9:293–313.

Alexander, Claire. 2000. *The Asian Gang: Ethnicity, Identity and Masculinity.* Oxford: Berg

———. 1996. *The Art of Being Black: The Creation of Black British Youth Identities.* Oxford: Clarendon Press

Alexander, Claire, and Knowles, Caroline. 2005. Introduction to Claire Alexander and Caroline Knowles, eds., *Making Race Matter.* London: Palgrave, 1–16.

Ali, Suki. 2003. *Mixed-Race Post-Race: Gender, New Ethnicities and Cultural Practices,* Oxford: Berg.

Amin, Ash, and Nigel Thrift. 2002. *Cities: Reimagining the Urban.* Cambridge: Polity.

Amin, Ash, Doreen Massey, and Nigel Thrift. 2000. *Cities for the Many not the Few.* Bristol: Policy Press.

Amit, V. 2007. "Globalization Through 'Weak Ties': A Study of Transnational Networks Among Mobile Professionals." In *Going First Class? New Approaches to Privileged Travel and Movement.* Edited by V. Amit. Oxford: Berghahn Books.

Amit, Vered, and Nigel Rapport. 2002. *The Trouble with Community,* London: Pluto Press.

Amit-Talai, Vered. 1996. "The Minority Circuit: Identity Politics and the Professionalization of Ethnic Activism." In Vered Amit-Talai and Caroline Knowles, *Resituating Identities.* Peterborough: Broaview Press, 89–114

Audit Commission. "Value for Money Study." November 2004. Http://esf.edu.hk.

Back, Les, and John Solomos, eds. 2000. *Theories of Race and Racism.* London: Routledge.

Bales, Kevin. 1999. *Disposable People.* Berkeley: University of California Press.

Basch, Linda, Nina Glick Schiller, and Christian Szanton Blanc. 1994. *Nations Unbound.* New York: Gordon and Breach.

BBC News Asia Pacific. Http://www.news.bbc.co.uk/2/hi/Asia-Pacific.

Beaverstock, Jonathan V. 2005. "Transnational Elites in the City: The British Highly Skilled Inter-company Transferees in New York City's Financial District." *Journal of Ethnic and Migration Studies* 31, no. 2: 245–68.

Bell, Daniel. 1998. "Hong Kong's Transition to Capitalism." *Dissent* Winter: 15–23.

Benjamin, Walter. 1999. *Illuminations.* London: Pimlico.

Berger, John. 1997. *Ways of Seeing.* London: Penguin.

Blunt, Alison, and Robyn Dowling. 2006. *Home.* London: Routledge.

Bonnett, Alistair. 2000. "Whiteness in Crisis." *History Today* December: 39–40.

———. 1998. "How the British Working Class Became White: The Symbolic Reformation of Racialized Capitalism." *Journal of Historical Sociology* 11, no. 3: 316–40.

———. 1996. "'White Studies': The Problems and Project of a New Research Agenda." *Theory, Culture and Society* 13, no. 2:145–55.

Bottero, Wendy. 2005. *Social Stratification: Social Division and Inequality.* London: Routledge.

Braman, Donald. 1999. "Of Race and Immutability." *UCLA Law Review* 46:1375–1463.

Calvino, Italo. 1997. *Invisible Cities.* London: Vintage.

Candy, Fiona. 2005. "The Fabric of Society." *Sociological Research Online.* Special issue, "Working Visually," ed. Susan Halford and Caroline Knowles. Http://www.socresonline .org.uk/10/1knowleshalford.

Cannadine, David. 2001. *Ornamentalism: How the British Saw Their Empire.* London: Penguin.

Carby, Hazel. 2005. Foreword to Claire Alexander and Caroline Knowles, *Making Race Matter* Basingstoke: Palgrave.

Castells, Manuel. 2000. *The Rise of Network Society.* Vol. 1. Oxford: Blackwell.

Clarke, Nick. 2005. "Detailing Transnational Lives of the Middle: British Working Holiday Makers in Australia." *Journal of Ethnic and Migration Studies* 31, no. 2: 307–22.

Clifford, James. 1997. *Routes.* Cambridge: Harvard University Press.

———. 1994. "Diasporas." *Cultural Anthropology* 9, no. 3: 302–38.

CNN Asia Now. February 2005. Http://www.asiaweek.com.

Cohen, Philip. 1998. *The Last Island.* London: Centre for New Ethnicities Research.

———. "Labouring under Whiteness." In *Displacing Whiteness.* Edited by Ruth Frankenberg, 244–82. Durham: Duke University Press.

Cohen, Robin. 1995. Prologue to *The Cambridge Survey of World Migration.* Edited by Robin Cohen, 1–6. Cambridge: Cambridge University Press.

Colley, Linda. 2002. *Captives: Britain, Empire and the World. 1600–1850.* London: Jonathan Cape.

Collins, Jane. 2003. *Threads.* Chicago: Chicago University Press.

Conradson, David, and Alan Latham. 2005. "Transnational Urbanism: Attending to Everyday Practices and Mobilities." *Journal of Ethnic and Migration Studies* 31, no.2: 227–33.

Constable, Nicole. 2003. *Romance on a Global Stage.* Berkley: University of California Press.

———. 1997. *Maid to Order in Hong Kong.* Ithaca: Cornell University Press.

Cuthbert, Alexander R., and Keith G. McKinnell. 1997. "Ambiguous Space, Ambitious Rights—Corporate Power and Social Control in Hong Kong. *Cities* 14, no. 5: 295–311.

Dant, Tim. 1999. *Material Culture in the Social World.* Buckingham: Open University Press.

De Certeau, Michel. 1989. *The Practice of Everyday Life.* Berkeley: Los Angeles.

Dyer, Richard. 1997. *White*. London: Routledge.

Eade, John. 1997. "Reconstructing Places." In *Living the Global City*. Edited by John Eade, 127–45. London: Routledge.

Editorial. "Hong Kong Targets Foreign Women in Wage Cuts." 2005. Http://www.asiaweek.com, February.

Editorial. "Minimum Wage." 2005. *The Standard. Greater China Business Paper*, 17 February.

Edwards, Jack. 1990. *Banzai You Bastards*. Honk Kong: Corporate Communications.

Elias, Norbert. 2000. *The Civilizing Process*. Oxford: Blackwell.

English School Foundation Web site. February 2005. Http://www.esf.edu.hk.

Fanon, F. 1986. *Black Skin White Mask*. London: Pluto Press.

Feuchtwang, Stephan. 2004. "Theorizing Place." In *Making Place: State Projects, Globalization and Local Responses*. Edited by Stephan Feuchtwang. London: UCL Press.

———. 1992. "Policing the Streets." In *Where You Belong*. Edited by A. X. Cambridge and Stephan Feuchtwang, 94–107. Aldershot: Avery.

Findlay, Allan M. 1995. "Skilled Transients: The Invisible Phenomenon?" In *The Cambridge Survey of World Migration*. Edited by Robin Cohen, 515–22. Cambridge: Cambridge University Press.

Flowerdew, John 1998. *The Final Years of British Hong Kong: The Discourse of Colonial Withdrawal*. Basingstoke: Macmillan.

Frankenberg, Ruth. 1993. *White Women, Race Matters: The Social Construction of Whiteness*. Minneapolis: University of Minnesota Press.

Gallagher, Charles A. 2004. "Racial Redistricting: Expanding the Boundaries of Whiteness." In *The Politics of Multiracialism: Challenging Racial Thinking*. Edited by Heather M. Dalmage. Albany: State University of New York Press.

Giddens, Anthony. 1990. *The Consequences of Modernity*. Stanford: Stanford University Press.

Goswami, Manu. 1996. "'Englishness' on the Imperial Circuit: Mutiny Tours in Colonial South Asia." *Journal of Historical Sociology* 9, no. 1: 54–84.

Government of Hong Kong. February 2001. "Population Census, 2001." Http://info.gov.hk/population.

Grant, Stephanie. 2006. "GCIM Report: Defining an 'Ethical Compass' for International Migration Policy." *International Migration* 44, no. 1: 13–19.

Hall, Stuart. 1991. "Old and New Identities, Old and New Ethnicities." In *Culture, Globalization and the World-System: Contemporary Conditions for the Representation of Reality*. Edited by Anthony King. Minneapolis: University of Minneapolis Press, 1991.

Hammerbeck, Brigadier Christopher. June 2002. Interview, *English People Daily on line*. Http://www.english.people.com.cn/200206/10/.

Hannerz, Ulf. 1996. *Transnational Connections*. London: Routledge.

Hardt, Michael, and Antonio Negri. 2000. *Empire*. Cambridge: Harvard University Press.

Harper, Douglas. 2001. *Changing Work: Visions of a Lost Agricultures*. Chicago: University of Chicago Press.

———. 1987. *Working Knowledge*. Chicago: University of Chicago Press.

———. 1982. *Good Company*. Chicago: University of Chicago Press.

Hartigan, John Jr. 1997. "Establishing the Fact of Whiteness." *American Anthropologist* 99, no. 3: 495–505.

Held, David, Anthony McGrew, David Goldblatt, and Jonathan Perraton. 1999. *Global Trans-formations*. London: Polity.

Helena May information booklet. 2000. Hong Kong: n.p.

Hesse, Barnor. 1999. "Reviewing the Western Spectacle: Reflexive Globalization through the Black Diaspora." In *Global Futures: Migration, Environment and Globalization*. Edited by Avtar Brah, Mary Hickman, and Maitrin Mac an Ghaill, Maitrin, 122–43. London: Macmillan.

Hirst, Paul and Graham Thompson. 1995. "Globalisation and the Future of the Nation State." *Economy and Society* 24, no. 3: 408–42.

Hodge, Sir James. Interview, April 2001. Http://www.feng.peopledaily.con.cn/english/200104/10print20010410.

Hoe, Susanna. 1991. *The Private Life of Old Hong Kong*. Oxford: Oxford University Press.

Hong Kong America Center. Mission statement of the. Http://www.cuhk.hk/hkac/about/mission.

Hong Kong Public Housing Authority. Undated. *From Shelter to Home: 45 years of Public Housing Development in Hong Kong*. Hong Kong: Public Housing Authority.

Hong Kong Trader. March 2002. Http://www.hktrader.net/200203/200101/200101s3.

Hughes, Donna M., Laura Joy Sporcic, Nadine Z. Mendelsohn, and Vanessa Cirgwin. 1999. Fact Book on Global Sexual Exploitation: China and Hong Kong. Http://www.humantrafficking.org www.uri.edu/arts ci/wms/hughes.

Ingold, Tim. 2004. "Culture on the Ground: The World Perceived through Feet." *Material Culture* 9, no. 3: 315–40.

———. 2000. *The Perception of the Environment*. London: Routledge.

International Press Service. "Hong Kong: For the Money, Foreign Workers Cross Over to the Sex Trade." Http://www.aegis.com/news/lips/2002.

Kay, Diana, and Robert Miles. 1992. *Refugees or Migrant Workers?* London: Routledge.

Klosson, Michael. 2002. U.S. Consul General's speech to the Washington State China Relations Council. April 11, 2002. Http://www.usembassy-australian.state.gov/hyper/2002/0411/epf416.html.

Knowles, Caroline. 2005. "Making Whiteness: British Lifestyle Migrants in Hong Kong." In Claire Alexander and Caroline Knowles, eds., *Making Race Matter*. London: Palgrave.

———. 2003. *Race and Social Analysis*. London: Sage.

King, Russel. 2002. "Towards a New Map of European Migration." *International Journal of Population Geography* 8: 89–106.

Lam, J. T. M. 1997. "Sino-British relations over Hong Kong during the Final Phase of Political Transition." *International Studies* 34, no. 4: 425–44.

Lipsitz, George. 1998. *The Possessive Investment in Whiteness: How White People Profit from Identity Politics*. Philadelphia: Temple University Press.

Massey, Doreen. 1999. "Imagining Globalization: Power Geometries of Time-Space." In *Global Futures*. Edited by Avtar Brah et al., 27–44. London: MacMillan.

———. 1993. "Politics and Space/Time." In *Place and the Politics of Identity*. Edited by Keith Michael and Steve Pile. London: Routledge.

Mauss, M. 1992. "Techniques of the Body." In *Incorporations*. Edited by Jonathan Crary and Sanford Kwinter, 455–77. New York: Zone.

McClintock, Anne. 1995. *Imperial Leather.* London: Routledge.

———. 1994. "The Angel of Progress: Pitfalls of the Term 'Postcolonialism.'" In *Colonial Discourse/Postcolonial Theory.* Edited by Francis Barker, Peter Hulme, and Margaret Iverson. Manchester: Manchester University Press.

McGee, Derek. 2005. *Intolerant Britain? Hate, Citizenship and Difference.* Milton Keynes: Open University Press.

Mills, C. Wright. 1970. *The Sociological Imagination.* Harmondsworth Penguin.

Lam, Jermain T. M. 1997. "Sino-British Relations over Hong Kong during the Final Phase of Political Transition." *International Studies* 34, no. 4: 427–44.

Lefebvre, Henri. 1996. *The Production of Space.* Oxford: Blackwell.

MacGaffey and Bazenguissa-Ganga's. 2000. *Congo-Paris: Transnational Traders on the Margins of the Law.* Oxford: International African Institute in Association with James Currey; and Bloomington: Indiana University Press.

Maffesoli, Michel. 1996. *The Time of the Tribes.* London: Sage.

"March Art at the Helena May—A Celebration of Women and the Arts in Hong Kong." 2000. Hong Kong: n.p.

Martin, Phillip, and Susan Martin. 2006. "GCIM: A New Global Migration Facility." *International Migration* 44, no. 1: 5–8.

Migration News. 1995. Http://www.migration.ucdavis.edu.

Nahm, H. Y. 2008. "Susie Wong Revisited." *Asian American* (July). Http://www.goldsea.com.

Omi, Michael, and Howard Winant. 1994. *Racial Formations in the United States.* New York: Routledge.

Ongley, Patrick. 1995. "Post-1945 International Migration: New Zealand, Australia and Canada Compared." *International Migration Review* 24, no. 3:765–93.

O'Reilly, Karen. 2000. *The British on the Costa del Sol: Transnational Identities and Local Communities.* London: Routledge.

Parrenas, Rhacel Salzar. 2000. "Migrant Filipina Domestic Workers and the International Division of Reproductive Labour." *Gender and Society* 14, no. 4: 560–581.

Paul, James, and Martin Spirit. 2002. "The Hong Kong Riots." Http://britains-smallwars.com/RRGP/HongKong.

Pearson, V., and B. Leung. 1995. "Perspectives on Women's Issues." In *Women in Hong Kong.* Edited by V. Pearson and B. Leung. Hong Kong: Oxford University Press.

Richmond, Anthony. 1992. "Immigration and Structural Change: The Canadian Experience." *International Migration Review* 24, no. 4: 1200–1221.

Roediger, David. 1992. *The Wages of Whiteness: Race and the Making of the American Working Class.* London: Verso.

Said, Edward. 2003. *Orientalism: Western Conceptions of the Orient.* London: Penguin.

Sandoval, Chela. 1997. "Theorizing White Consciousness for a Post Empire World: Barthes, Fanon and the Rhetoric of Love." In *Displacing Whiteness.* Edited by Ruth Frankenberg, 86–106. Durham: Duke University Press.

Sassen, Saskia. 2002. *Global Networks, Linked Cities.* New York: Routledge.

———. 2000. "New Frontiers Facing Urban Sociology at the Millennium." *British Journal of Sociology* 51, no. 1: 143–60.

———. 1990. "U.S. Immigration Policy towards Mexico in a Global Economy." *Journal of International Affairs* 43, no. 2: 369–383

Schueller, Malini Johar. 1999. "Performing Whiteness, Performing Blackness: Dorr's Cultural Capital and the Critique of Slavery." *Criticism* 41, no. 2: 233–56.

Scott, David. 1999. *Refashioning Futures.* Princeton: Princeton University Press.

Scott, Sam. 2006. "The Social Morphology of Skilled Migration: The Case of the British Middle Class in Paris." *Journal of Ethnic and Migration Practice* 32, no.7: 1105–1130.

Sinha, Mrinalini. 2001. "Britishness, Clubability, and the Colonial Public Sphere: The Genealogy of an Imperial Institution in Colonial India." *Journal of British Studies* 40: 489–521.

Skeldon, Ronald. 1997. "Hong Kong: Colonial City to Global City to Provincial City." *Cities* 15, no. 5: 265–71.

Smith, Michael Peter. 2005. "Transnational Urbanism Revisited." *Journal of Ethnic and Migration Studies* 31, no. 2: 235–44.

Spivak, Gayatri Chakravorty. 1999. *A Critique of Postcolonial Reason.* Cambridge: Harvard University Press.

Sriskandarajah, Dhananjayan, and Catherine Drew. 2006. *Brits Abroad: Mapping the Scale and Nature of British Immigration.* London: Institute for Public Policy Research.

Stiglitz, Jospeh. 2002. *Globalization and Its Discontents.* London: Penguin.

Stoler, Laura Ann. 2002. *Carnal Knowledge and Imperial Power: Race and the Intimate in Colonial Rule.* Berkeley: University of California Press.

Tatsuyuki OTA. 2003. "The Role of Special Economic Zones in China's Economic Development as compared with Asian Export Processing Zones, 1979–1995." Htpp:// www.iae .univ-poitiers.fr.

Twine, France Winddance. 1999. *Race-ing Research, Researching Race: Methodological Dilemmas in Critical Race Studies.* New York: New York University Press.

Verdery, Katherine. 1994. "Ethnicity, Nationalism and State-making." In *The Anthropology of Ethnicity: Beyond Ethnic Groups and Boundaries.* Edited by Hans Vermeulen and Cora Govers, 33–58. Amstedam: Het Spinhuis.

Walsh, Katie. 2006. "'Dad says I'm tied to a shooting star!': Grounding Research on British Expatriate Belonging." *Area* 38, no. 3: 268–78.

Ware, Vron, and Les Back. 2002. *Out of Whiteness.* Chicago: University of Chicago Press.

Washington Times. International report on Hong Kong, 6 April 2000. Http://www .internationalreports.com/asiapacific/00/hongkong.

Watts, Jonathan. 2004. "Democracy on the Retreat." *Guardian Unlimited.* 14 January.

Winant, Howard. 1994. *Racial Conditions.* Minneapolis: University of Minnesota Press.

Wu, Yiching. 1999. "Prelude to Culture: Interrogating Colonial Rule in Early British Hong Kong." *Dialectical Anthropology* 24: 141–70.

Zhensheng, Li. 2003. *Red-Color News Soldier: A Chinese Photographer's Odyssey through the Cultural Revolution.* London: Phaidon.

Zlotnik, Hania. 1999. "Trends in International Migration since 1965: What Existing Data Reveal." *International Migration* 37, no. 1.

Yeoh, Brenda S., and Katie Willis. 2005. "Singaporean and British Transmigrants in China and the Cultural Politics of 'Contact Zones.'" In *Journal of Ethnic and Migration Studies* 31, no. 2: 269–85.

INDEX